The Primitive Mind and
Modern Civilization

The Primitive Mind and Modern Civilization

By

CHARLES ROBERTS ALDRICH

With an Introduction by
BRONISLAW MALINOWSKI

and a Foreword by
C. G. JUNG

AMS PRESS
NEW YORK

Reprinted from the edition of 1931, New York
First AMS EDITION published 1969
Manufactured in the United States of America

Library of Congress Catalogue Card Number: 79-98401

To

GEORGE FRENCH PORTER

1931

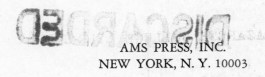

AMS PRESS, INC.
NEW YORK, N. Y. 10003

CONTENTS

v

PREFACE

NEARLY six years ago I began work on a book that was meant to be a presentation of the theories of the modern ' psychology of the depths ' as these are found scattered through the writings of Dr Jung of Zurich. The title I chose was *The Thought of Carl G. Jung*. In spite of the fact that from then until now I have worked upon psychology and have been most of the time in personal contact with Jung and other members of what is known as the Zurich School, that volume remains unfinished.

For books have an odd manner of going their own way. The father of one may think that he can guide his offspring's steps from the beginning to completion, from conception to maturity; but a book is disconcertingly like a real child. Freud and Jung, and all the host of minor writers upon the phenomena of conscious and unconscious psychic activities, constantly refer to a man who represents the common stuff of human nature. They call him the primitive. Upon him as upon a foundation various savage, barbarous and civilized cultures have grown, diverting his interests and altering his manners; but he himself survives unchanged. The idea that human nature is the same the world around is expressed in popular saws; and all legal systems are based upon the theory that people placed in certain situations will and ought to act in a certain way : without a general uniformity in human nature there could be no law. Of course if human nature were absolutely uniform we should not need law or lawyers. There would be, for lack of contrast, neither good people nor bad, neither sane nor insane, neither intelligent nor stupid; there would be no individuality.

It seemed to me that the logical course in studying human nature was to begin with the part of it that is common to all human beings, just as one would commence the study of botany by learning what is characteristic of all plants—in other words, with the psychology of the primitive. I began therefore to gather the material for a few chapters on the primitive, to serve as an introduction to the study of individual peculiarities as these are treated in that department of modern psychology which interests me most. But here the child of my mind began to live his own life, and to resist my attempts to mould his character. He would be a book on primitive psychology, and nothing else; and after a while I gave in, and let him grow along his own lines and according to his own nature. Now he has reached maturity, and must face the world for himself.

I cannot say that I regret the turn of events. I am more sure than ever that the fundamentals of human nature must be clearly seen before the variations of it can be grasped and understood. All the ways of the primitive are fascinating to me, whether they occur among savage tribes or in cultured Christian homes: they are full of *mana*. Once I realized that I had to write a book about the primitive I threw myself into the work with joy, regretting only that the unavoidable limitations of time and space and my own understanding made it impossible to explore the dark continent of the primitive psyche more deeply. Being practically forced into these investigations in the manner I have described, I had no preconceived notions to expound nor any positions to defend.

One of the greatest satisfactions in writing a book is the way that help and co-operation flow in alike from old friends and from strangers who make themselves friends: this might be used as an illustration of one of the main theses of my book. I most gratefully remember

what has been done for me, without which I could not
have finished my work, by Jung himself, by my wife,
by George French Porter, by Miss Toni Wolff and Harold
McCormick, and by Rowland Hazard.

CHARLES ROBERTS ALDRICH.

INTRODUCTION

By Professor B. MALINOWSKI, Ph.D., D.Sc.

University of London

As the scientific spirit enters more deeply into his studies, the anthropologist becomes ever less of the antiquarian and his discipline loses its museum character ; anthropology is no longer the mere collection of queer implements and outlandish customs. The modern anthropologist tries to discover and establish the laws underlying cultural process. He tries to show how customs, institutions and beliefs are related to one another and to define their place in the culture in which they are found, and by so doing he seeks to understand the structure of human civilizations. But this remains an incomplete study until the relations of culture to man's physical environment, on the one hand, and to man's biological equipment, on the other, have been determined.

In thus trying to place culture in its context of Reality, the anthropologist is brought into ever closer touch with specialists in many other fields. Of these, geography, biology and psychology are, perhaps, the three which are most intimately associated with the science of man proper.

Between the spheres of psychology and anthropology, there is today a No-man's-land. Whether or no this will ever be claimed by a special branch of science, it must for the present be filled by workers in both fields making excursions towards the other's province. Nor should the serious worker in either field ignore or resent such excursions, for they may have much of value for him in indicating new lines of research.

Psychology today is divided into many and opposing schools, each holding its own views and developing its own theories. Until these schools have settled their mutual differences, the anthropologist must consider all of them impartially, without aligning himself with any one. It is possible, even, that anthropological criticism and evaluation of the excursions into the Science of Man made by these various schools will do something towards clarifying the psychological atmosphere. And from the other side, each school may have, not only its special contribution to make to psychology, but also, something of value to offer the anthropologist.

It is with this in mind that we should read Mr Aldrich's book. Mr Aldrich, himself, viewing the subject from the standpoint of the psychologist, turns the tables on Anthropology, when he claims that into the welter of ethnographic facts and observations, order can be brought only by the psychological approach. This is perhaps a slight overstatement *pro domo sua* for the discovery and formulation of sociological principles has already done much to sort out and explain these facts and will yet do much more. But undoubtedly, established psychological principles will have more and more to be taken into consideration in the Science of Man.

Two hypotheses, the existence and activity of a racial unconscious as the fundamental basis of cultural phenomena, and the overwhelming importance of a gregarious instinct in the development of society are presented in this book. Now those acquainted with my own work will realize that, in my opinion, there can be no Racial Unconscious nor indeed any mental phenomena of a collective nature ; and again, that there is no such thing as a Gregarious Instinct, but that in fact, human beings are not in any sense gregarious, nor yet moved by instincts alone. Consequently, when I am prepared to regard this book as most useful and clarifying to my mind, this is not a partisan statement. Very often far greater profit can be derived from a book which moves us to violent disagreement, than from one which elicits lukewarm acquiescence. And in this case, though I am not able to follow Mr Aldrich in the solutions which he propounds, the questions which he raises, and which centre round the two concepts of Racial Unconscious and Gregarious Instinct—these questions are real and they have to be considered and solved by psychology and anthropology in a joint effort.

The book is also of great informative importance to the anthropologist, in that the two principles are not only the author's personal contentions, but form also the foundation of the Zürich School of Analytical Psychology. The contributions of this School cannot be ignored by any anthropologist. And the main concept of this School—Racial Unconscious—challenges anthropological criticism for, though it is put forward as a psychological principle, it is so dependent on cultural evidence that it is perhaps not claiming too much to say that in its final establishment or rejection, the anthropologist will have the last word. Mr Aldrich in bringing this directly into anthropological discussion has rendered a great service to both sciences.

B. MALINOWSKI.

FOREWORD

By Dr C. G. JUNG, *formerly of the University of Zürich*

THE author of this book, who studied analytical psychology in Zürich a few years ago, has asked me for a few introductory words to his work. I follow his request with all the more pleasure, as I was not bored but decidedly delighted by reading his book. Books of this kind are often of a very dry, though learned and useful, character. There are indeed not a few of them, because, together with the discovery of a new empirical psychology, the modern scientific mind has become interested in what were formerly called " Curiosités et superstitions des peuples sauvages," a field formerly left to missionaries, traders, hunters, and geographical and ethnographical explorers. A rich harvest of facts has been gleaned and gathered up in long rows of volumes even more formidable than Sir James Frazer's *Golden Bough* series. As everywhere in the science of the nineteenth century, the collection type of method has prevailed, producing an accumulation of ill-connected and undigested facts, which in the long run could not fail to make a survey almost impossible. Such an ever increasing accumulation, here as well as in other sciences, has hindered the formation of judgment. It is a truism that there are never facts enough, but, on the other hand however, there is only one human brain, which only too easily gets swamped by the boundless flood of material. This happens particularly to the specialist, whose mind is trained to the careful consideration of facts. But when judgment is required the mind must turn away from the impression of the fact and should lift itself to

a higher level, from which a survey is possible. One
might almost say : As a rule the higher standpoint is
not given by the specialized science but by a convergence
of view-points from other scientific realms. Thus the
understanding of primitive psychology would have
remained an almost insoluble task without the assistance
of mythology, folklore, history, and comparative religion.
Sir James Frazer's work is a splendid example of this
combined method. It is rather astonishing that among the
co-operating sciences psychology seems to be lacking.
It was, however, not completely absent. Among the
many who tried to tackle the problems of the primitive
mind, no one has done so without psychology. But the
psychological point of view employed by each investigator
was his own—just as if there were only one psychological
standpoint, viz. the author's own psychology. From
Tylor's point of view, Animism is quite obviously his
individual bias. Lévy-Bruhl measures primitive facts by
means of his extremely rational mind. From his standpoint it appears quite logical that the primitive mind
should be an " état prélogique." Yet the primitive is far
from being illogical, and is just as far from being " ani-
mistic." He is by no means that strange being from
which the civilized man is separated by a gulf that cannot
be bridged. The fundamental difference between them
is not a difference in mental functioning, but rather in the
premises upon which the functioning is based.

The reason why psychology has hitherto yielded so little
assistance to the efforts of the explorer in the vast field
of primitive psychology arises, as a matter of fact, much
less from the natural disinclination of the specialist to
appeal to principles outside his particular domain than
from the fact that a psychology which would be really
helpful simply did not exist. The psychology that is
needed must be a psychology of the complex functions,
i.e. a psychology that does not reduce the complexities
of the mind to their hypothetical elements, which is the
method of experimental or physiological psychology.

The first attempt at a complex psychology was made by Freud, and.his essay on *Totem and Taboo* was one of the first direct contributions of the new psychology to the investigation of the primitive mind. It matters little that his attempt is nothing more than an application of his sex-theory, originally gleaned from morbid minds. His essay nevertheless demonstrates the possibility of a " rapprochement " between psychology and the problem of the primitive mind. Sometime before the work mentioned, I undertook a similar task that eventually led me to the primitive mind, but with a very different method. While Freud's method consisted in the application of an already existing theory, my method was a comparative one. I have reason to believe that the latter yields better results for both sciences. The main reason is, that our new psychology is in no way advanced enough to present a theory of the mind that would have universal application. With modesty we can assert no more than the possession of sound facts and some rules of thumb which might prove useful in any attempt at mastering the problem of the primitive mind.

Mr Aldrich, I observe, has made use of his studies in analytical psychology, to the advantage of his research. His sane and balanced opinions, equally distant from the Charybdis of dry empirical enumeration of facts and the Scylla of deduction from arbitrary premises, owe their life and colour to no small extent to the consideration of analytical psychology. I am sure that the analytical psychologist will welcome Mr Aldrich's book as one of the most vivid and clear presentations of the primitive mind in its relation to civilized psychology. I may also express the hope, that the co-operation of the psychologist will prove its usefulness to all students of primitive psychology who approach their subject from the ethnological standpoint.

C. G. JUNG.

PRIMITIVE MIND
AND MODERN CIVILIZATION

CHAPTER I

THE METHOD

THE common course of perception, psychologists are agreed, proceeds from mass to details. A little serving-maid once came to work for us in Zurich ; on returning home to dinner I noticed that she was dark, slender, and of medium size ; that she was neat and held herself well ; that, in fact, she came nearer to having *chic* than one would expect. This much perception brought a sense of relief, and my attention immediately transferred itself to the dishes that were set before me. Days passed, and other details were perceived—not all at once, but a few at a time or even one at a time, and mostly when they were pointed out to me by my wife, who is far more observant of human features than I am. With such competent guidance I came to see her features one by one : I analysed the general *en masse* impression of pleasurableness. And a further process followed, a synthesis of the perceived details that gave me another mass-impression that went beyond the mass-perception first received of a tidy, presentable medium-sized, dark girl. One afternoon my wife said, ' I wish you would take a look at Paula, and tell me what she looks like to you. She is in your room." I made an excuse of getting a handkerchief. Paula sat sewing in the pale slanting sunshine, her dark head inclined over the golden-yellow antique brocade that spread across her knees and fell in gleaming billows of gold upon the floor beside her. All at once Paula's face seemed strangely familiar. The rounded high forehead, the fine eyebrows, the downcast eyes, the little pointed mouth with the firm little chin beneath it, the nape of the neck, the smooth dark hair gathered to a small knot upon her neck, the slender bare arms—it seemed as though I had known these pure outlines all my life. I went back to the studio and told my wife that Paula looked medieval, like a portrait by one of the Italian primitives. ' She looks like a Madonna,' said my wife. That was it : Paula sewing in the slanting afternoon sunshine, bending meekly over a flood of golden-yellow brocade, might have sat as a model for a painting of the Virgin. That was why it had seemed that I must have known this figure all my life. Paula was enough like the image that was so familiar to me that the sight of her had evoked the image, and none the less surely because I had not been able consciously to recognize the likeness until another person had spoken the revealing word.

From the perception of the mass the observer proceeds to the perception of details ; and from the perception of details he proceeds to the welding of these into a new and different perception of the totality. Because this is the natural way that objects present themselves to our perceiving senses and finally to our critical judgment it would seem that psychology should begin with a presentation of humanity in the mass, of the common elements of human nature, and should proceed afterwards to discuss the factors that differentiate one human being from another. And after the analysis, in turn, the new synthesis should come.

Such a presentation of psychology would begin with the primitive psyche, as we see it manifested in existing savages and peoples of simpler cultures than our own, in children who have not yet put on the veneer of modern civilization, in defectives who are not able to put it on, and in the sick and old from whom the faculties latest acquired are the first to fall away ; it would take up one by one those phenomena that are most widespread, and thus analyse our primitive man or woman. After this, we might try to combine these details into a new synthesis. Thus we should get a juster picture of the primitive than the one usually painted, and in the process the bewildering mass of details found in local savage cultures would be eliminated, or at least arranged in simple classes. The veil of illusion which we project upon the primitive because of our unthinking acceptance of received notions would also be thinned, if not completely lifted.

The reader will observe that I am assuming that there is no difference in kind between our psychic structure and processes and those of the savage and the primitive ; also that the primitive psyche and all its ways survive in the most highly cultured modern man and woman. The evidence in favour of these assumptions will appear later. It is but fair to note that the first assumption is disputed by some authorities.

After a general survey of those modes of behaviour which are usually found among savages, regardless of their racial affiliations and geographical location and the degree of culture they have attained, and an attempt to account for them psychologically, we should have a reasonably fair idea of human nature in general. From this, except that lack of space makes it impossible in this book, we might go on to a study of individual psychology. It is my hope that the present investigation of the primitive will be helpful both to those who wish to understand the modern psychology of the individual, and also to those anthropologists who are not content merely to record the facts of savage life but who wish to interpret the psychological tendencies behind them and their results in the life of the group and the lives of the members composing it.

One sometimes hears it said that we cannot know anything about primitive psychology for the simple reason that really primitive man is extinct, and that no people exist who have no culture. A great authority, Sir James Frazer, declares that the gap between the man of no culture and the lowest existing savage is greater than that which separates the latter from the man of the highest type of modern civilization. But, on purely theoretical grounds, it may be assumed that any psychic element, whether an instinct or a less sharply-defined tendency to action, which is common to all civilized and living savage races was also a characteristic of primitive mankind. This assumption would be fortified if an analogous element appeared in man's cousins, the great apes. If the characteristic under discussion was found to be highly developed among the civilized in comparison with the savage, we should conclude that it was still more rudimentary in the primitive ; while if the reverse was the case we should take it that the given characteristic was stronger in the primitive than in the savage of today. An example of the first class would be the logical, purposeful reasoning, technically known as directed thinking ; and a sample of the second class would be the power of summoning up memory-images with such clearness as to amount to hallucinations. Another example of the first class would be found in the modern man's greater power of intellectually discriminating between two objects both of which call up the same emotional response. Again, the second class is illustrated by the tendency of savages to disregard physical causes in situations evoking strong emotions and to attribute the result to some mystic agency : the death of a fellow member of the group is an example of this. In other words, the difference in culture between the modern civilized man and the savage is sufficient to enable us to judge whether a given tendency is developed and brought to the fore by culture, or whether culture represses it : we can see whether the line of increasing culture means the growth or shrinking of the tendency under discussion. And, in the absence of evidence to the contrary, we are bound to assume that the same cause—culture—operated with like effect all along the line from primitivity to

civilization. The fantasy-pictures of primitive man—
Freud's, for instance—which disregard this simple rule
violate a fundamental law of all reasoning.

If we apply the comparative procedure here indicated
the nature of our difficulty is changed : instead of being
hampered by a lack of material we are appalled by its
vastness. The records of savage customs, religious ideas,
laws, inventions and arts make up a literature which one
man, even if he loved the topic, could hardly read through
in a lifetime. Luckily this literature has been sifted and
classified by scholars such as Tylor and Frazer : within
the compass of the latter's *Golden Bough* series alone there
is ample material for any ambitious anthropological or
psychological theorist to labour upon. Professor Lucien
Lévy-Bruhl, working upon material gathered by others,
has written two fascinating volumes of psychological
deductions as to savage and primitive human nature : it
is hard to overestimate the importance of these books if
one is alive to the value of trial-and-error in scientific
theorizing.

Today we have anthropologists of a new kind, men who
are thoroughly trained in the science of anthropology and
who in addition have lived with savages and studied their
ways at first hand. Among such men the names of
Boas, Seligman, Malinowski and Rivers come to mind.
The tremendous advantage of combining acquaintance
with the literature and intensive training in anthropological science with actual intimate experience of savages
is obvious. Most of the available accounts of savage
ways were written by missionaries, explorers or traders :
they are not the work of trained observers. Usually
the writers did not even speak the language of the tribes
they described, and they were full of prejudices and
preconceived notions. Frequently they describe only the
startling and outlandish details of savage customs, and
omit the more revealing story of the savage's humdrum
daily existence. But such men as those I have named
see and record facts to which the lay writer pays no

attention, or does not perceive at all. In fact, these men themselves often seem to think that this is the greatest, perhaps the sole, advantage of their sharing of the daily life of the natives—the recording of more facts. But no one who has had a training in psychology can fail to note that living among savages has given them something even more important, a sympathy which enables them to understand the meanings that underlie the otherwise incomprehensible ways of people of simpler cultures. When, in addition to their other equipment for their work, such anthropologists have studied psychology their interpretations become truly illuminating. Facts alone are but building-materials of the sciences : it is only after they have been sorted out and related to each other that the structure of a science begins to rise, and the meaning of the facts themselves to be revealed. The meaning of anthropological data can never be understood without the help of psychology, and psychology must always remain vague and fanciful unless it takes into account the solid facts of anthropology. Apart, these two branches of knowledge are like the half-people of the Nigerian folk-story ; united, they make a whole. Malinowski, for instance, writing as an anthropologist has done psychology a great service in showing that the father-complex which, according to orthodox Freudian doctrine, is part of the psychic heritage of every boy and man, cannot be discovered in a society where kinship is reckoned exclusively through the mothers [1] and that the real envy, jealous distrust, and hatred of the youth is directed against the person in authority—here the mother's brother. This shows that the so-called father-complex might better have been termed the authority-complex or the complex against being controlled. It is mere metaphor to speak of the boy's complex against his father, seeing that his rebellion is really directed against the authority for which his father happens in most social organizations to stand. This is exactly parallel to Jung's contention that the

[1] Malinowski, *Sex and Repression in Savage Society.*

constellation of longings which the Freudians call the boy's incest-complex for his mother is a mere metaphor expressing his desire for those things for which the mother is a symbol—childishness, avoidance of labour and pain—which, in turn, is a psychologist's contribution toward an understanding of such anthropological material as initiation and mother- and sister-taboos. A deeper understanding of all human nature comes out of such work as this.

CHAPTER II

SOME PSYCHOLOGICAL DETAILS

As we are to take up a number of primitive and savage
ways in the light of the analytical psychology of Jung
and his co-workers, noting whether similar tendencies
appear in our cultured selves, it is necessary to give a
brief description of some of the tools with which we
shall explore.

The basic concept of the new psychology is that the
mind must be studied as a dynamic whole. The parts of
this whole cannot be studied separately *in vacuo* but must
be examined in action in their relation to one another
and to the whole. Sometimes it finds it convenient to
regard aspects of the psyche one by one; but always
these are treated as parts of the living, acting, ever-
moving organism, as ways in which the psyche manifests
its energy.

This energy is called libido by Freud, Jung, and Adler.
The English psychologists often employ a better word,
interest. A value is any object tangible or intangible,
another person or an idea for instance, upon which the
subject's interest is directed. There is some reason to
suppose that psychic energy and physical energy are really
different manifestations of the same energy. This is
however a very controversial hypothesis. Certainly
psychic and physical changes in the organism often accompany each other; but which is to be regarded as cause
and which as effect is disputed. It is even denied by some
psychologists that either is the cause of the other.

The new *Tiefpsychologie* (for it is important to insist
upon its youth, and that it is far from being a complete

8

science with indisputable conclusions) deals with life and behaviour as manifestations of interest, or libido : it is essentially dynamic, not static. The bases of the new psychology will be much firmer theoretically when we are able to measure libido, as is done with other forms of energy ; but so far this has not been accomplished. Everyone knows that some of his psychic processes are of low potential and not fatiguing, while others are very intense and produce great fatigue ; so that we all recognize that much or little libido may be discharged in the same period of time. We all recognize also that there is an average potential at which psychic energy is consumed in various kinds of activity, so that we are able to estimate what is a fair day's work in terms of time. It is generally considered reasonable for a bookkeeper to work eight hours ; the lawyer's day, when occupied with actual research or writing, is five hours ; and an author doing serious creative work can seldom write more than three hours in a day— his work, after three hours, shows a noticeable deterioration in quality. Thus, in the practical affairs of life, we do measure libido even if this measuring is only approximate. It seems likely, therefore, that the problem of exact measurement is not insoluble.

For the purposes of our discussion libido may be taken in the same way that, in daily life, we use the concept 'energy'. Whether energy has an objective existence or not, whether it is a reality or not, is still a philosophical question. Each man is free to affirm or deny its reality, according to that subjective predilection which determines his philosophical theories. But no one can deny that we use the concept 'energy' as a factor in our thinking and other behaviour : energy has a psychological actuality, a value, for us whether it has objective reality or not. So is it with libido : it is a psychic actuality, and a convenient one. Analytical psychology studies human beings through their behaviour, regarding mind and body as aspects of one entity—not as separate entities in themselves ; and, in order to mark off the field of its investigations from other sciences, it finds it convenient to confine itself chiefly to that aspect of the life-energy which is not the object of bio-chemical or bio-mechanical science ; that is, to the aspects of life-energy manifesting libido, interest, or psychic energy.

CHAPTER III

INSTINCTS AND COMPLEXES

THE United States is a federal republic, composed of states which came together for mutual protection and to enable themselves to work out their own destinies in freedom and security. Before the Constitution was adopted in 1779 each of these states was a sovereignty, governing of its own authority and subordinate to no other government. When the states entered into the Union, they each and all delegated to the new central government certain enumerated powers, and by implication the powers necessary to carry the specified powers into effect. Thus each state surrendered much of its sovereignty to the nation. Each state, in turn, contains subordinate governmental organizations such as counties and townships. The simple units from which all these governments are built up are the citizens ; and in theory all governmental authority and power is derived from them and rests upon their free consent. This means that each citizen renounces absolute freedom of conduct, and submits to a measure of control through various governmental units. Theoretically, the citizen parts with a portion of his freedom to rule himself in the hope of making himself more secure in life, liberty, and the pursuit of happiness.

This delegated energy of government is sovereignty. It is not a formless acquiescence in being governed. Sovereignty is always manifested in a definite organization of government—in organic divisions such as townships, counties, states, and the federal government ; in functions such as law-making, law-interpreting, and law-enforcement ; in weapons such as army, navy, and police. Each of these is really an aspect of one entity, government, manifesting one energy, sovereignty. Sovereignty is not a force : it is, rather, the authority which puts in motion the physical forces of government.

The body politic is healthy when each governmental unit receives and properly employs the amount of sovereignty necessary to carry out its functions. It becomes diseased when any unit is denied the necessary sovereignty, or when it usurps more sovereignty than is rightfully its own.

It will be clear, of course, that I have introduced this illustration—the working of a federal state—in order to draw an analogy between libido and sovereignty. As this analogy is used only suggestively to bring out certain salient features of the human psyche, it must not be carried too far. An objection might be raised that whereas the mind is a natural organism, government is artificial. Whether or no this classification is valid in itself, the objection does not really hold so long as the analogy remains such and is not transformed into argument.

Roughly, then, the psyche may be compared with a federal state. The instincts may be likened to the political states composing the federation. There are many and contradictory definitions of instinct. To the behaviourist an instinctive act is a series of reflexes which are always performed in the same sequence.[1] McDougall finds that an instinct is a hereditary disposition to pay attention to objects of a certain class, to experience a certain emotion in respect to them, and to react to them (or to experience a tendency to do so) in a definite manner.[2] All authorities agree that an instinctive act is common to all members of a given species, or to all males or all females of the species ; that it is hereditary, and does not require to be learnt although its performance may be improved through practice. Since an animal which is not conscious (in the sense in which this term is used in analytical psychology,

---

[1] Watson, *Behaviorism*.
[2] McDougall, *An Introduction to Social Psychology*, 29.

i.e., does not relate its experience to a definite ego) performs instinctive acts, an instinct is primarily a subconscious or unconscious urge. In man such an urge may or may not rise into consciousness. Often, when it does rise, it comes into consciousness in a disguised form.

McDougall does well in emphasizing the element of ' paying attention ' in his definition of instinct. There are certain classes of objects which sometimes fascinate one's interest, willy-nilly, through a mysterious compulsive power that seems to be inherent in them : such is a woman to a man, for example. If there were any uniformity in this fascination it would tend to show that (in this case at least) man is a mechanism which merely reacts to a stimulus reaching him from without. But it is notorious that a man does not react with uniformity even to the same woman in exactly the same environment : the reaction five minutes before sexual intercourse is entirely different from the reaction five minutes afterwards. Therefore, it would seem to the naïve mind, there must be something more involved than mere mechanical reaction : the nature, need, condition, and a host of other details concerning the subject must also be taken into account. So, also, must the entire pattern or configuration of the subject's situation.

Though McDougall does not attribute omnipotence to things to the extent that the behaviourists do, his definition nevertheless errs in that it puts too much weight upon the object, takes too little account of the subject, and is too extraverted. According to McDougall a man could not walk along a street, where pretty women abound, without being in a continuous state of erotic excitement ; he could not pass the windows of the restaurants and food-shops without experiencing a tendency to eat—and this in spite of the fact that he had just stuffed himself to his uttermost capacity, *ad nauseam*.

Jung uses the word instinct very rarely : usually he employs *Naturtrieb*, meaning simply a natural urge. But when he wrote a paper in English entitled *Instinct and the*

Unconscious [1] he took pains to emphasize the subjective elements, treating instinct as a definite organized charge of libido gathered in the unconscious and making itself perceptible as a need or desire. Every man knows from his own experience that he can be in the presence of women or of food without feeling any desire for either, without having any tendency to behave toward them in an instinctive manner, and in fact without paying any conscious attention to them. Conversely, he knows that the entire absence of woman or food does not prevent his thinking about them, sometimes obsessively even. The sexual instinct or the instinct to eat affect him with tremendous force at times, in spite of the fact that his environment contains neither food nor a woman. Clearly, the motive energy of the instinct comes from the subject himself ; and without this libido the object might affect him differently or not at all. Analytical psychology fully recognizes the importance of the object ; but it prefers to concern itself more with the subject.

Jung calls especial attention to the fact that each instinctive act involves a recognition of the situation or the object in respect to which the act is appropriate. As the tendency to perform the act and the ability to do it are hereditary, it is obvious that the recognition involved is also hereditary. That is, the repeated experiences of the race have left each individual with an inherited memory-image of the suitable object of each instinctive activity. As memory is supposed to depend upon the linking-up of cells in the nervous system, this means simply that certain cells link up with each other as part of the process of individual growth, without requiring individual experience. Jung illustrates this by describing the way the Yucca moth deposits its eggs and provides for the nourishment of the larvæ. This moth lives in symbiosis with the Yucca plant ; and in this biological partnership the plant depends upon the moth for fertilization, repaying the services of the moth by furnishing food and a safe

[1] Jung, *Collected Papers on Analytical Psychology*, II.

habitat for the latter's offspring. The plant blooms during but one night in the entire year. On that particular night the moth gathers pollen from one plant, and kneads it into a ball. Then it flies to another plant, cuts open a pistil, lays its eggs inside, and pushes the ball of pollen down upon them. Without this complicated procedure on the moth's part the plant could not reproduce itself ; and without thus using the plant, the eggs of the moth could not hatch and the larvæ survive. Clearly the moth is impelled to lay eggs by a subjective unconscious urge ; and clearly it selects the place to lay them through a hereditary image, an unconscious racial memory.

Analytical psychology is content to note and to use certain elements of the instinct, without trying to make an immutable hard-and-fast definition. Those elements which interest us most are the facts that the instinctive urge comes from the unconscious ; that it manifests itself as an impulse or need to do a definite act to a definite object, often regardless of whether the object is present or not ; that the proper object is recognized through an inherited memory-image ; and that the whole process and all the elements involved in it are collective, racial, and not individual. This last is none the less true in spite of the fact that each instinctive act is always performed by individuals.

Regarding the human psyche as a polity, it is obvious that its welfare depends upon a system of checks and balances. Instincts conflict, desire opposes desire. Hospitals, asylums and prisons are provided by society to take care of persons who allow any one instinct to usurp too much sovereignty ; and nature has her own penalties for those who allow themselves to become onesided through devoting too much libido to one instinct. A natural punishment also follows the refusal to allow any instinct to exercise the limited sovereignty that is its right under the psychic constitution.

Complexes are governmental organizations in the psyche somewhat analogous to voluntary associations of citizens in the state. A complex is an association of psychic elements—sensations, intuitions, thoughts, feelings, tendencies to action, or some of these ; and it may be either conscious or unconscious, or partly conscious and partly unconscious. Some of our complexes are collective : that is, they are handed to us ready-made by our social environment. The home-and-mother complex is an example. Others we build up for ourselves, usually employing material furnished us by society. Thus a girl may be taught that sex is evil and disgusting, and later some man may cause her a severe psychic shock by making sexual advances to her. Often this is followed by rationalization, or alibi-thinking, and projection on her part : she assures herself, ' There is no sexuality in me—the fact that I was so terribly upset proves there is none. But Mother was right : there is a beast, a dreadful beast, in every man. All men are disgusting and hateful.' Here may be the beginnings of a complex that will affect her whole later life.

One famous complex is the father-complex, which Malinowski's researches in Melanesia enable us to see as a resistance to being made to work, disciplined, tamed— the youthful animal's resistance against culture, in short. In most societies the father stands for these distasteful necessities ; but among the Trobriand Islanders, where descent is reckoned exclusively through the mother, it is the mother's brother who is used as the symbol. Here the boy has an uncle-complex, not a father-complex.[1] Jung, as has been mentioned, has shown that the equally noted mother-complex is really the libido in regression from life and its difficulties toward the childishness for which the mother is the symbol. The man who has a mother-complex longs to be his majesty the baby, a petted irresponsible despot. This seems to be an infantile form of the will-to-power. It might be said that the father-complex and the mother-complex are different aspects of the same tendency : in the former the symbol of duty is hated ; in the latter the symbol of escape from duty is loved.

[1] Bronislaw Malinowski, *Sex and Repression in Savage Society*.

The complex may be useful in the psychic common-wealth. It may give a definite orientation to a life which, without it, might be spent in aimless drifting. Complexes of this character, embracing the whole point of view toward life, are called attitudes. Like a voluntary organization of citizens banded together to accomplish something which the regular government neglects or does inefficiently, the complex can carry on work which the hereditary units of the psyche are not organized to do easily. But just as voluntary organizations of citizens often usurp powers which are not rightfully theirs, and proceed to undermine and endanger all constitutional government, so the complex often drains the energy of normal psychic functions and upsets the healthy balance of the psyche. We read more in the papers about abnormal and anti-social organizations than we do about those which are quietly carrying on constructive work ; and similarly it is those complexes which are anti-biological, which work for destruction, that strike our attention most forcibly.

The healthy psyche is the balanced, evenly developed psyche ; no libido-organization can absorb too much psychic energy without upsetting the psychic balance ; and no rightfully constituted libido-organization can be denied its functioning without crippling the entire psyche. This is especially true of those great expressions of energy, the fundamental instincts or urges, which have been built into our very psychic structure by the immemorial habits of the race. Human life is not limited to the expression of any single instinct ; it expresses them all ; all are indispensable and hence equal in importance. Neverthe-less, when we come to examine some of the facts of the lives of savages, we shall find it hard to avoid the con-clusion that there is one urge to which all the others are subordinated—one urge that is easily first among equals. It is precisely this one which is denied due expression among ourselves. We suffer from this self-mutilation.

B

CHAPTER IV

UNCONSCIOUS AND CONSCIOUS

CONSCIOUSNESS, as this term is used in analytical psychology, means more than that sensitivity which some biologists regard as the distinctive characteristic of animal protoplasm. It means more than awareness of an object. Animals consisting of a single cell move toward food and away from irritating substances. These two responses are simple illustrations of the positive and negative interest of all animals, of libido directed toward the object and libido directed away from the object; but they do not involve consciousness. Being awake is not the same as being conscious; for one may be awake and still have an incomplete realization of what is going on. A man may be walking across the street sunk in his own thoughts, and an automobile may be approaching within his field of vision; yet he may not be conscious of the danger. The eyes report the approach of the automobile; but, because of his preoccupation, the pedestrian does not relate the moving vehicle to himself. He is awake; he sees the object; but he is not conscious in respect to it. If he were conscious he would grasp the relation of his perception (of the automobile) to himself. The perception is a psychic content of the subject, but unless that psychic content is brought into relation with the ego there is no full consciousness. The essential element in a definition of consciousness is then the relation by the ego of psychic contents to itself.[1] The ego is the centre of consciousness.

Thus consciousness involves awareness of the subject

---

[1] Jung, *Psychological Types*, 535.

as well as awareness of the object. It necessarily includes self-consciousness.

One of the soundest of psychologists and sanest of philosophers, William James, in the famous lectures that he delivered in 1902–1903 upon *The Varieties of Religious Experience*, expressed his conviction that the most important discovery in the field of psychology during the preceding quarter of a century was that of the ' subliminal field ' and its influence upon what goes on in consciousness. Later discoveries have amply justified his judgment. The explorations of this field have made it possible to find the causes of many obscure nervous troubles and, for the first time in history, to cure a large proportion of them ; they have illuminated the workings of the healthy psyche as well as the diseased ; they have suggested new aims in education ; and they have humanized such studies as law, mythology, anthropology, philosophy, religion, and ethics. Morality, for instance, in the past has rested upon expediency, conventionality, or supernatural authority ; and the attempts to build a rational basis for it have resulted in peculiarly lifeless ethical systems ; but there is reason to hope that modern science, in revealing to man his own nature, will show us a new morality resting upon firmer foundations. Doubtless we shall have to be modest in our demands upon the coming scientific morality : there is no indication at present that it will operate as a general policy of insurance covering the repair and maintenance of hypothetical souls in a hypothetical future life ; but we can reasonably expect that it will aid the individual and society to be healthy, efficient and happy in the life of the present. Most of the sciences continually approach the truth about things ; psychology is striving toward the truth about ourselves ; and from the two kinds of truth we are learning facts that will help us in the conduct of life. But so far we know only a small fraction of human nature, much of which is incomprehensible and aimless so long as our psychological knowledge is limited to conscious manifestations.

The earlier investigators of the hidden reality called this the subliminal field, or the subconscious. Either term is far more apt than the unconscious. A lump of clay is truly unconscious ; but the subconscious is continually alert, aware, paying attention. Not only this, but the attention, the awareness, is not of objects alone : it is definitely of the subject also, and of the relation between subject and psychic contents. So here is a paradox, an absurdity even. What is called the ' unconscious ' has an awareness equivalent to consciousness—the only difference being that it is not related to the conscious ego— and hence, by definition, the consciousness of the unconscious is not conscious at all. Such foolishness would be avoided if we had kept to the words subconscious and subliminal. It is at least comprehensible to assert that there is a subliminal consciousness.

All psychic contents are unconscious, except those which at the present moment are conscious. Stating the matter thus, it is at once evident that the contents of consciousness are few indeed in comparison with the contents of the unconscious. The psyche is often compared with an iceberg, of which one-tenth is visible and nine-tenths are below the surface of the sea. The contents of the unconscious are doubtless many thousand times greater than the contents of consciousness. Consciousness plays like a searchlight upon an exceedingly small portion of the psychic field that it can reach at all : where its illumination falls is the present moment of one's conscious life, even though it falls upon memories of the past or dreams of the future.

The theory of the unconscious mind has been elaborated and the phenomena in which it is based have been investigated in a systematic and scientific manner only during the last half century. But though as a scientific theory it is so new, some inkling of the truth can be found both in the common lore of peoples and in the works of artists and philosophers throughout the ages. It may not be amiss to quote by way of introduction from one of the earliest of these. Plato speaks of ' the wild beast in our nature, gorged with meat and drink ' which when we are asleep ' starts up and walks about naked, and surfeits at his will ; and there is no conceivable folly or crime—not excepting incest or parricide—of which such a nature may not be guilty. . . . In all of us, even in good men, there is such a latent wild beast nature which peers out in sleep.'

It is to Freud that we owe the re-discovery of the latent wild beast nature through the study of dreams. Freud dealt almost exclusively with pathological cases, in which the illness involved the forgetting—generally by the forcible pushing out of consciousness called repression—of thoughts and memories arising from personal experience which could not be retained in consciousness without causing distress. Shameful desires, humiliating experiences, unrealized hopes, and duties evaded, all are likely to be banished from consciousness. These, along with perceptions and other psychic contents of so little intensity that they have never registered in consciousness at all or else have faded away, make up the unconscious to which Freud has devoted his great genius. These are all based upon personal experience and hence this part of the subliminal field is known as the ' personal unconscious.'

Jung has attempted to investigate the catacombs which lie beneath the cellars of the personal unconscious. We human beings are psychically like buildings. The house of consciousness is built above ground, in the free air and the sunshine ; each of us sees his house from within, and his neighbours' houses from the outside. Beneath each house is its own cellar, the personal unconscious, where many things are stored so as to be easily accessible and other articles are so well hidden that it takes a special technique to find them and bring them upstairs. In each cellar there is a trap door that leads down into a subterranean labyrinth, which is no individual's property but underlies all the houses. Here all is incredibly ancient—how ancient we are about to see—and all is the common heritage of our race. Jung calls this, in order to distinguish it from the ephemeral personal unconscious, the collective unconscious. The common structure of the psyche is here, *in esse* and *in posse*. All those habits of our human and pre-human ancestors which have persisted so long as to mould the configuration of the psyche belong to the collective unconscious. So, too, do those purely human responses to given situations which have occurred so often in the history of the human race that engrams, imprints, have been left upon the psychic structure—making the race-habitual response the path of least resistance ; and insuring that the response will occur unless blocked by the conscious processes or by a stronger unconscious tendency. Here again, as with the instincts, a hereditary recognition of the situation is involved, an unconscious hereditary image—an archetype of behaviour in an archetypal situation.

The distinction between the personal unconscious and the collective unconscious may be made clearer by illustration. We periodically desire food, the desire for food being the form in which the unconscious need for food rises into consciousness. But eating is not an individual habit, and hunger has nothing individual about it except that we feel it for ourselves and not for others ; these are common to all humanity and, so far as we have any means of knowing, to all our pre-human animal ancestors ; they are collective. On the other hand, Dr Rivers noted that he could remember all of a house in which he lived when a young child except a certain part ; and he concluded that some disagreeable experience must have taken place in that part of the house, and, when this was repressed from memory, the memory of the environment (which might have recalled the disagreeable episode) went along with it. This was a purely personal experience of Dr Rivers', and the memory of it went to swell his personal unconscious.

In educating nervous people back to health it is often important to explore the personal unconscious. But just because it is personal, relating to one subject's experience only, it has little to do with what is common to all human nature. For that reason we shall call rather upon the collective unconscious to furnish explanations of those institutions and ideas which anthropology shows us are common to whole races or to many peoples of simple culture. Here we are not interested in individual men, but in man.

CHAPTER V

TIME AND THE PSYCHE

It is relevant to glance briefly at the periods of time that have gone into that process of unfolding from within (literally translated by the single word ' evolution ') through which man has passed. Here one must remember that man, in common with every living creature upon the earth is a growth, an accretion, a structure reared upon immemorial foundations. Evolution buries the past, compressing and distorting it sometimes, rather than abolishes it : in fact, by burying the past it preserves it. I have seen wooden houses in Constantinople upon stone foundations that seemed disproportionately firm and strong ; and a closer examination has revealed the fact that this foundation was itself a building, buried by the street-litter of centuries until only the tops of the ancient walls were visible. So is it with the modern rational mind : it is a recent and somewhat flimsy addition built on top of a buried pyramid that reaches down, ever broader, firmer, more changeless, into an unknown antiquity. The medieval psyche shows somewhat in all of us, and so does the primitive ; but below that is a man more ancient than even the primitive. Below the oldest aboriginal man come the ape-like ancestors ; then animal forms that endured for æons on the land ; then fish ; and so on down, to an antiquity at which we can only guess, until the simple one-celled organisms, the protozoa, were the only living animals on earth.

It is well to get some idea of the rate at which the ocean of time has laid down these accretions :

An individual man reaches full physical manhood in

about twenty years, and full psychical manhood in about twenty-five years. Calling fifty years a full lifetime will give us a convenient measuring-rod.

In reviewing the psychic development of the race, we notice first that modern science, and the use of purposeful, willed, conscious, directed thinking, have developed and spread side by side. Science is the objective result of the subjective process of directed thinking, when such thinking or reasoning proceeds from facts that have been ascertained from actual observation.

Jung says that if we go further back into history than the Schoolmen, we shall find that which we call science dissolved into an indistinct cloud. The modern culture-creating mind is incessantly occupied in stripping off all subjectivity from experience. It would be absurd if we were to assume that we are more intelligent than the ancients. Our materials for knowledge have increased, but not our intellectual capacity. Our knowledge has increased, but not our wisdom. The main focus of our interest is transferred wholly to material reality. But the ancients focussed their interest upon myth ; they grasped the world of objects by intuition, and expressed it by fantasy. So ' we see the antique spirit create, not science, but mythology and art.' [1] Other writers, such as Boas and Goldenweiser, are also convinced that the modern man has not improved his capacity for thinking beyond that of the ancients : they even go further, and assert that people of the lowest existing cultures have as much intellectual ability as we have.

So this modern science of ours, which has changed the whole face of the earth for us, is not to be taken as the result of our superior powers, but as the result of a change of attitude on our part. This change consists in turning the attention from the subjective to the objective, from creating art and myth to discriminating objects one from another by actual observation and then classifying them conceptually, and finally to classifying the concepts them-

[1] Jung, *Psychology of the Unconscious.*

selves so as to form further concepts. This process has inevitably emphasized the importance of material things at the expense of the things of the spirit, such as myth, religion, and art, at least in its beginnings ; for the interest employed in conquering our material environment has had to be withdrawn from other aims.

Civilization can hardly be attributed to our ancestors of Northern Europe of one thousand years ago. There were here and there instances of city-life, with the amenities and developed social organization possible only in a compact, permanent community ; but these were exceptional. Most of the population was scattered over the land and through the forests, defending their lives with their own muscles and weapons, and inhabiting rude hovels, or even caves and holes dug in hillsides. They were barbarians in their mode of living, and intellectually the vast majority of the inhabitants of Europe are barbarians still.

Written history takes us back only about five thousand years. Two hundred generations of lives, each twenty-five years long, suffice to cover the period that is covered by recorded history—and most of this period is but imperfectly recorded, at that.

Homo Sapiens has existed some twenty thousand or thirty thousand years.

But for half a million years man has been Man, walking erect, with the same structures of bones and muscles, with the same organs and presumably with almost the same psyche, that we have today. He has had, during all this period, ten fingers ; and if those fingers were not as agile and delicate instruments as those of the modern surgeon, musician, or typist we must attribute this to the fact that he never trained them to these special uses. He had a brain and nervous system also ; but before assuming that these were inferior to our own we must remember that no child comes into the world capable of fine sense-discriminations or able to think. These psychic functions must be acquired. He must be especially forced by parents and teachers if he is to learn to think with any persistence or accuracy. It may well be that the man of half a million years ago had an intellect potentially as good as our own. But probably there was nothing in his environment to start him on the way to conscious reasoning : for this was before the Ice Age forced him to struggle for his food, and to co-operate with his fellows more closely than had ever yet been necessary. His instincts, born with him, each accompanied by a characteristic emotion, and by an inherited memory-image of the objective situation in which it was appropriate for the instinct to take possession of him, were quite enough. Thinking would perhaps have been a superfluity, a sad gift ; and if it had led him to weighing choices, to hesitation and indecision (as it does us) it might have caused the extermination of the human race. For if food was abundant in the Pliocene times, so also were dangerous animals with which man, naked and unarmed, could not cope ; and when one of these approached it was no time to hesitate.

The separate line of human ancestry running back to some form from which both apes and man descended is so long, about two million years, that the figures already given seem small in comparison. Man is not descended from any known form of ape, either living or fossil. But that man and ape had a common ancestor is an undoubted fact.

To sum up these figures as to antiquity of man, and the length of time it has taken him to reach his present physical and psychic development, let us take an individual life of fifty years as the unit of measurement. On this basis, six lives is the period during which a new form of thinking, which Jung calls *directed* thinking, has come into general use, and has created science ; before this only occasional gleams of directed thinking flash out here and there, at rare intervals, among mathematicians and philosophers. And, in the case of the philosophers, this directed thinking was far from pure : it was based upon primordial images of an intuitive and poetical character, and much of it was in the nature of special pleading, as Dewey has shown, designed to bolster up the existing social order by offering intricate rationalizing in place of a dying faith in religion. So we can say that practically all of the intellectual side of our present civilization, based upon the observation of facts and directed thinking, all our scientific knowledge of the world in which we live, and all the concrete results of this knowledge, has been achieved in the space of six human lives. Six lives ago the affairs of this world were carried on by supernatural powers, by gods, devils, fairies, and witches ; and the concept of law-regulated natural processes had little influence upon the people's thought. We cannot suppose that such a brief period of time had sufficed to bring about any evolutionary changes or developments in the human psyche. All we can say is that the period of six lives has developed a change of attitude, a turning of interest into new channels, and consequently the discovery of new values.

Neither have we any reason to think that the period that civilization has existed in Northern Europe, about twenty lives long, can have brought forth any new psychic faculties. Or the period of partly recorded history, which covers some one hundred lives.

For mankind has had so slow a growth that these periods are almost inconsiderable. *Homo Sapiens* has lasted five hundred times fifty years, and Man himself ten thousand times as long. Since we and the apes parted company, and man started his own family tree, the term of fifty years has passed forty thousand times.

By rights, in order to picture as completely as possible the ratio that modern civilization bears to all the growth and evolution that went before it, we should go into our animal ancestry : for every human being in his physical growth traces his way up from the single-celled protozoa. This is guessed to have been about one hundred million years in the making, or two million times fifty years. And, since physical organs, physical functions, and psychic functions are all concomitants, it is a reasonable hypothesis to assume that we probably contain in our present psychic structure the psychic elements of all our ancestors, including those that came before the common progenitor of man and apes. But the lineage of our own race gives figures that are stupendous enough. To point out that the ratio of duration of our somewhat over-praised modern civilization is to our separate human lineage as 1 to 6666 seems quite sufficient.

Or (to put the matter still more graphically) let us suppose that a man fifty years old and six feet tall is standing beside a bush six feet high. The fifty years that have elapsed since the man was born represent all of his personally-acquired psychic equipment, both that which is accessible to consciousness and that which has fallen or been repressed into unconsciousness. Pictorially the length of this personal experience may be represented by his own height, and that of the tree beside him, six feet, while the experience of the race and the individual's hereditary psychic equipment may be represented by the root of the tree. The hidden root nourishes the tree. The hidden psychic structure of the race supports and supplies with energy the personality of the man, as this has been manifested during his brief fifty years of personal existence —one-third of which has been spent unconscious in sleep, by the way. If, in our pictorial representation, the root of the tree is proportional in length to this collective, racial psychic structure of the man, then this root penetrates the earth for eleven miles and still is human. It goes down into unexplored strata of antiquity for more than forty-five miles before it reaches the lost ancestor of apes and man. In all, it descends half-way to the centre of the earth, more than two thousand miles.

It is a well-known psychological law that the oftener an action is performed, the easier and the less conscious it becomes, and the greater is the tendency to repeat it.

Conversely, the more frequently the act is done, the more difficult is it to avoid. This is the law of *habit*, and it applies both to the individual and to the race. Now since so little of the life of the race has been passed under civilized conditions—that is, taking the word civilized broadly and literally as ' dwelling in cities '—it is clear that the race-habits developed during man's long infancy must be biologically and psychologically more vital and basic in the race than those which have cropped up during the last two, six, or one hundred lives. Habit is more than second-nature : it is nature. Therefore whatever is vital and basic in the race itself, is vital and basic in each individual member of the race. And this is true in spite of the fact that no two individuals ever put exactly the same interest upon the same *conscious* values—a fact that frequently misleads us into thinking that Jones and Smith are very different from each other all the way through, whereas they differ only in consciousness and in the masks they show to society.

The analytical-psychologist contends that just as we find the physical evolution of man from protozoa to *Homo Sapiens* recapitulated in the prenatal development of each individual, so the psychical development of the human race is lived through by each individual in infancy and childhood.

This condensation of vast periods of early racial evolution into such brief periods of the individual's recapitulatory development is probably due to the law of habit : the processes of the nine prenatal months have been carried through so often in the life of the race that they can be speeded up in the individual. Later-acquired powers, like directed thinking, require a greater proportion of the individual lifetime to reach maturity. New ways of behaviour, new habits, are not so ' natural ' as old ones.

CHAPTER VI

THE PRIMITIVE PSYCHE

It is very difficult to distinguish the character attributed by some students to primordial man, sometimes picturesquely called the Caveman, from that of our old acquaintance, the Devil. Not only is he the first murderer and (according to Freud) the original parricide, as well as the inspirer of crime and what look like cases of demoniacal possession, a lover of cruelty for its own sake, and totally devoid of any virtue whatever, but even his fondness for practical jokes (usually of an unpleasant nature) and his natural stupidity are the same as that of the devil of legend and folk-stories.

Ernest Jones, a very able exponent of the Freudian psychology, has written,[1] 'The pleasure-principle represents the primary original form, and is characteristic of the earliest stages of human development, both in the individual and in the race. . . . Its main attribute is a never-ceasing demand for immediate gratification of various desires of a distinctly lowly order, and literally at any cost. It is thus exquisitely egocentric, selfish, personal, anti-social.' The Caveman gives himself up unrestrainedly to the pleasure-principle.

Miss Barbara Low[2] tells us that the unconscious is perpetually leaking through into consciousness, where ' It may manifest itself in direct form in such states as insanity, delirium, dream, trance ; in the actions regarded as criminal, intense, uncontrollable, murderous anger,

---

[1] Ernest Jones, *Papers on Psycho-Analysis*, 3.
[2] B. Low, *Psycho-Analysis*.

31

mysterious, intuitive cunning, obscene curiosity, unveiled exhibitionism.'

So far as Freud himself is concerned, his position in regard to primitive man is not entirely clear. During most of his writing career he went upon the theory that the unconscious consists entirely of buried personal material, and it is only recently that he has come around to the view that beneath this personal unconsciousness lies the collective unconscious. According to his earlier view, derived mostly from the study of psychic abnormalities, the unconscious (the personal unconscious, that is) is generally a trouble-maker. Not, perhaps, in and of itself, but because some of its contents come into conflict with consciousness : there may be painful and humiliating memories that have been forcibly pushed down into forgetfulness, or shameful desires that have met the same treatment. They have been repressed, these ' incompatible ' elements ; but they remain alive none the less, gathering energy to themselves, and striving to break into expression. Given a suitable occasion, and they do break forth in a symptomatic form. And the result is abnormal nervousness (a neurosis), if not something worse.

All this is perfectly understandable, and doubtless true. But it seems to have fixed a bad reputation upon the whole personal unconscious. So when Freud, stimulated by the work of Wundt and by Jung's *Psychology of the Unconscious* (as he himself tells us [1]) turned his attention to racial psychology, he carried over his judgment of the personal unconscious—that it is a maker of disease, a storehouse of incestuous and parricidal fantasies—to the entire history, social as well as psychological, of the race. In that most fascinating book, *Totem and Taboo*, Freud has sought to link up primitive customs and religious rites of atonement and communion with the hatred of the son for the father—a hatred which according to him arises from the son's desire to possess the mother sexually. So far as it goes, there is certainly at least a metaphorical

[1] Freud, *Totem and Taboo*, 1.

connection here. But the implication is that these items comprise the most important part of our psychic inheritance, if not all of it. By thus dwelling upon the Original Sin, which Freud interprets to have been parricide committed in order to have incestuous intercourse with the mother and sisters, Freud's own book does nothing to incline us to be at all proud of our ancestors.

Freud believes that the earliest form of human society was the family, consisting of one adult male and such females as he was able to gather around him, along with their offspring. The Old Man drove his sons out as soon as they began to show interest in the women and girls. This theory derives from Darwin, who supposed that early mankind lived very much as do the great apes, the gorilla, orang-utan and the chimpanzee. How these jealous and ferocious ancient Old Men ever united their groups, so as to form larger societies, is not explained and is difficult to imagine. Furthermore, it has lately been discovered that adult gorillas with their mates and offspring, sometimes go about in bands.[1]

One dissimilarity between the apes and man has been overlooked in formulating this hypothesis : the apes, by reason of the fact that they can travel rapidly through the trees, have little to fear from the great cats, and nothing to fear from dangerous beasts who cannot mount into trees at all ; and hence there is no apparent need for them to unite into groups. But mandrills, and other baboons, living upon the surface of the ground, are gregarious. They have to be, in order to defend themselves against other animals. Yet the mandrill is fleeter than man, can run up rocks that naked man cannot climb, has natural weapons that man lacks, and is far more powerful than man. If the mandrill needs to be gregarious in order to survive, then *a fortiori* we may be sure that his physically inferior relative, man, needed it even more. It would therefore seem certain that our ancestors must have been gregarious for at least as long a period as they have had

---

[1] B. Burbridge, *Gorilla.*

C

approximately the same physical structure that we have now : that is, for so long as they walked erect. In fact, the growth of the gregarious instinct could not have come later than learning to live upon the surface of the ground—the transferring of interest from arboreal locomotion to walking would have been possible only if our ancestors were already gregarious. If this be true, then it is likely that the family arose within the homogeneous troop : the gregarious group probably came first, and families were organized within it. In this theory—which I believe to be true—there is no room for the terrible Old Man, for the incestuous longings of his sons who saw no woman except the mates of their father, or for the Original Sin whereby the sons made away with the father.

But, be this as it may, the evil reputation of our ancestors—with all the unconscious theological suggestions that cling to the Freudian mythology, such as the implied origin of mankind from a single family, the original sin, the brothers taking their sisters to wife, and perhaps also a hint that the nearer man is to the animal the further he is from God—has become firmly fixed in the popular mind. Literature shows this, as in the following example [1] :

> I am, they say, a darkling pool
> Where huge and cunning lurks a fool
> Childish and monstrous, untaught of time ;
> Still wallowing in primeval slime.
> All powerful he with fang and claw
> To fill his red capacious maw
> And not a thousand thousand years
> Have eased his belly, stilled his fears.
> But ever with dim, consuming fire
> Swirl the slow eddies of desire
> About his sprawling limbs and lull
> The torments of his brutish skull.
> He is most merciless, lone and proud,
> There in the scaly darkness bowed,
> And sleeps, and eats, and lusts, and cries,
> And never lives, and never dies.

---

[1] Barrington Gates, *Abnormal Psychology*, in *London Mercury*, June 1921.

Such was the character of our ancestors, according to the Freudian assumption. And such is the oldest, most persistent and most vital part of the nature of each civilized man and woman of today, by the same theory ; while children, far from being the innocent angels that humanity has so long mistaken them to be, are little monsters of viciousness and perversity. This is good literary material : it is picturesque, exciting to the imagination. But—is it the truth ?

The question has a good deal of practical importance ; for it involves a problem that has to do with the here and now, with the business of living our daily lives, and not only with the speculations concerning the dim antiquity of the race. Is it true that fundamentally we are evil, obscenely, blood-thirstily evil, through and through ? If so, then the deepest layers of the unconscious contain an alien demon who lies hidden below the floor of our brightly-lighted, orderly, and civilized consciousness, a devil that is eternally the enemy of ourselves and all the values we most cherish, and who must continually be fought. Somewhere between this demon-ancestor of ours, and ourselves, there must have been a great break or jump in the evolutionary process, and an ethical element opposed to self-interest as well as to immediate sensual self-gratification must have been injected. Thomas Huxley was mightily puzzled to account for the appearance of altruism and self-sacrifice among mankind ; and even today the French sociologists, with Professor Lucien Lévy-Bruhl at their head, maintain that the mental processes of peoples of low cultures must be radically different *in kind* from those of the civilized white man. The great break in the evolutionary process (if it ever occurred) in respect to reason, the putting away of superstition, and in perceiving natural phenomena began about three hundred years ago ; though admittedly there might have been some manifestations of altruism and social virtues even earlier. Such a theory is difficult to swallow. Even though it represents mankind as day by day, in every way, getting better and better, one cannot overlook the fact that it goes counter to commonsense, and needs a good deal of evidence to prove it. This has not so far been offered.

Jung and Freud agree that our psychic structures and tendencies are chiefly determined by inheritance, and that our ancestors—primitive, primordial and pre-human—live and work within us all. If the ancestral element is as immoral as the Freudians would have us believe, then we are indeed children of the pit by inheritance. Our morals are nothing but recent, and therefore insecure, artificial additions to our hereditary structure.

It is only recently that it has dawned upon students that there is a morality in nature, and that every enduring relationship between living organisms involves a moral element. W. Trotter has expressed this modern view in these words :

' If we now assume that gregariousness may be regarded as a fundamental quality of man, it remains to discuss the effects we may have expected it to produce upon the structure of his mind. . . . What will be done here . . . will be to mention a few representative writers who have dealt with the subject, and to give in a summary way the characteristic features of their exposition.

' As far as I am aware, the first person to point out any of the less obvious biological significance of gregariousness was Professor Karl Pearson.

' He (Pearson) called attention to the enlargement of the selective unit affected by the appearance of gregariousness, and to the fact that therefore within the group the action of natural selection becomes modified. This conception had, as is well known, escaped the insight of Haeckel, of Spencer, and of Huxley ; and Pearson showed into what confusions in their treatment of the problem of society these three had been led by the oversight. For example may be mentioned the famous antithesis of the " cosmical " and the " ethical " processes expounded by Huxley's Romanes Lectures. It was quite definitely indicated by Pearson that the so-called ethical process, the appearance, that is to say, of altruism, is to be regarded as a directly instinctive product of gregariousness, and as natural, therefore, as any other instinct.' [1]

[1] W. Trotter, *Instincts of the Herd in Peace and War*, 25–26.

If one considers the long infancy of human children, it is hard to avoid noticing that they need care and protection for a period that seems out of proportion to the comparatively short infancies of most of the other animals ; and if they need it in order to survive, the fact of survival shows that they have received it. But care and tenderness and protection are not afforded by stocks and stones : it is humanity itself that is tender to its young. We lose ourselves in materialistic philosophy if we think of existence simply in terms of competition. It is certain that the ' competition for existence ' has had much less to do with the survival of the most successful animal, man, than the co-operation for existence has accomplished. Man, as a unit in society, has the society of his fellows as the supreme factor of his environment ; and it is his adaptation to society that makes for a secure and happy life—not his adaptation to freezing weather, wolves and great cats. All that is past for the more civilized races : and except in American cities so long as they do not murder each other at the behests of their rulers, men are reasonably safe from being murdered at all.

That there is an individual morality, just as there is an individual consciousness, must be kept in mind : what is one man's meat is another man's poison. But here we are not discussing individual morality. We are trying to decide whether there is a morality in nature, and if so of what it consists. Besides individual conscious morality there is a collective conscious morality, which is purely conventional, varying according to the stage of culture, the race, the times, the locality, the religious sect, the philosophical theory, even according to the profession or trade to which one happens to belong. What is moral according to the conventions of one group may be hideously immoral according to the conventions of another group : the ancient Greek attitude toward homosexuality is a good example. The collective conscious morality is a matter of the passing fashion : it is really not being moral at all to be in the ethical mode that happens to prevail where one lives, for the same person who is a Quaker merely by chance would have been a head-hunter and cannibal (also by chance) if he had been born and reared in another environment.

But there seems to be one kind of conduct concerning which there is a morality in Nature—and this is the matter of co-operation, of paying one's way in life by giving services for services received. This is not collective conscious morality, but *collective unconscious* morality : it is bio-morality, inherent in the laws of life. The earthworm cultivates the soil for the plants on which it feeds, even plants co-operate. Existence and progress in development are made possible by co-operation ; and, as Reinheimer shows, each act of co-operation involves self-restraint and self-sacrifice, actual creative work, on the part of the partners. The higher up one looks in the evolutionary scale the more intricate, extensive, and vitally important this natural social urge is seen to be. In man it is beyond all imagination : for not only does man live in symbiosis with many plants and animals, which he protects, breeds, and uses, but the intricacy of his relations with his fellow men is endless. No human being even produces everything that he uses—no civilized human being produces one in a thousand of the articles that he employs.

Nevertheless, the greater part of our co-operating together is blind. We obey an inner impulse, and the pressure that others put upon us. Our social instinct of co-operation is still, with most of us, part of our collective unconscious. Where, in a few highly developed men and women, this bio-moral urge has been raised to full consciousness and is given a place in living commensurate with its importance, we see the finest and most valuable type of individual morality. So we may leave this discussion by noting that, whatever else may be right, virtuous, or good, there is one rule that Nature has made valid among plants, animals, and men ; and that is, ' Help one another.'

CHAPTER VII

CONCERNING SAVAGES

IF order is ever to be brought into the wilderness of facts that have been accumulated concerning savages, it will have to come, I am convinced, through psychological classification of their habits and customs. These habits and customs themselves are too various to permit a purely descriptive classification. But psychology furnishes classifying concepts that serve to relate phenomena of the most disparate objective appearances. Thus the Christian goes to communion, some savages eat the heart of a slain enemy, a lover gently bites his beloved, a totemite kills and eats his totemic animal : all these acts, taken objectively and descriptively, seem entirely separate and unrelated. Yet psychologically they are closely allied ; for through them all runs the idea of assimilating into oneself the desired qualities of the loved, admired or feared one, the seeking for a mystical union, for atonement.

Astonishingly little has been achieved in this field, in spite of the sincere and laborious efforts of such scholars as Wundt, Durkheim, and Lévy-Bruhl. One great difficulty seems to lie in a lack of definiteness in the terms that must be used : how translate into psychological language the actions of the savage, when no two schools of psychology agree as to the terminology of their own science ? Take the psychological term ' thinking ' : to the Zurich school this means reasoning ; to the Behaviourist it means a special form of the speech-habit ; to others it includes the mere stringing together of images, such as ' Rabbit, fur, fur coat, cold, winter, skating.'

Moreover, the terms used in describing the actualities

of savage life, as they are found in the books, are frequently woeful misfits. Most of the accounts we possess were written by missionaries, traders, explorers, and adventurers, who naturally did not have any training in recording anthropological or psychological facts—who, indeed, never heard of psychology—and who naïvely assumed that the speech-signs which stand for things, words, mean the same to savages as they do to the civilized.

Thus we read of 'shell money' that is in circulation among the natives of some of the islands in the Pacific Ocean. This term gives the impression that these people have actually thought out and put into operation a medium of exchange equivalent to the coinage used in civilized countries. But when, in the fifth or perhaps the fiftieth heavy volume that mentions shell money, we discover that shells are used only to buy wives and to pay for spilt blood, while pigs are *de rigueur* to pay for ceremonial feasts, we see that the term money is wholly inappropriate, and that the notion that these savages possess a true medium of exchange is merely projected into their minds and customs by the white observer. Pigs for eatables, shells for a woman—the inexorable code, formed on some sense of fitness that precedes or even contradicts reason, prescribes these things.

This same inappropriateness of the words which, perforce, the white observer uses to describe the facts of savagery distorts his whole picture. Take the word 'soul.' To the average easy-going Christian his soul is an indefinite something which he feels he ought to worry about, but does not ; it gets somewhat better or somewhat worse, according to his moral behaviour ; certain acts are so taboo that he would be mortally afraid to do them, lest his soul be irreparably damaged thereby ; when he dies he will somehow become his soul ; his individuality will pass into his soul ; the soul is difficult to define—but, after all, why define it, seeing that everybody knows exactly what is meant by the word ? This, I take it, is about as completely as most of us could describe the collective representation designated *soul*. If this is the case, what chance have we of making clear, by the use of the word soul, the collective representations of pagan savages of the non-material part of man ? The Hausa of Northern Africa has five or six souls—for so we must call them, simply for lack of another word.

And so it is with almost every really vital actuality in the life of the savage. Energy, power, matter, life, death, time, space, cause, effect, spirit, animal, god, marriage, impregnation, the tribe—to say nothing of custom, law, morals, justice, punishment, religion, magic—every one of these words stands for such a definite representation to us that, for the affairs of daily living, we should never think of defining them. We are just as sure that the word death, for instance, conveys the same meaning to every one of our fellows that it does to ourselves as we are certain that the words ' President Hoover ' mean the same person to them as to us. But death means something entirely different to many savages, if not to all of them. If a vampire, sorcerer, or spirit, devours the ' life ' of a man during his sleep, the ' dead ' man may go about for a long period, eating, drinking, and generally acting as though he were alive. Death really takes place only when the soul leaves the body : the body-spirit may carry on the usual functions of lungs and heart, but the savage is dead nevertheless [1] and the preparations for disposing of the body may be proceeded with. If the body-spirit persists in thus imitating life, the survivors are entitled to become annoyed ; the ' dead ' person may be quieted by medicine, and made to act as dead as he really is. Here it is clear that not only does our word death fail to express the savage's idea, but that often it really amounts to almost an antithesis of his notion.

Another source of confusion in much of the literature about primitives can be traced to Tylor's magnificent work, *Primitive Culture*, which was published in 1871. At the time when Tylor wrote it was not realized that most

---

[1] Lévy-Bruhl, *Primitive Mentality*, 69.

savage races believe in a mysterious form of energy that
resides in objects—mana—very much as electricity resides
in a charged Leyden jar, an energy which flows from the
charged object into other objects that come into contact
with it, or into persons, often to their extreme detriment
if they themselves are not also charged with mana of
nearly the same potential. For example, among the
Malays a chief has mana of very high potential. Priests
and persons of high rank can safely touch the chief or
his belongings, for they also have mana at a high tension,
and so there is no destructive flow of the dangerous energy
from the chief to them. But with a commoner the case
would be different : even the blanket in which the chief
has wrapped himself is so charged with his mana that
a commoner would surely die if he slept in it. It sounds
fantastic, but one cannot help wondering whether there
really is not some connection between mana and static
electricity : the Australians rub pieces of wood and stone,
called churingas, in order to charge themselves with
energy ; and it might very well be that pieces of wood
diligently rubbed would give off a spark. However this
may be, the savage is firmly convinced that certain objects
are charged with energy, sometimes a sort of energy of
holiness and therefore beneficial, and sometimes an energy
that is hurtful and that makes the object taboo—that is,
sacred and unclean.

Tylor seems to have confused this savage concept with
what he calls animism. Crawley says that ' Tylor describes
animism as " a belief in the animation of all nature, rising
at its highest pitch to personification." This belief is
" bound up with that primitive mental state where man
recognizes in every detail of his world the operation of
personal life and will " and is, in short, a conception of an
all-pervading " life and will in nature." ' [1]

The more the savage's theory of mana has been studied
during recent years, the more Tylor's theory of animism
has been discarded by scholars ; but it remains in many

[1] Crawley, *The Idea of the Soul.*

excellent books, confusing the student. Even more misleading than animism itself, however, is Tylor's explanation
of how primitive man came to his belief in it. Tylor's
primitive seems to have been a man who enjoyed abstract
thought, and who was tormented by metaphysical problems : he strongly resembles the theologian who was so
formidable an enemy to the new sciences of Darwin's,
Spencer's and Tylor's own day. This primitive (we are
told) was mightily perplexed by the difference between
the quick and the dead, and by the causation of waking,
sleep, trance, disease, and death. Naturally he was also
puzzled about the beings, animal and human, that
appeared to him during sleep, and at the travels and feats
that he himself performed while his body lay motionless
at night.

The reality of such questionings is so great to ourselves
that it is easy to picture the noble savage—Eskimo or
kinky-haired black cannibal—sitting so rapt and lost in
his philosophic labours as never to hear his wife, or wives,
calling him home to dinner ; until, perhaps, the Arctic
cold took him painlessly away to the land of eternal
feastings, or a lion crept up and carried him off into the
jungle. Such questionings would be natural to a very
highly educated modern Englishman ; therefore they are
natural to the savage—so runs the implied argument.

From such abstruse meditations primitives, the world
over and with practical unanimity, concluded that man
possessed a ' life ' and a ' phantom ' which at last combined
into a ' soul ', and that these three were somehow responsible for the phenomena mentioned. Such is the course of
Tylor's reasoning : it rests upon the assumption that the
savage delights in philosophy and spends a good part of
his time worrying about transcendental problems.

But, as Crawley points out, the savage has no love for
thinking : rather he has a ' naïve distrust and fear of
thought.' [1] Cosmic problems do not exist for him : he
is a ' quick, alert, and hardy animal, whose senses were

[1] Crawley, *loc. cit.*, 267.

sharpened by hunger, and experienced in the continual search for food and in the avoidance of danger. In animals and children philosophical rumination and introspection do not occur ; they are rare in the lowest and highest savages alike.' [1] Curiously enough—for so difficult is it to give a picture of the savage mind except in terms of the one mind we are acquainted with, which is our own—one finds that Crawley and Tylor seem to adopt each other's positions at times. Thus Tylor himself implies in one place that there is no such thing as a savage philosopher, while Crawley infers that the primitive's fear of thought arose from the fact that he recognized ' that the most powerful of all influences is that of ideas. . . . For the way of ideas is the way of temptation. The tendency to realize an idea in action . . . is irresistible (to the primitive), except for the inhibition of fear.' [2] Lévy-Bruhl confirms Crawley's contention that people of low cultures have a positive aversion from the labour of thought, with many examples. Among these he cites the case of an Eskimo who was annoyed when a white man asked him what he was thinking about.[3] This is the story :

' All the ideas of the Eskimo centre round the whale fishery, hunting, and eating. For anything beyond that, thought, to them, is generally a synonym for boredom or annoyance. " What are you thinking about ? " I said one day, when out hunting with an Eskimo who appeared to be deep in thought. My question made him laugh. " Oh, you white people, you are always thinking so much. We Eskimo think only of our stores of food ; shall we have enough meat for the long winter or not ? If the meat is enough, we have no need to think about anything else. As for me, I have more food than I really need." I realized I had offended him in attributing any " thoughts" to him.'

The truth is that people of low culture have a most enviable capacity for being completely idle, a divine laziness that many of us have lost. They do not fatigue

---

[1] Crawley, *loc. cit.*, 15.   [2] Crawley, *loc. cit.*, 267.
[3] Lévy-Bruhl, *Primitive Mentality*.

themselves with thought when they can avoid it (and they usually find some way to avoid thinking) or worry themselves with problems unless they are actually cold or hungry, or feel the immediate pricking of some other desire. But the abstract-thinking, metaphysical primitive of Tylor keeps cropping up everywhere just the same. He appears as a maker of statute law in Sir J. G. Frazer's four-volume work on *Totemism and Exogamy* : Frazer is convinced that prehistoric primitive ' sages ' among such races as the Australians recognized the evil effect of too close inbreeding, and, by an intellectual effort, invented the immensely complicated system of exogamous classes— and this in spite of the facts that inbreeding has never been proved to be harmful in and of itself ; that the Australians do not know that sexual intercourse has anything to do with producing children ; and that their social organization does not include any chief or other despot who could force a manufactured statute upon the people. Probably the Primitive Philosopher, like the Caveman and Santa Claus, will live on in literature for a long while, simply because he is just as interesting as he is imaginary.

But Tylor made a contribution to the subject of primitives which is hardly ever noticed, but that seems to me to be of great importance :

' A poet of our own day has still much in common with the minds of uncultured tribes in the mythologic stage of thought,' says Tylor.[1] This is so very true that, to understand the savage, one should so far as possible put oneself into the attitude of listening to poetry or looking at a ballet—critical analysis may come later, but primarily appreciation is a matter of mood. The savage must first of all be perceived, like a landscape or an antique statue or music. ' Wanting the power of transporting himself into this imaginative atmosphere the student of the mythic world may fail so pitiably in conceiving its depth and intensity of meaning, as to convert it into stupid

---

[1] Tylor, *Primitive Culture*, I, 315.

fiction. Those can see more justly who have the poet's gift of throwing their minds back into the world's older life, like the actor who for a moment can forget himself and become that which he pretends to be. . . . Fully to understand an old-world myth needs not evidence and argument alone, but deep poetic feeling.' [1]

But it is not savage myth alone which must be so approached : all the savage's ways, his strangely-linked thoughts and strong emotions, his conventional ways of seeing things, his mystic identity with his totem and his group, his magic and his fears, can be most truly grasped only by putting ourselves into his place and rôle, and feeling them. Any attempt to find a logical explanation of individual acts, or of social institutions or customs, that originated in the ' mythologic stage of thought ' is bound to result in error in so far as we suppose that these acts, customs, or institutions were the consciously intended results to any considerable extent of reasoning processes on the part of the primitive. All lawyers realize that the great body of the common law of England grew up through custom, and that legislative interference with the common law was very infrequent before the abolition of the feudal system. The law merchant, governing negotiable instruments, still is mostly the international usage of merchants, and has not been much changed by the inventions of legislators. When the laws of ancient Rome were put into writing, it was no new system that was devised by reasoning but a codification of old customs. If this has been the course of the evolution of law and social institutions among races as advanced as the Romans and our own forefathers, it is clearly absurd to attribute to savages and primitives such law-manufacturing processes as civilized races today find themselves burdened with. The primitive's intellect must be left practically out of account when one seeks to understand his social psychology, and the customs, social organizations, and actions that result from his psychic processes.

[1] Tylor, *loc. cit.*, I, 305.

In fact, if one investigates any institution among races of lower culture, as marriage for example, it is a good deal safer to avoid speculations as to its origin, and to confine one's attention to the *results* that it brings to the social group. Still, in spite of its dangers, speculation as to causes has an almost irresistible charm.

CHAPTER VIII

PERCEPTION

IF order is to be brought into the chaos of anthropological facts and observations by classifying and explaining them on a psychological basis, it becomes necessary to examine and establish the character of the primitive psyche. For it is this psyche which is the co-ordinating factor; which, in fact, is responsible eventually for the customs, beliefs and institutions of the human race in all their diversity, but particularly of that section of humanity which is still in a savage state.

First let us inquire whether we moderns, the so-called civilized, have a psychic structure really different from existing peoples of simpler cultures, the so-called backward or inferior races? Is our hereditary 'faculty' higher?

It is one of our conventional assumptions, our *représentations collectives* as Lévy-Bruhl calls them, that savages have far more acute senses than the civilized. It is said that the Australian can tell which member of his group has passed merely by looking at the print of naked feet upon the ground. Every American boy has read how our Indians can recognize faint sounds in the forest that the white man does not even hear, and notices a myriad of slight signs that the white man does not perceive, signs that give him important or even vital information as to food, friends or danger. Out of stories of these extraordinary powers of observation and deduction has grown up a highly conventionalized representation of the American Indian, and of savages in general. The man of the woods (I use the word savage in this, its literal meaning) does appear to the city-dweller to possess almost miraculous powers of 'noticing'; but the white savage does not appear to be inferior to the Redskin in acuity of perception. It must be remembered that to one who dwells out of doors in wild places, accurate and minute perception of nature is one of the chief interests of life. In fact, it is a vital necessity. In so far as a wild animal yields food or fur, it represents a value to the child of nature; and so it is also with animals that must be avoided. But beyond this purely utilitarian observation, and the æsthetic perception that is also strong in primitives, there is little interest : a Fabre sees more of insects than any savage ever did. Conversely, take the white man in his own environment, and it is clear that he has here the more acute perceptions. The Eskimo can detect numerous varieties of blubber by taste, all of which the white man classifies under the one term putrid. But how about the professional tea-taster, or the connoisseur of wines ? How about the mechanic who listens to the sound made by the engine of an automobile, and knows at once what is not running smoothly in its complicated mechanism ? What savage could discriminate tones as does a civilized musician, or shades of colour as does a portrait painter ?

Each excels at his own work, in the work that is his own profession, and each is a bungler and seemingly dull-sensed in the speciality of the other. The Cambridge Expedition to Torres Straits endeavoured to discover differences in sensory capacities between the natives and Europeans by the use of delicate psychological instruments. ' So far as these experiments might have been expected to show a marked difference between wild folk and civilized folk as to sense-endowment—for instance, in respect to acuity of vision—the results were largely negative. In other words, it turned out that, whereas experience might teach the savage to interpret his sensations more accurately than we should *in contexts more important to him than to us*, the actual sensations were

D

much the same in both cases.' [1]   We have to conclude, therefore, that so far there is no evidence that the savage and the civilized have different powers of sense-perception, except in respect to the particular objects upon which they habitually direct their interest.   Each perceives better those objects which are important to him in the conduct of life, and to which he is in the habit of paying attention, than he does objects which are meaningless to him.

Since our contact with the world of reality is by way of the senses, sense-perception is an indispensable element in the subject-object relation.   The senses ' present ' objects to us, or, to speak more accurately, through the senses we receive impressions that (we are in the habit of assuming) correspond to perceived objects.   Most of us know that what the eye reports is really light, that what the eye is sensitive to is really light-waves of various lengths.   We know that we have only to put on coloured glasses, and the report of the eyes as to objects becomes different : colour does not exist in objects, but is purely subjective ; it is in the observer.   The process of seeing is not at all direct but consists chiefly in a series of inter-pretations and assumptions on the part of the person who sees.   We *read* the light-waves that reach our eyes by reflection from a face just as truly as we read a printed page.   Even the question whether the object which we say we perceive is real or not cannot be definitely answered ; for we never directly perceive more than our own psychic processes, and never perceive objects themselves.   If two or more persons agree that there is a snake in the corner of the room, then the presumption is that the snake is real ; but if only one person sees the snake, while others regarding the corner do not see it, the presumption is that there is no real snake there.

Yet even these presumptions never amount to absolute

---

[1] R. R. Marett, a paper on *Psychology and Anthropology*, 35 (contained in *Psychology and the Sciences*, a symposium by a number of leading specialists).

proof ; for crowds of people as well as individuals are subject to illusions and hallucinations. Gustave Le Bon relates that all the Crusaders saw St George upon the walls of Jerusalem. Another instance of collective illusion given is this :

' The frigate, the *Belle Poule*, was cruising in the open sea for the purpose of finding the cruiser *Le Berceau*, from which she had been separated by a violent storm. It was broad daylight and full sunshine. Suddenly the watch signalled a disabled vessel. The crew looked in the direction signalled, and everyone, officers and sailors, clearly perceived a raft covered with men towed by boats which were displaying signals of distress. . . . Admiral Desfosses lowered a boat to go to the rescue of the wrecked sailors. On nearing the object sighted, the sailors and officers on board the boat saw " masses of men in motion, stretching out their hands, and heard the dull and confused noise of a great number of voices." When the object was reached those in the boat found themselves in the presence simply and solely of a few branches of trees that had been swept out from the neighbouring coast.' [1]

Collective illusions similar to these related by Le Bon are not at all rare. When the direct testimony of the sense which we use most and upon which we most depend, sight, is capable of playing such tricks it is obvious that sense-presentations which are re-presented by memory must be still more liable to subjective distortion, colouring, and misinterpretation. Psychologists have repeatedly demonstrated this experimentally : they have assembled their students, have told them to watch carefully what was about to happen, and then to write down immediately what they have just seen. Thereupon some simple action is staged : perhaps someone mounts the lecture-platform, blows his nose three times, lays a bunch of keys upon the desk, takes an umbrella out of the corner, and walks out. One would think the audience would one and all agree as to what had just taken place. As a matter of fact there

[1] Le Bon, *La Foule*, English translation, The Crowd, 46, 48–49.

are invariably many and varied conflicting reports. This means that there is really no such thing as a ' pure ' sense-perception, determined exclusively by the object : every sense-perception is largely subjective. In fact, it would not be far wrong to say that the object merely stimulates *a* perception, and that *what* perception arises depends upon the subject.

Further, that any object excites a perception at all—that it is perceived—depends to a greater extent than is customarily recognized upon the object's meaning for the subject. What is devoid of meaning is generally over-looked. Koffka's researches into the psychology of babies is in point here. It used to be assumed that the very young infant perceived a chaos of sights and sounds which it learned, as time passed, to fit together like a mosaic into associations. This, Koffka shows, is not the case.[1]

' If the theory of original chaos were correct, one would expect " simple " stimuli to be the first to arouse the reaction and interest of the child ; because single stimuli ought to be the ones first to be singled out from the chaos for association with one another. This, however, contradicts all our experience. . . . The first differentiated reactions to sound are aroused by the human voice, the stimuli (and " sensations ") of which are very complicated, indeed. Nor is the interest of a suckling aroused by a single colour, but by human faces, as Miss Shinn has expressly reported to be the case with her niece after the twenty-fifth day. Think what sort of experience ' (here Koffka refers to inner or psychological experience, as contradistinguished from outer, observable behaviour) ' must parallel the process of distinguishing, among an infinite variety of chaotic images, the father's from the mother's face (and more than this, a friendly from an unfriendly countenance), the sensations of which are constantly undergoing change. . . . According to the chaos-theory the phenomena corresponding to a human face can be nothing but a confused mass of the most varied light-, dark-, and colour-sensations, all in a constant state of alteration—changing with every movement of the

1 Koffka, *The Growth of the Mind*, 125–142.

person observed, or of the child itself, and likewise subject to every change of illumination. Yet the child recognizes its mother's face as early as the second month, and in the middle of the first year it reacts quite differently to a " friendly " face than it does to an " angry " face.'[1]

Scheler says that ' of all the external objects apprehended by man, " expression " is the very first.'[2] But the expression which a child reads upon (or, more exactly, reads into) a face is its value and meaning to the child ; and this is surely more dependent upon the psychic pattern of the child than it is upon the face perceived. That is, there is inherent in the nature of the baby a sensitiveness to the moods of nearby members of its own species which cannot be accounted for by personal experience. This is no mere ' reaction ' to a stimulus : rather, the baby reaches out and explores other human beings to ascertain whether they are friendly or unfriendly. This is an active process just as much as kicking its legs, making vocal noises, or seeking the breast. It would be strange if this were not so ; for other human beings (especially the mother) are by far the most important and meaningful objects in the baby's world. The baby has a hereditary interest in human beings : human beings are the chief inherited values in its primitive psychic life.

I think Koffka goes too far in assuming that the baby's discrimination between friendly and angry persons is a matter of sense-perception only, depending entirely upon the expression of a face or a voice. To me it looks more like an intuition—intuition being a function generally described as a mass-perception, or (better) a judgment unconsciously arrived at—as to whether the person perceived is to be liked and trusted or distrusted and feared. Dogs, and even horses, make similar discriminations as to human character ; but one could hardly assert that the only process by which they arrive at their judgments is a simple perception of facial expression.

[1] Koffka, *loc. cit.*, 133–4.
[2] Scheler, *Sympathie*, note 16, p. 275, quoted by Koffka.

But even if we follow the generally accepted opinion, and classify these discriminations by a baby as perceptions and not as intuitions ; it is at once apparent that such discriminations are not yet fully explained. The difference between a friendly expression and an angry one is not usually very pronounced in the case of a father bending over his child's cradle : the father does not manifest dangerous-looking horns or spectacular tusks when annoyed, but merely changes the tension of certain facial muscles. If the child had to learn the meaning of these slight muscular variations from observation alone it is obvious that a very considerable amount of experience would be required. Learning by experience involves a number of factors, including the vividness of the stimulus, the frequency with which it is repeated, and the length of time that the training lasts. Now the actual stimulus in the first place (the visual perception of the father's face) is, in itself, a very weak stimulus indeed : it is not nearly so strong or distinct as the perception arising from folded arms, crossed legs, or a bright necktie would be. It cannot be compared with the vividness of a stimulus causing pain, as the sting of a bee or a scratch from a cat, or a weak blow. Second, babies who are under the observation of trained scientists like Miss Shinn, Koffka, or Watson, are not children of the slums but belong almost always to enlightened families ; they are often related to the psychologist ; and it is very rarely indeed that they are present at family brawls wherein the father loses his temper. Enlightened people do not often expose infants to the nervous strain of seeing their elders angry. So we can take it as certain that the angry-face stimulus is a very infrequent one. The third and last item is the duration of the training. ' By the middle of the first year,' according to Koffka, the child discriminates between the friendly countenance and the angry one. So here we have an exceedingly weak stimulus occurring very infrequently during the first six months of the infant's life.

To me it seems incredible that so little experience of

such a low-tensioned kind could teach a child to make so subtle and meaningful a discrimination as that between a friendly and an angry person. I think we have to assume here an inherited tendency to perceive and pay attention to such moods of another person, and to react to them in a definite manner, or at least to experience a tendency to do so. There must be a hereditary sensitiveness to another's moods, a hereditary recognition of such definite moods as friendliness and anger, an archetypal or primordial memory-image that is part of the child's inherited psychic structure. If not instinctive, the baby's discrimination is at least quasi-instinctive.

This theory tends to break down any hard-and-fast barrier between instinctive and non-instinctive, in so far as it is possible to erect one. Watson says that the word instinct already has so many meanings that it practically has none ; and he thereupon assigns the term a new meaning of his own.[1] With so distinguished an example, we may be permitted to note that, in the language of analytical psychology, any action or process is deemed ' instinctive ' to the extent that it is motivated by the collective unconscious—to the extent, that is, that it depends upon the inherited psychic structure.

According to analytical psychology, inherited capacities to recognize an object or a situation, ' primordial images,' arise from the same sources as do individually learned memory-images. It is not doubted that an act which by the narrowest possible definition must be taken as instinctive (as a baby's sucking the breast) results from the fact that generation after generation infants have done this, so that a habit has been established in the race. The extreme opposite of such a race-habit is a habit that is personally acquired in one lifetime. But between these extremes an infinite variety is possible of acts which are, as it were, *en route* from being personal to becoming racial : were such a transition not possible there is no conceivable way in which racial habits might become established at all.

[1] Watson, *Behaviorism*, Ch. I.

The more a pattern of behaviour in respect to a given object or situation comes to be racial, the greater is the relative importance of the subjective factor in such behaviour and the less can we say that the objective stimulus is the effective cause of the behaviour. In a strictly instinctive act we see a complicated structure of subjective tendencies loaded with energy and pressing to operate, which the object merely releases. The object bears about the same relation to the instinctive act as the gunner's pull on the lanyard bears to the firing of a gun and the delivery of the projectile.

The foregoing discussion is not so irrelevant to the topic of perception as it might seem ; for though an object may be perceived by a person for the first time in the race's existence, such a case would be a rarity. Most objects, and most of the situations in which a man can find himself, have been perceived innumerable times during the racial life. The most vitally important objects and situations that could be perceived by any man are precisely those which have been experienced by all or nearly all our ancestors : the mother, father, family, the social group ; strangers ; the sex-object ; the love-object ; angry persons and dangerous animals ; trees, bodies of water, the heavenly bodies ; storms, darkness, lightning ; fire, food ; the coming of death to others, the gruesome changes death works ; and many other incidentals of daily commonplace life. It would be a strain upon commonsense to suppose that the universal, almost infinite repetition of such experiences has not left imprints upon human nature, has not greatly moulded human nature in fact. We must assume, until evidence to the contrary is offered, that we have a hereditary disposition to perceive such objects, and to pay attention to them, to recognize them, to read meaning into them, and to be emotionally stirred by them.

Not only is an object *what* it is to us by reason of our psychic inheritance ; even its existence often seems to depend upon the subjective factor. This is not an unconscious excursion into philosophy on my part : I am not considering ontology, but am remaining within the field of psychology proper. We see colours lying between infra-red and ultra-violet ; and we feel differences in temperature of objects within a very small range, approximately that between the freezing and boiling points of water ; and our range of hearing is also very limited. That is, our perceptions operate within hereditary fields with enough accuracy to meet the needs of everyday life. They are not adapted to objects outside these fields. So far as perception goes, ultra-violet does not exist : we know of its existence only indirectly.

On the other hand, among the objects which inheritance has fitted us to perceive, which we are by nature inclined to pay attention to, which, indeed, seem to possess an inherent power or mana to compel our attention, there are few if any that are emotionally indifferent to us. There is not one of the nineteen objects which I mentioned a couple of paragraphs above that always leaves me cold when I perceive it ; and I invite the reader to decide for himself how many of these familiar objects he perceives as a ' pure ' perception, with no emotional content whatever. Take each of them in turn, and ask yourself whether you would ordinarily contemplate it with complete emotional aloofness.

The question of whether a perception is simply a quasi-mechanical reaction to a sense stimulus, or whether it may be full of subjective elements such as value and meaning is highly important. It is obvious that the more subjective human perceptions are, the more is the external world of objects in which we live a world of our own creating. Moreover, memory is chiefly the re-presenting of past perceptions ; and our intuitions, feeling-judgments, and reasoning can never be less subjective than the perceptions on which they are based. It is characteristic of primitive psychic processes that they are massive and undifferentiated. In the child and the savage not even the basic process of perception is unemotional. The highly-developed adult learns to a certain extent to keep his emotions from colouring his perceptions ; but there always remain many objects, and these the most meaningful and important in his life, of which he cannot have a ' pure ' perception. Certainly there is no difference in kind between the perceptions of the savage and the child on the one hand, and those of the most highly differentiated individual on the other. The difference is in the degree of the subject's psychic development alone.

CHAPTER IX

REPRESENTATIONS

PERCEPTIONS, as we have seen, are greatly influenced by the subject's own psychic pattern. When the object is unimportant to the subject the perception may not even reach consciousness. When it does reach consciousness, the more meaningful it is to the subject the less can the perception be said to depend upon the external stimulus of the object : the greater the meaning of the perception, the greater is its subjectivity. The stimulus from without is usually (but not always, since some stimuli are solely subjective) the incentive to a perception ; but the external stimulus does not determine the vividness, the clearness, the content or the nature of the perception, or its effect upon the subject. How little the perception can be regarded as a reaction to a stimulus dependent only on the stimulating object is seen from the fact that witnesses of a simple series of events so seldom agree as to what has taken place that lawyers and judges know, as a practical matter, that witnesses whose stories are the same have almost surely been instructed as to what they are to testify.

This being the case, it is essential to study the subjective factors which determine the character of the perception. To examine the mechanisms of the psychic processes is not sufficient. Psychic activity is truly illuminated only when it is seen in relation to the psychic whole, when its meaning to the psyche is investigated.

To us who study the psychology of the depths, the *Tiefpsychologie*, whether we favour more the theories of Jung, Adler or Freud, it is this factor of meaning which

59

is all-important.   We see meaning in every form of
psychic activity, and are likely to underestimate the
importance of the mechanisms of experimental psychology.
I am conscious that I must make an effort to be just to
the Behaviorists, seeing that my interest does not turn
naturally to their hypotheses and that this seems anything
but a mechanical universe to me.   I know that I am not
the scientist of tradition, aloof, equally interested (or
equally indifferent) to all facts, making up my mind as to
the validity of this or that theory without emotion or
prejudice and solely by pure, cold reason.   I *care*.   The
subjective element has very much to do with my conclusions.   And, it seems to me, the Behaviorist is just
as human as I am in this respect ;   though perhaps he
does not realize the fact.

Now, if sense-perceptions are so little determined by
the objective fact, how about re-presentations, in which
the sense-perceived object or scene is worked up again
by memory, or in which it is transmitted to another
person by description ?   The subject's perception was, in
the first place, conditioned by his own subjective peculiarities.   Then this inaccurate perception is recalled and
further distorted by memory.   Then comes an attempt
to put the memory-image into words, whereby the original
fact becomes still more distorted.   The listener then
perceives the tale according to his own selective tendencies.
All this distortion occurs anew with every fresh repetition.
It throws some light on fundamental human nature to
look at the character of the changes which a fact undergoes
when it is handed about by word of mouth.

Jung has published a psychological study of a case of
rumour that demonstrates very clearly how memory-
representations are modified when a story that contains
situations that arouse emotions or that excite the imagination is started on the rounds of oral repetition.   A thirteen
year old schoolgirl told three friends that she had dreamed
that she went swimming with their teacher, a man, far
out in the Lake of Zurich ;   that they were picked up by

a passing steamer, landed at a place where a wedding was going on, and passed the night in a barn. There were a few other details in the dream, which, it is to be noted, was related by the little girl as a dream, and not as an actual occurrence. But here is a piquant situation, although imaginary : Marie goes swimming with the teacher, and spends a night in a barn with him. As the girls passed the story on from one to another the little gossips altered it. Dream became fact, and the story became a full-fledged sexual adventure with very thrilling details. Marie was expelled from school because the story that reached the authorities in its elaborated, re-presented form was highly indecent.[1]

Huxley pointed out that the more ignorant a people were, the more common were the reports of miracles among them. This is true, but it does not go far enough. Even among people of high culture dull fact fades and wonders grow when a tale is told and retold. The universal human love of the marvellous, the shocking and the indecent comes out all the more when the gossip passes through the lips of the cultivated and refined, to whose daily lives a wholesome Rabelaisian savour is denied. When old maids of a congregation find an indiscretion of the minister and a woman member of the choir, they often build up an extraordinarily satisfying myth upon it. The love of miracles is indeed a primitive characteristic, and on this account it is found in everybody. In re-presentation by word of mouth the subjective element is enormous, while the objective fact is generally negligible.

All this is by way of introduction to the topic of collective representations, which are conventional, generally accepted views. Savages often have such strange collective representations of an object, views so different from the white man's perceptions of the same object, that advocates of the hypothesis that the psychic processes of the primitive are different in kind from our own confidently rely as proof of their hypothesis upon such facts as that (for

---

[1] Jung, *Collected Papers on Analytical Psychology*, I, 176.

instance) a deer and a feather are the same thing in the view of certain Indians, or that other Indians do not distinguish between themselves and red parrakeets. In general, it is the French sociological school of anthropologists, of which Professor Lucien Lévy-Bruhl is the most distinguished exponent, which regards the mental processes of the primitive as being of an essentially different kind from those of the modern European. The English and American school of psychological anthropologists, denying that there is any difference in kind, hold that it is with the mental (or intellectual) processes as it is with the sense-perceptions : it is where the interest is turned that determines which functions reach high development, and which remain more or less in abeyance. Professor Boas, one of the most scholarly and convincing advocates of the theory that psychologically the peoples of various races and cultures are alike, or so nearly alike that the most earnest efforts have so far failed to discover any differences between their hereditary capacities, has developed this thesis very competently in his book, *The Mind of Primitive Man*.

To go into all the evidence and the arguments advanced by the adherents of the two doctrines would take us too far afield. If Lévy-Bruhl is correct, those peculiar processes which he cites to prove that the primitive is psychologically different in kind from the civilized will not be found in the civilized ; but if these processes are seen to occur in civilized persons, even in educated people, then Lévy-Bruhl will have disproved his own theory. Lévy-Bruhl has published two admirable books, which have been translated under the titles *How Natives Think* and *Primitive Mentality*. The second is the later and more satisfactory of the two, and I shall follow the order of its presentation to some extent both for my own convenience and in order that the reader may examine the French theory conveniently and fairly.

Lévy-Bruhl remarks that savages have minds more like those of children than of adults. He notes that a representation is classified in the current parlance of psychology when the civilized psyche is under discussion as an intellectual phenomenon, and not as emotional or motor in nature : that is, a representation is ' a matter of cognizance, inasmuch as the mind simply has the image or idea of an object.'

' It is not in this way, however,' writes Lévy-Bruhl, ' that we must understand the collective representations of primitives. Their mental activity is too little differentiated for it to be possible to consider ideas or images of objects by themselves apart from the emotions and passions which evoke these ideas or are evoked by them. Just because our mental activity is more differentiated, and we are more accustomed to analyzing its functions, it is difficult for us to realize by any effort of imagination more complex states in which emotional or motor elements are *integral parts* of the representation. . . . By this state of mental activity in primitives we must understand something which is not a purely or almost purely intellectual or cognitive phenomenon, but a more complex one, in which what is really " representation " to us is found blended with other elements of an emotional or motor character, coloured and imbued by them, and therefore implying a different *attitude* with regard to the objects represented.' [1]

Lévy-Bruhl finds that the basic difference between the attitude of the civilized and the primitive lies in this : to the civilized this is a world in which all that takes place occurs according to natural laws which invariably operate in the same manner, so that events are predictable when they are not too complicated for our understanding—the same cause always produces the same result. Theoretically, in this view of Nature, there is no room for accident or chance ; each and every event results from a cause, and the accidental is merely the unforeseen. But do we really live according to this neat and useful theory ? I should like to point out that we have not dropped the words

[1] Lévy-Bruhl, *How Natives Think*, 36.

' chance ' and ' accident ' from our daily speech, and often we conduct ourselves as though these were objective realities.   Perhaps this is because there is a very plain and indisputable failure on the part of Nature to conduct herself like a perfect clock : in a general way there is, for instance, a synchronicity or coincidence in time between the warmth of spring and the growth of vegetation ; but we are all painfully aware that there is no mechanical exactness about this—often when the fruit-trees are in blossom there comes a frost that blights the flowers.   It is only for the purposes of reasoning that we find it con- venient to assume that Nature is a machine that conforms to human logic : in the business of living we often have to take her as a despotic mistress full of whims.

The primitive, according to Lévy-Bruhl, lives in a world that has a richer content than ours.   For it is peopled with ghosts and vampires, with demons, witches, sorcerers, with men and women who have animal familiars, and with people who can change themselves into animals.   It is a magic, mystical world.   The primitive believes even more firmly than we that all events have their cause : to him there is absolutely no such thing as chance or accident ; but he does not think of the course of events in nature or in his own life as being regulated by a mechanical cause- and-effect process.   It is the mystic powers by which he is surrounded that bring about the fertility of the fields, the fall of rain, the abundance of game, or periods of want, as well as all that we should classify as unusual or as the results of chance or accident.   The ordinary course of events comes from no immutable natural law that is beyond all interference from man : quite the contrary, things occur because of the dictates of the mystic powers, and these powers in turn are aroused to beneficent or vengeful action according to whether they are pleased by the performance of customary rites or angered by their neglect.   No congregation of farmers earnestly praying for rain is more confident that natural processes can be interfered with by mystical means than is the primitive.

In fact, it might be considered a mistake to speak of the primitive's having any notion of the regularity of natural processes at all if it were not for the fact that he conducts his ordinary activities with a practical commonsense that seems to imply that he has glimmerings of such an idea.

Goldenweiser, on the other hand, tries to prove more than I should care to attempt : he refers to the very ingenious harpoon used by the Eskimo in hunting seals as proof that these people actually reason, where their ordinary activities are concerned, just as a civilized inventor reasons when he sets out to devise a machine to meet a need.[1] By this argument the Australian savage has higher powers of reasoning than we have ; for the boomerang could hardly have been devised purposefully by a white inventor. Goldenweiser completely overlooks the rôle played by intuition and lucky chance in such achievements. Lévy-Bruhl is more correct when he says that the primitive is distinguished by a great aversion from following a chain of directed thinking. This extends so far that it has been noted that some Africans, the Thonga for instance, easily master the senseless intricacies of the English systems of weights and measures, but make difficulties over learning the rational metric system : indeed it is the fact that the metric system is rational that makes them turn away from it. 'Why is it,' asks Lévy-Bruhl, 'that primitive mentality shows such indifference to, one might almost say such a dislike of, the discursive operations of thought, of reasoning, and reflection, when *to us they are the natural and almost continuous occupation of the human mind?*' For, 'In short, the entire mental habit which rules out abstract thought and reasoning, properly so called, seems to be met with in a large number of uncivilized communities, and constitutes a characteristic and essential trait of primitive mentality.'[2]

I have italicized the phrase in this quotation which

[1] Goldenweiser, *Early Civilization.*
[2] Lévy-Bruhl, *Primitive Mentality*, 29.

E

seems to me to reveal the weakness of Lévy-Bruhl's whole theory that there is a difference in kind between the mental processes of the civilized and the uncivilized. F. C. Bartlett [1] has hit the nail exactly upon the head : ' The error here as in much recent social and abnormal psychology, is not that the primitive or the abnormal are wrongly observed, but that the modern and normal are hardly observed at all.'   Bartlett is also right when he says that ' Lévy-Bruhl's antithesis is not between the primitive man and the ordinary member of a modern social group, but between the former and the scientific expert at work within his own field.'

Where is the educator, I wonder, who believes that reasoning is the ' natural and almost continuous occupation of the human mind ' ?   Doubtless the power of reasoning is latent or active in every healthy mind ; but in any mind this power comes late in life to full development, and in all but the very few it remains during life mostly latent, mostly unconscious and undeveloped.   For every European or American who can reason keenly, accurately and without becoming soon fatigued, there are thousands in whom reason is infantile or hardly to be detected at all. Some inherent honesty makes this show even in our speech :   the Englishman says ' I expect ' or ' I fancy,' while the American says ' I guess,' instead of saying ' *I think.*'   This is an expression of the exact truth :   the vast majority of mankind reasons but rarely, and then only when there is no escape from doing so ; it is only a numerically insignificant minority that reasons, and these do so only intermittently.   We must remember that the pick of our American youth, the conscripts for the latest war, showed an average mental development of a child of thirteen years, and that the moving-pictures (which constitute the preferred recreation of such a vast proportion of our supposedly intelligent and educated classes) are deliberately adjusted by the producers to come within the comprehension of a child of nine or ten

---

[1] Bartlett, *Psychology and Primitive Culture*, 284.

years. The truth is that reasoning is not a natural endowment except in rudimentary form. On the contrary, it is a highly artificial accomplishment. To teach a child to reason accurately and persistently is an extremely laborious task ; it is very rarely accomplished, because, in addition to the toil involved, there are few parents and teachers who can themselves reason. And even if the rare man or woman does learn to reason, it remains the most exhausting of all forms of psychic activity. Lévy-Bruhl should acquaint himself with his own countrymen —who generally admit that they use reason more widely and fearlessly than any other race—and note the inconceivable stupidity of most of them concerning all matters which do not come within what Anatole France called their ' own shop-window.' [1]

But let us be fair to Lévy-Bruhl : however mistaken he may be in believing that reason is common among the general public in civilized countries, he admits—or at least implies—that primitives also possess the power of directed thinking in situations important to them that require reasoning. He cites a Jesuit missionary's observations of the Iroquois, written in 1672-3 :

' " We are forced to the conclusion that the Iroquois are incapable of reasoning like the Chinese and other civilized races to whom we set forth the belief in God and his truth. . . . The Iroquois is not influenced by reason. His direct perception of things is the only light that guides him. . . . They usually believe only what they see. . . . *Although there are minds among them quite as capable of scientific thought as those of Europeans* [italics mine], yet their up-bringing and their need to hunt for a living has reduced them to a state in which their reasoning power does not go beyond what pertains to their bodily health, their success in hunting and fishing, their trading and their warfare ; and all these things are like so many principles from which they draw all their conclusions, not only as regards their homes, their occupations and their way of life, but also their superstitions and their deities." '

[1] Anatole France, *Le Lys Rouge.*

This passage admirably states the most modern view of the use of reason among primitives : Their mode of life determines their psychic values, *i.e.*, the objects upon which they habitually direct their attention and interest (libido). Concerning these values they do reason ; and we have no evidence that their reasoning is different from or inferior to our own. Their reasoning, however, tends to become ' like so many principles '—that is, their opinions concerning health, hunting, fishing, trading, and warfare tend to become crystallized in a series of ways of looking at these matters which are generally accepted as being correct and proper, as being conventional ; in short, they become what Lévy-Bruhl calls ' collective representations.' And when a collective representation has been formed concerning primary values, such as health, hunting, fishing, trading, and warfare, the opinions concerning secondary values are made to conform.

That this process of the primitive mentality survives in ourselves cannot be doubted. Individuals form leading ideas that guide them through life, some *Weltanschauung* or general view of the world and of life : indeed, it can be said that anyone who lacks this is psychically deficient, an aimless drifter in life. Such a leading idea may be a complicated philosophical theory, or it may be very simple, as when a man says to himself that he will make himself a millionaire before he dies, or that there is nothing so good as to indulge the senses to the uttermost, or that he will do his duty every day and leave the result to God, or that he will do unto others as he would be done by. Such leading ideas are not confined to individuals : whole societies have them. Germany had one before the outbreak of the world war, an idea that it was the destiny of Germany to conquer and rule the world by force of arms. England used to have a collective representation of her destiny of Empire, an empire to be held by trade and justice when possible, with armed force always ready in case of need. We Americans used to have a leading idea of a sweet land of liberty, before the world war. It is interesting to note that these collective representations have all been discarded now, and that so far no clear national aims have emerged to take their place.

Lévy-Bruhl, then, is decidedly weak in assuming that the primitive psyche is distinguished by a lack of reasoning, and still weaker in his hypothesis that the civilized psyche is distinguished by reasoning naturally and almost continuously. But at first glance he seems to be upon firmer ground when he points out the primitive's indifference to the law of contradiction. That the same physical object can be in several places at the same time seems to most educated moderns a manifest absurdity ; but, one cannot help wondering, would this multipresence seem an absurdity to an uneducated Swiss, Frenchman, or American ? My own opinion is that it would not, considering some current religious beliefs according to which God has the form of a man and yet is present everywhere at the same time ; but I must admit that I have no evidence upon this point. Be that as it may in the case of the uneducated, it is certain that indulgence in metaphysical thinking, if carried far enough, can bring the educated intellect to a degree of flexibility (and invalidity) that makes it admit the possibility of multipresence. The primitive, according to Lévy-Bruhl, is not in the least averse to believing that a person can be here and there at the same moment.

' The event I am about to relate involves yet greater difficulty, unless we admit that the experience of these Indians is arranged in a setting more elastic than our own, and allowing, at one and the same moment, of data which to our minds would be mutually exclusive. " This man arrived at my village from a place about a hundred and fifty miles off. He asked me for compensation for some pumpkins which I had recently stolen from his garden. I was thoroughly surprised, and told him that I had not been near his village for a very long time, and so could not possibly have stolen his pumpkins. At first I thought he was joking, but I soon perceived that he was quite serious. It was a novel experience for me to

be accused by an Indian of theft. . . ." The latter '
(the Indian) ' does not in fact doubt that he has seen the
missionary himself ' (in his dream)—' When Grubb asserts
that he was a hundred and fifty miles off at the time, the
Indian concurs in the statement. Yet the logical incon-
gruity between the two is not enough to make him abandon
the statement based on his dream, and he maintains both
facts, particularly the one which rests upon what he saw
with his own eyes while dreaming. He prefers admitting
what the Schoolmen call the " multipresence " of the
same person, to doubting what seems a certainty to him.
That is the necessary result of his experience, which,
beyond and above the realities which we term objective,
contains an infinity of others belonging to the unseen
world. Neither time, nor space, nor logical theory, is of
use to us here, and·this is one of the reasons which cause
us to regard the primitive's mind as " prelogical." ' [1]

It seems to me that this case might be explained without
invoking any belief in multipresence. The Indian in this
case did not claim that the missionary had corporeally
entered his garden, but only that Grubb's soul had come
in to steal pumpkins. Moreover, it is well known that
many primitives hold a man responsible for what he
dreams—which has sound psychology behind it—and even
for actions that a third person has dreamed that he committed. Lévy-Bruhl himself cites numerous instances of
this. This faith in the objective truth of dreams survives
among moderns in the country, and among the lower
classes in our cities : books on how to interpret dreams
are sold in enormous numbers in every civilized country,
and the interpretations given are quite concrete—to
dream of lice means that there is money coming to you,
to dream someone is dead means a marriage, and so forth.

' The multipresence implicitly admitted by the Indian
just cited,' says Lévy-Bruhl, ' is not an isolated case. In
a great many primitive peoples the natives thus picture
to themselves the multipresence of the man who has just
died, who, to the European's great perplexity, inhabits

[1] Lévy-Bruhl, *Primitive Mentality*, 106–7.

the tomb where his body lies, and at the same time is haunting the neighbourhood where he passed his life.' [1]

But, in the words of Prof. Jean Larguier des Bancels, ' This perplexity is a perfect stranger to certain occulists of Europe. They admit that a living person can be in at least two places at the same time. And, to designate this curious phenomenon, they have created a new word : they talk of " bilocation." ' [2]

If we were to stop here it would, I think, be clear that Lévy-Bruhl has not proved his main contention that there exists a difference in kind between the primitive's way of thinking and our own. Whoever breathes a prayer that danger may be averted from himself or from one he loves believes in mystic causation, however dogmatically he may assert that this is a world where natural law rules supreme. Sensible men provide in their contracts against their own responsibility for ' acts of God.' The unusual and unforeseeable, such as earthquakes, the burning or sinking of a ship at sea, are regarded even in our legal systems as acts of the great mystic power, God. For the vast majority of moderns there are still ghosts : on the night of All Souls' Day, all over Europe, food is still placed on the graves for the ghosts to eat. There are witches, too : when the Swiss peasant finds that his cow is sick he very often consults a witch-doctor to find out who has laid a spell on her, and to obtain a magic remedy. It should be remembered that the late Mary Baker Eddy once sued a neighbour for practising witchcraft against her. It is admitted that the primitive lives in a double world, the tangible and the mystic ; but how does this differ from the double world of the religious modern, which is at once a world of things and a spiritual world ?

I think we shall have to admit, before we finish our studies, that the entire primitive psyche survives in the modern, and is merely obscured by our very recent change of attitude—by our turning our interest away from art,

---

[1] Lévy-Bruhl, *Primitive Mentality*, 106–7.
[2] des Bancels, 77 *Archives de Psychologie*, 6.

myth, and religion, to the concrete realities of Nature. It would be difficult otherwise to account for the fact that psychic illness often removes the values which have grown up during the last three hundred years, whereupon the ancient mystic, myth-making interest is revealed to be still alive and flourishing riotously. An insane and entirely uneducated Swiss peasant sees a tube hanging down from the disc of the sun, and out of this tube comes the wind—such was one of Jung's cases. This is an ancient Gnostic myth. The same thing is found in children who have not yet reached the modern scientific attitude : Prof. des Bancels cites a boy of seven years who remarked, ' The wind that makes the trees sway—that is thought.' [1]

[1] des Bancels, *loc. cit.*, 10.

CHAPTER X

MYSTIC CAUSATION AND MYSTIC PARTICIPATION

Two of the most striking facts of primitive psychology, which are especially relied upon by Lévy-Bruhl in his effort to show that the primitive psychic processes are different in kind from those of the modern and civilized, are the prevalence of the belief that human affairs and natural phenomena are influenced or directed by occult supernatural beings and powers, and the failure of the primitive to see differences between things that, to the modern mind and perceptions, are absolutely distinct and often not even related. These two characteristics are aptly named mystic causation and mystic participation. In the view of Jung these both result from the fact that primitivity is, as the name implies, an early stage of development, a racial childhood ; and the primitive has not progressed far enough toward complete consciousness to be able to discriminate accurately between objects, or to see how regularly a given result follows an immediate given cause. Childlike, he takes his own fantasies for objective realities, and quite frankly turns away from the labour of collecting facts and reasoning about them to the more attractive dreamy world of myths and fairy-tales. Each modern child passes through this stage on his way to the world of real objects and later—in case of the minority—to the world of ideas. We cannot well doubt that in this the child is recapitulating the development of the race. We know too that even the adult individual does not shed the love of fiction as he does his milk teeth, but retains it usually during life, a welcome retreat from both things and thoughts. This older world of fantasy is with us the world of art, in which man was at home long before the stern taskmaster, consciousness, put him to work upon such tiresome pursuits as science and philosophy.[1]

On the face of it Lévy-Bruhl seems to have taken a somewhat formidable task upon himself in endeavouring to prove that these important characteristics of racial childhood have become extinct in the modern. In so far as we can unearth in the civilized psyche any characteristic that he specifies as distinguishing the primitive from the modern, as dividing the cultured and the savage into different *kinds* of humanity, Lévy-Bruhl's argument must fall. If these primitive characteristics are found in the civilized, we can go further than merely saying that the burden of proof was upon Lévy-Bruhl and that he has failed to offer convincing evidence : we can justly claim that his contention has been affirmatively disproved.

Mystic participation may be taken up before mystic causation, seeing that perception usually precedes thought : the child perceives before it thinks. In actual living, however, the two are thoroughly mingled, as the examples to be given will show. An instance of mystic causation often might just as well be cited as an illustration of mystic participation, or *vice versa*.

Lévy-Bruhl gives many instances of mystic participation. He observes that ' the mentality of inferior peoples, though not so impenetrable as it would be if it were regulated by a logic different from our own, is none the less not wholly comprehensible to us. We are led to imagine that it does not exclusively obey the laws of *our* logic, *nor possibly any laws which are wholly logical.*' [2] Here are some instances in which the mystic participation involves mystic causation :

' " A certain drought at Landana was attributed to the missionaries wearing a certain kind of cap during the services, the natives said that this stopped the rain ; a

---

[1] Cf. Wittels, *Sigmund Freud.*
[2] Lévy-Bruhl, *How Natives Think*, 71–73.

great outcry that the missionaries must leave the country was raised." '

' " After the Catholic missionaries had landed, there was a scarcity of rain, and the plantations were suffering from drought. The people at once took it into their heads that this was the fault of these clerics, and especially due to the long robes they wore, for such had never been seen before. There was besides a white horse which had recently been landed, and it had prevented trading, and occasioned many troublesome discussions. . . . A shiny mackintosh coat, an unusual hat, a rocking-chair, any instrument whatever, can give rise to disquieting suspicions. The entire coast population may be disturbed by the sight of a ship with unfamiliar rigging, or a steamer which has one more funnel than the others." '

' " At Tanna, in the New Hebrides, " it can hardly be said that there is any sequence of ideas, properly so called. . . . A turtle came ashore one night and laid a nestful of eggs. It was captured in the act. Such a thing had never taken place in the memory of the people. The conclusion was that Christianity was the cause of the turtle coming ashore to lay its eggs, and the right thing to do was to offer the turtle to the missionary who had brought the worship of Jehovah." '

' " Ideas are linked up in the same way in North America. One evening, when talking about the animals of the country, I wanted to let them know that we had rabbits and leverets in France, and I showed them to them by making the shadow on the wall in the firelight. It happened quite by chance that they caught more fish than usual the next morning ; they believed that the shadow-pictures I had made for them were the cause of this, and they begged me to do this every evening and to teach them how, a thing which I refused to do, as I would not minister to this foolish superstition of theirs." ' [1]

Had the good Father Sagard, who in 1632 wrote this last passage,[2] understood better the psychology of the

[1] Lévy-Bruhl, *How Natives Think*, 71–73.
[2] Sagard, *Le grand voyage au pays des Hurons*.

Indians, he might himself have believed that they would catch more fish if they made shadow-pictures of a rabbit the night before. For the primitive is not blessed with any theory that it is desirable to keep busy all the time ; on the contrary, he dreads work as much as does any healthy child ; and he likes to feel certain that he will see results from whatever labour he may be obliged to perform. Consequently he goes through various rites intended to bring success. The primitive mind assumes that these rites have a concrete, objective potency : if you make a shadow-picture of a rabbit in the evening, the fish are sure to bite or to linger in the way of your spear the next morning. Thereafter it is the old story between the different results of attacking a task with confidence and enthusiasm, or doubtfully and sluggishly. Naturally making the rabbit causes them to catch more fish : the fact that they have performed this rite acts as a summons that awakens energies dormant in the unconscious. This is one good reason why primitive peoples have fixed rites, rites that group-experience has proved to be efficacious, which must always be performed before undertaking anything at all important. The war-dance, dramatizing the slaying of the enemy and all the prowess the performers are about to exhibit in battle, is one of the most striking examples.

' To the natives,' writes Lévy-Bruhl, ' there is no such thing as chance. Occurrences which are close together in point of time, even if widely removed in space, readily appear to them to be linked by a causal relation.' [1] The fallacy of *post hoc, ergo propter hoc* is as current among primitives as among the civilized—even more so, in fact.

But, according to Lévy-Bruhl, the primitive is ' impermeable to experience ' and ' incapable of learning from experience.' For instance, neither disease nor a wound, nor poison nor old age, can ever be the actual cause of the death of a human being. These are seen only as intermediate phenomena, interposed between some supernatural actor and the death he causes, exactly as we

---

[1] Lévy-Bruhl, *How Natives Think*, 74.

disregard the tearing of tissues, the energy of the flying bullet, the explosive action of gunpowder ignited by the percussion-cap, the fall of the hammer, and a host of intermediate details, and hold the man who fired the gun responsible for the murder. Spencer and Gillen tell of an Australian native who was badly wounded when a spear that a comrade had thrown at a tree glanced from its mark. This to the savages was no accident, but indisputably the work of a wizard.[1] Among the Abipones the same direct and self-evident relations between a spear-wound and death are not comprehended.[2] No matter how often the natives see a wound followed by death, they never attribute the latter to the former. Hence, says Lévy-Bruhl, they do not invariably apply the hypothesis of *post hoc, ergo propter hoc.*

' Let us then no longer endeavour to account for these connections either by the mental weakness of primitives, or by the association of ideas, or by a naïve application of the principle of causality, or yet by the fallacy *post hoc, ergo propter hoc* ; in short, let us abandon the attempt to refer their mental activity to an inferior variety of our own. Rather let us consider these connections in themselves, and see whether they do not depend upon a general law, a common foundation for those mystic relations which primitive mentality so frequently senses in beings and objects. Now there is one element which is never lacking in such relations. In varying forms and degrees they all involve a " participation " between persons and objects which form part of a collective representation. For this reason I shall, in default of a better term, call the principle which is peculiar to " primitive " mentality, which governs the connections and pre-connections of such representations, *the law of participation.*' [2]

Thus blacksmiths are a hereditary caste among the Hausas of Northern Africa, and participate mystically with iron. Iron has special virtues : it drives away Bori, as demons and evil spirits are called. In fact, if one is pursued by

[1] Spencer & Gillen, *The Northern Tribes of Central Australia.*
[2] Lévy-Bruhl, *How Natives Think,* 75.

Bori it will be enough to call out the name of the metal. On the night of the marriage of a blacksmith's daughter a piece of red-hot iron is bound to her back. If she is a virgin this does not burn her.[1]

Lévy-Bruhl is careful to say that the law of participation cannot yet be exactly formulated. Tentatively, he would express it thus :

' I should be inclined to say that in the collective representations of primitive mentality objects, beings, phenomena, can be, though in a way incomprehensible to us, both themselves and something other than themselves. In a fashion which is no less incomprehensible, they give forth and receive mystic powers, virtues, qualities, influences, which make themselves felt outside, without ceasing to remain where they are.

' In other words, the opposition between the one and the many, the same and another, does not impose upon this mentality the necessity of affirming one of the terms if the other be denied, or *vice versa*. This opposition is of but secondary interest. Sometimes it is perceived, and frequently, too, it is not. It often disappears before the mystic community of substance in entities which, in our thought, could not be confused without absurdity.' [2]

Then our author goes on to give the much-quoted instance of the Bororó, a tribe of Northern Brazil, who claim that they are red araras—a kind of parakeet.[3]

' This does not signify that after their death they become araras, nor that araras are metamorphosed Bororós, and must be treated as such. It is something entirely different. " The Bororós," says von den Steinen, who would not believe it, but finally had to give in to their formal affirmations, "give one coldly to understand that they are araras *at the present time*." It is not a name they give themselves, nor a relationship that they proclaim. What they desire to make understood, is an essential identity. That they can be simultaneously the

---

[1] Tremearne, *The Ban of the Bori*, 120.

[2] Lévy-Bruhl, *How Natives Think*.

[3] Lévy-Bruhl *loc. cit.*, 77 (citing K. von den Steinen, *Unter den Naturvölkern Zentralbraziliens*, 305–6).

human beings that they are, and at the same time birds with red plumage, von den Steinen judges to be inconceivable. But, for a mentality ruled by the law of participation, there is no difficulty whatever. All societies of totemic form yield collective representations of the same kind, implying a similar identity between the individuals of the totemic group and their totem.'

Here I should like to call attention to the definition of *identity*, given by Jung : ' Identity is unconscious equality.' [1] Identity occurs when consciousness has not yet developed to the point where subject and object are discriminated one from the other. It is an unconscious manifestation, often of great importance in securing the survival of a species—as when a mother, animal or human, takes an attack upon her offspring as though it were an attack upon herself, or the male defends his female as though she were part of himself. Identity is a form of mystic (that is, unconscious) participation between the subject and object. That ·the Bororós consider that they are araras is hardly more incomprehensible than that a mother feels that her new-born child is herself. Primitive tribes rarely move away from their own territory unless they are driven out of it, so that in all probability the Bororôs have no memory of ever living in a land that was not inhabited by araras ; and they have not yet become sufficiently conscious to discriminate between themselves and the red-feathered inhabitants of their country.

It has often been remarked that the greatest confusion of primitive thought, which especially strikes the observer, is this failure to distinguish between subject and object.

Mystic participation has a broader meaning than identity, as the latter term is used in analytical psychology ; for it embraces also the essential sameness of objects with each other, objects between which more conscious observers would immediately discriminate.

Here is a case of mystic participation from my own

----

[1] Jung, *Psychological Types.*

experience. I became acquainted with an old squatter who lived near the Rio Grande in Texas. This man had no Spanish, Indian or Negro blood. He had been born in New England, and had gone out west when a boy. He was decidedly shrewd ; one could even have said that he had a superior intelligence in most respects although in many ways he thought as border Mexican. I always imagined that he must have come from good stock, for he spoke a very pure simple English ; but this may have been due to the fact that he had mastered one book, the Bible. The old man told me one day that he must get either a Mexican hairless dog or else, if he could not obtain the dog, a horse-chestnut. Either would serve his purpose, but one or the other he must have immediately.

That I could see no connection between the shivering, repulsive little beast and the nut plainly excited the old man's contempt, but he condescended to enlighten me. It seems (according to what he said) that disease is caused by a malignant agency that gets into the body. It is a perfectly tangible entity, not merely a condition. He himself had rheumatism. The rheumatism-body roamed about his joints and muscles at will, and delighted in giving him pain. There was only one way to get rid of it, and that was to offer it a dwelling that it would prefer to his own racked frame. Rheumatism preferred to inhabit a horse-chestnut rather than a man ; if he carried one in his pocket it would leave him to go into the nut ; then after he was free he could take the afflicted nut so far away that the rheumatism could never find its way back, and leave it there. Or, more than any other abiding-place in the world, rheumatism loved a Mexican hairless dog. If he owned a Mexican hairless dog he would have the unlucky creature sleep with him ; and thereupon the rheumatism would pass into the dog, which would swell up and become too stiff to walk. Then the dog could be taken far off into the mountains or the desert and left to perish. According to this theory the horse-chestnut and the hairless dog were practically equivalents, if not in the accidentals of appearance, at least in essential nature and function. This sounds primitive enough for a white American of the twentieth century ; but an actual savage would probably never have felt any need to rationalize the common (and only important) nature of the two objects. He would simply have said, ' A Mexican hairless dog *is* a horse-chestnut.'

The instance I have just cited is psychologically and philosophically simple. A philosopher might point out, as Kant did with respect to the idea of the existence of God, that the verb *to be* is a mere copula that serves only to unite two ideas in spoken representation. Here nut and dog are already united in mental representation, and in speaking one may use the copula to connect the word-signs for the two objects, if Kant's reasoning is sound. Also it would be correct to say that a Mexican hairless dog *is* a horse-chestnut, if each is defined in terms of human use—which is one of the commonest ways of defining an object. For instance, a razor, according to the Oxford Dictionary, is ' an instrument used in shaving hair from the skin ' ; and the unromantic editors define a bed as a ' thing to sleep on.' The dog is a cure for rheumatism, the horse-chestnut is a cure for rheumatism : therefore the dog is a horse-chestnut.

Obviously, however, an isolated instance such as my old squatter, who had reverted to a primitive manner of living and who had been surrounded for nearly all his life by densely ignorant and superstitious Mexicans, is not enough to prove that mystic participations and mystic causation are modes in which the ordinary modern mind still functions. But I do not see how anyone who examines the facts without having committed himself irrevocably to the hypothesis that there is a difference in kind between our mental and other psychic processes and those of the primitive can fail to observe that not only the ignorant among us but also the cultured do, to some extent at least, think mystically, and are sensitive to mystic participations between some objects.

F

Take, for instance, the phrase 'home and mother.' These two nouns represent one emotionally-coloured image for most Americans : where home is, there is mother ; where mother is, there is home. They are not quite separate entities, the home and the mother, even for the most cultivated grown-ups ; not quite completely discriminated one from the other : they form one complex image. They *are* a complex, psychologically speaking, since the interest that goes to them is not clearly divided between the home and the mother, but is directed in an undivided stream upon both. In innumerable cases, where what Jung has called the ' psychic umbilical cord ' uniting the mother and her child has not been severed (the mother-fixation, as it is called), there is also a failure to discriminate between subject and object : the child—he may be a child fifty years old—still is in a condition of mystic participation with the mother, a condition of identity. Naturally, the degree of these mystic participations is the converse of the degree of consciousness attained by the individual subject : I am not arguing that the modern is as greatly given over to mystic participations as is the primitive ; his more developed consciousness and rationality preclude that ; but I do insist that exactly the same unconscious confusion of subject with object, of one object with another, is to be detected in moderns, though to a less degree, as is revealed among primitives.

The difficulty which the Romans had in freeing themselves from the notion that a man's property was part of himself, and that he could not divest himself of it by selling it, is another case in point. Among primitives a weapon that has caused the death of a human being (people not belonging to one's own tribe are scarcely rated as being human) participates in the guilt of the murderer. Similarly in English common law such a weapon is a deodand, *deo dandum*, a thing to be given to God, and is forfeit to God's representative, the king. In India the British had considerable difficulty in doing away with the practice of suttee among the Hindus : not only was it the duty of the widows to be burned alive, along with the corpse of their late husband ; but it was also their privilege, which they themselves insisted upon, that his death should not sever their mystic participation with him.

William James refers to the famous ' vulnary ointment ' attributed to Paracelsus. This contained (among other ingredients which James cites) the fat of a bull. A splinter of wood, dipped in the patient's blood, or the weapon that wounded him, is to be immersed in this ointment. The bull's fat, being full of ' secret reluctancy and vindictive murmurs ' dating from the time of his slaughter communicates its excitement to the blood of the wounded man on the splinter or weapon, which thereby gets a commission to cure its cousin-german, the blood in the patient's body.[1]

Modern mind-cure literature, observes James,[2] is full of sympathetic magic ; and he refers to the works of Prentice Mulford as an example of this. Sympathetic magic depends upon mystic participation. So does the efficacy of charms. Some charms are very difficult to account for : how in the world did the American Negro learn that the left hind foot of a graveyard rabbit brings luck ? One can, however, understand why the wearing of an image of St Anthony hung about one's neck prevents one from losing anything ; for it is an especial duty of this good saint to see that his human friends do not suffer such misfortune, or, if they have mislaid something, to see that they find it again ; and the saint is always present, through mystic participation, where his image is. It is the same with the holy images of the Catholic Church : cultured Catholics do not worship the carved figure that hangs upon the cross, but the image is holy nevertheless because it participates mystically with the Divine Hero.

Among primitives, the name of a person is so mystically identified with the person that a child is often given two

[1] W. James, *The Varieties of Religious Experience*, 496.
[2] W. James, *loc. cit.*, 497.

names. One of these is secret, and may not be revealed for fear that an enemy or a sorcerer might learn it and so have its owner in his power, while the other name is used freely because it is not the true one. Among the Hausas of Northern Africa not even the parents may know the true name until the child is three or four years old.[1] For children are universally supposed to be sensitive to mystic influences, bad and good : Heaven lies about us in our infancy, and so do the dark powers. Babies are only trying life, to see if they are going to like it : if they happen to be born in a household where there is quarrelling and scolding they are likely to leave life and wait for a chance to be born again in a more peaceful environment.[2] They might leave if their true names were carelessly handled.

Even the rationalist who has convinced himself that there is no supreme maker and ruler of the universe is often shocked and offended by blasphemy. God is where his name is uttered, for his name is God, or at least mystically participates in him. In all countries where the English common law prevails it is a criminal offence to use the name of God blasphemously.

Even a dog, one knows, connects his name with himself. If I wished to refer to my dog without attracting his attention I had to speak of ' my four-footed friend ' or use some other description ; for if I uttered his name, Joggi, even in the most conversational tone, he usually came to see what was doing, or to beg me to play with him. It is a common superstition that one of the wild denizens of the forest or mountains is likely to appear if the name is spoken. Very many savages consequently fear speaking the names of dangerous beasts.

Love brings out very clearly the fact that the modern has not outgrown the primitive sensitiveness to mystic participation. Mothers cherish the first little shoes that their child wore. The lover guards jealously a flower that

[1] Tremearne, *The Ban of the Bori*, 120.
[2] Talbot, *In the Shadow of the Bush.*

his beloved has carried, a lock of her hair, or a handkerchief that gives off traces of her favourite perfume : her
mana is in these, they participate mystically with her in
his half-conscious fantasies. The power of a perfume to
bring up a vivid memory-image of the one who used to wear
it has often been noted in literature. In this connection
one thinks of the dog, in whose world odours play such a
great rôle. Odours represent more to the dog than do
sights or sounds. An unusually intuitive woman insisted
to me that, other things being equal, a woman's falling
in love with a man depended upon whether his personal
odour repelled or attracted her. This might very well be
the case with a woman of the intuitive type, since an
intuition is a perception or judgment formed in the
unconscious and thence transmitted to consciousness. Her
theory not only fits in with the power of an odour to
evoke the image of his beloved in the lover's mind, but
also with the fact that yellow and black races smell
offensive to us, and these people in turn declare that they
are repelled by the corpse-like odour of the whites. These
instances show that mystic participations may often be
based upon the subject's own emotion : if two otherwise
distinct objects each arouse the same emotion in the
subject they are often not distinguished from each other.
This will be more fully discussed later on. And the
emotion may be aroused by a subconscious perception.

In referring to love as a form of identity or mystic
participation between subject and object, I must make
a detour to point out that in my opinion love is wholly
distinct from sexual desire. The frequently found phenomenon called sadism shows this, where the same person
serves as the object upon which another directs both
sexual desire and hatred or a desire to dominate or to
humiliate. There are many sadists whose sexual satisfaction is not complete unless they inflict pain upon their
sexual partner. Sometimes this perversion is so strong
that nothing short of mutilation or death will satisfy it.
The case of Jack the Ripper is perhaps the best known

example of this. This man would go with a prostitute, and the end of his sadistic passion was to disembowel her : the number of his victims, if I remember correctly, ran above a score.

Many women are sadists, varying in degree from the woman who makes her lover miserable by teasing him to the woman who sets out to destroy his happiness entirely and bring him to financial and social ruin. A very large number of women have ideas of mutilating and unsexing their lovers flash unbidden into their minds. An extremely vivid picture of sadistic fury in women is given in the Ulysses of James Joyce.[1] Conversely, there are masochists of both sexes, whose sexual desire demands that their companion should torture them.

It is thus clear that sexual desire can coexist with desires that are absolutely incompatible with love. The two bear no necessary relation to each other. Sexual desire can function even in the presence of love's opposites, of hatred and the desire to torture or kill. And love can exist without there being present the slightest sexual desire. The mother of a baby girl most surely can love her child with the intensest ardour without a trace of sexuality entering into her love. Even, I feel sure, the sexual desire of the man who loves a woman truly is something far more complicated than the simple sexual urge, which would be satisfied—probably better satisfied— by the skill of a professional prostitute than by the bodily possession of the beloved. It is not sensation alone that the real lover wants, nor what Havelock Ellis calls detumescence of loaded glands : he desires to assimilate her, to be assimilated by her, to be at one with her in the communion of love. His longing is that they shall participate mystically each with the other.

Mystic participation, like mystic causation then, is in no wise alien to the modern psyche : if these two hall-marks of primitivity do not so much influence the psychic processes and the conduct of civilized individuals with

[1] James Joyce, *Ulysses*, 407–565.

trained intellects it is simply because these persons have
been educated to discriminate, and to detect and repress
these primitive tendencies ; the collective representations
of educated people often do not admit that it is the correct
thing to allow these tendencies to operate. The presence
in thinking of mystic causation and mystic participations
is primitive, ' natural ' : the removal of them is the work
of increasing consciousness, ' culture ', a work which is
never completely done.

CHAPTER XI

INDIVIDUAL, GROUP, AND TOTEM

AMONG primitives the supreme mystic participations are those that exist between the individual and his group, and the participation between the group and all its members with the totem, the symbol of the group. Among moderns these are paralleled by a person's participation with the various groups to which he belongs—his family, his trade or profession, his club or secret society, his church, and his nation—and by his mystic relation to God.

Many learned volumes have been written about totemism, and the theories which have been put forward to account for it are various and contradictory : the reader who is interested in this fascinating topic had better take up Frazer's comprehensive work, *Totemism and Exogamy*. It seems superfluous to add to the number of explanations that are now current another one still. But I cannot help believing the matter is simpler than it appears. We know that primitives do not always remain on the same level of consciousness, and that their customs change— very rapidly when a stronger race, especially the whites, come into contact with them, and so slowly when they are left in peace that there is every reason to suppose that the primitives themselves are unaware of these modifications. Now, even among animals there are many which have an intuitive, unconscious recognition of their own group as distinguished from strangers of their own kind. Köhler has given an interesting account of the enmity shown by chimpanzees to another chimpanzee newly introduced into their enclosure, and of the measures which had to be taken to prevent the group from killing the stranger.[1] If a new pig is put into a pen with a herd that are accustomed to each other, the group gives him no peace but chases him about until he is so exhausted that he lies down and lets himself be devoured by his persecutors : this I have seen with my own eyes. The pariah dogs of Constantinople, my Turkish friends there told me, were divided into packs each of which occupied its own territory ; and if a strange dog entered this territory the pack set upon him and killed him. There must have been a time when the ancestors of totemistic tribes discriminated between the members of their own troop and strangers in this same instinctive, unconscious way—as the baby also discriminates between strangers and the familiar members of the household.

Later this distinction began to come into consciousness. Jane Harrison writes of primitive groups ' choosing ' names for themselves,[2] implying (inadvertently, I am sure) that this was done in the same conscious fashion that a group of modern men form associations and call themselves Elks, Moose, or White Rats. But the primitive does not pass thus from subconscious recognition of a somewhat complicated fact (as that we form a distinct group, united in interest, well known and friendly to each other, and all other human beings are strangers and objects of suspicion) to a full consciousness of it, saying, ' For convenience, let us hereafter call our social unit the Red Parakeets.' The original psychic state is not even an assumption that ' we are red parakeets '; it is simply a failure to distinguish between oneself and the familiar objects, including others of one's group and the birds, which make up the home-complex. The ability to discriminate between familiar and strange persons comes early in the child's development, as we have seen ; it is in evidence among swine, dogs, and apes ; and in all probability our prehuman ancestors, long before speech appeared, discriminated thus—being at ease among familiar surroundings, and fearful of all that was unfamiliar,

---

[1] Köhler, *The Mentality of Apes.*
[2] Jane Harrison, *Epilegomena to the Study of Greek Religion*, 8.

including unfamiliar people. The discrimination between themselves and other elements of the home-complex, such as the red parakeets, must have arrived much later. ' We are Red Parakeets ' would survive as a group-designation long after the group had become conscious of the fact that they were not really birds at all.

Andrew Lang thought that a totem was originally a nickname bestowed upon a group by a neighbouring tribe, much as the French Canadians have been nicknamed ' Frogs ' by the inhabitants of Maine. With the theory that a totemic name is imposed from without, I must disagree. To my mind such names come from within. A totemic name means that a group has become conscious of the fact that it *is* a group, a band, a kind of large family, a brotherhood, that it exists distinct from all strangers. And, at first, it means that the members of the group are not yet conscious of the fact that they are distinct from some familiar object—usually an animal or a plant—which is also found in the home environment. The totemic name makes the fact of group-unity representable in speech. The totem is an emblem of the group, much as is a flag. Dr Paul Radin told me that during the latest war the Winnebago Indians spoke of the British as lions, and the French as cocks. The totem, then, means that the fact of group-unity has become conscious ; it serves as an emblem of the group ; and it is a convenient term to designate the group.

But the totem is also a deeply significant religious symbol. For very frequently the totem is regarded as the ancestor and creator of the group. Among the Australians and many other races ceremonials are performed to secure the propagation and abundance of the totemic animal. The kangaroo is sacred—taboo—to the members of the kangaroo clan, who may not partake of its meat except under exceptional circumstances. Members of other totems, however, are entirely free to eat kangaroo meat whenever they are lucky enough to get it. R. R. Marett deals thus with this aspect of totemism :

' So we reach by another path the view to which we
already inclined, namely, that the savage manages on the
whole to keep his sentiment and his science in separate
compartments of his experience.   He can distinguish the
kangaroo of the (sacred) dance from the kangaroo of the
hunt.   The one feeds his soul and the other his belly.
And it is the former only or at any rate chiefly that has,
as we say, supernatural attributes, standing for something
over and above mere nature in the sense of the food-value
which the beast represents.   Nay, in his effort to uplift
the matter to the plane of the symbolic, the totemite
formally negates the food-value.   For profane purposes
the kangaroo may not be eaten by him, though without
inconsistency he allows it to provide a symbolic meal
whereby a human brotherhood reinforces its sense of
communion.   For the rest of the tribe, who worship other
totems, let kangaroo mean mere butcher's meat, since
theirs is the profane and literal way of looking at it.
But for him, the totemite, the kangaroo is brotherhood in
the only sense that counts among initiates ; seeing that
kangaroo is their common name, their social essence,
their luck, their mystery, in a word, their sacred dance.' [1]

Marett does not make a division between religion and
magic analogous to the famous definition of orthodoxy
as my-doxy and heterodoxy as your-doxy.   ' If I have
seemed to argue upon the side of the defence,' he writes,[2]
' it must not therefore be supposed that I put primitive
science on a par with our own.   A narrower experience is
bound to afford a weaker hold upon the nature of things :
though indeed I believe that in this department of thought
the savage demonstrably relies upon the same logical
principles, the same method of trial and error, as does the
civilized man.   Here, however, I have paid attention to
that other department of his thought which is concerned
with what some call his magic and others—I think, more
suitably—his religion.   It is here especially that his
thought appears to be utterly wanting in logical quality.
My reply to this accusation amounts to this—that the

[1] R. R. Marett, in *Psychology and the Sciences*, 46.
[2] Marett, *loc. cit.*, 50.

psychology of symbolism bids us be cautious in judging the quality of the logic of the symbolist. Before we judge the logic, we must have got at the meaning; and the literal meaning of a piece of symbolism is never the right meaning.'

Tylor, and many other scholars after him, have been struck by the parallel between the primitive's idea of the totem and Plato's theory of the eternal perfect pattern or image of which each mundane object is only a transitory and imperfect copy. The modern Christian Scientist tells us that mortal man (the carnal man of the New Testament) is only a faulty imitation of the reality, the spiritual man who exists eternally perfect in the mind of God. American Indians of the beaver totem think of their totem as a magnified spiritual being, as large as a cabin, the creator of beaver-men and beaver-animals. The beavers of the present participate mystically with the Great Beaver, the spiritual ancestor, just as to the good Catholic the carved figure of Christ participates in the mana, the power and grace, of him whom it portrays. It is obvious that when a race has arrived at the idea of a spiritual creator, through mystic union with whom human brotherhood exists, they have arrived at the idea of God—regardless of whether they picture him as a greater man or a greater animal; for whether God is imagined anthropomorphically or theriomorphically is an unimportant detail. The psycho-logical fact is that the group has reached consciousness of its own symbiotic existence, of the inter-dependence of its members, and consciousness also that there is one supreme value or object of interest for all the members of the group, the God in whom they all have their being, their union, and their 'luck.' The symbiosis, naturally, existed long before it was consciously recognized through the symbol : unconsciously the fact of group-unity was known. The symbol, the totem, serves to bring the actuality of brotherhood to consciousness in a representable form. Brotherhood, a united front toward all dangers, now becomes a concern of consciousness as well as of the unconscious urges. That is the rôle of the symbol in human life : it acts as a focus for the interest, the libido, of both consciousness and the unconscious.

As might be expected from the fact that the symbol arouses unconscious processes to activity, the psychic reverberations it brings about are enormous. On the conscious side the idea of God may culminate in giving a direction to a hitherto drifting life, a fixity and tenacity of purpose that means morale, a degree of rising above the accidents of fate, a power to tear through ' the paper walls of circumstance.' Persons who are enslaved by the predominance of their rational thinking over their other, comparatively childish, psychic functions often delight in limiting the symbol by defining it, and so depriving it of its living potency. Such rationalizing is theology.

But the richness and vitality of the symbol of supreme value, call it totem or God, is best seen on the unconscious side. Here its ramifications are endless—it sends its libido-conducting roots into every instinct and other unconscious complex or organized libido. That there is a connection between religion and sexuality has long been recognized. All taboos, including sexual prohibitions, are usually put upon religious grounds. Among primitive peoples where the ritual allotment of women to men is made along totemic lines, the notion that it is impious for a man to have sexual intercourse with a woman of his own totem is perhaps connected with the idea of shedding the blood of his totem, since the woman may bleed. This would seem to be one of the main sources of the ' horror of incest ' that is so characteristic of primitivity, for the blood of the totem may not be shed except ritually, a taboo perhaps second in importance only to the taboo against returning to the mother and her environment— to returning to childishness, that is, after the manhood-imitation. Moreover, the supreme value, the totem or god, is full of mana, and so also are the sexual organs and objects that resemble them ; and this participation is enough for the unconscious ; forthwith a sexual symbolism evolves which, in Christianity, has reached a marvellous luxuriance. Unfortunately, Payne Knight's scholarly book on *Phallic Worship* is out of print ; but the reader will find Inman's *Ancient Pagan and Modern Christian Symbolism* as useful in tracing Christian symbols as it is astonishing.

The eating-instinct also mingles with the religious urge, manifesting itself in intense interest turned upon the totem and the totemic brotherhood. At times the totem-animal must be killed and eaten. By this sacrifice the mysterious virtue, the mana, of the totem is assimilated by the totemites, and the social bond uniting the totemites is solemnly affirmed and strengthened. It is impossible not to see at once the parallel in the Christian communion. Whatever Christ may mean to the consciousness of modern man—and to each of us he means something different, of course—there can be no doubt that to the primitive who survives in us he is the totem. To eat with others is, the world over, a way of seeking at-one-ment with them. It is a primeval celebration of unity and alliance, to be detected even among animals. If I went away for the day and left plenty of English dog-biscuits for my dog, Joggi would not touch them so long as he was alone in the house ; but just as soon as I returned he used to make extravagant demonstrations of joy, and an invariable part of his ritual was to bring a biscuit to me, to toss it into the air and roll over it, and, as a finish to this ceremonial of welcome, to eat it. Even when the maid had just fed him, and he was not in the least hungry, he always made this ritual meal when I returned from my work in the town. Conversely, when my wife and I have gone away for several days, and have left him with neighbours, Joggi did not eat until absolutely compelled by hunger : this was usually on the fourth day of our absence. Mourning is marked by fasting, joyful reunion by a feast.

The primitive when he makes a cannibalistic feast of his slain enemy, or when he is about to partake of some formidable animal such as the bear, has definite ends in view beyond the satisfaction of his hunger. There are two results to be accomplished : the qualities, such as strength and courage, that resided in the dead man or animal are to pass into the eater by assimilation ; and the spirit of the dead man or animal is to be placated, made friendly, at one with the slayer and the slayer's group. It is in atonement, in the literal sense of the word, that the head-hunter fondles his gruesome trophies, places cigars between their teeth, and begs the dead enemy to make himself at home in his new environment and to be a friend. The most civilized mother loves to bite her baby playfully, unconsciously strengthening the close bond between them by a symbolic assimilation ; and so it is also with the ' love bite ' exchanged by lovers, concerning which Havelock Ellis has written so learnedly. From all the line of those divine heroes who, seemingly overcome by the powers of evil, have conquered death, the *Pagan Christs* as Robertson calls them in his book of this name, have arisen brotherhoods, most if not all of which have celebrated their communion by a ritual meal together. Historically, the Christian communion is but one of these communions ; and psychologically it is precisely the same as all the earlier communions, including the eating of the totemic animal.

So long as we look at the mere outer aspects of custom and conduct, we are struck by the dissimilarity of savage ways from our own. But as soon as we penetrate to the psychic actuality embodied in these manners of acting, as soon as we reach the *meaning*, the unlikeness vanishes, and the fundamental similarity of mankind the world over, in every stage of culture, forces itself upon us. Variation, individuality, appears with consciousness : but even individuality depends upon what elements, arising from the common unconscious, are admitted into consciousness and there emphasized through the directing of conscious interest upon them. So far as can be seen, there is always a kind of balance in all living organisms between the tendency to maintain a standard pattern of structure

and the tendency to variation, to the throwing off of
' sports.' This is true of both physical and psychic
structures. The organ of psychic variation in man is
consciousness, while the remaining true to pattern comes
from the collective unconscious.

It seems curious that Lévy-Bruhl is apparently unaware
of the work of even his own countrymen—Charcot, Binet,
and Janet, for example—to say nothing of Jung, Freud,
Adler, Mason, Prince, Myers, and a host of others who are
not of the Cock Totem, upon the existence and workings
of the unconscious. It is more than a quarter of a century
since that eminently sane man, William James, pronounced this discovery ' the most important step forward
that has occurred in psychology since I have been a
student of that science ' ; so it is fair to say that Lévy-
Bruhl is at least that far behind the times. By ignoring
the progress of science, Lévy-Bruhl does not thereby
abolish it ; but he does limit the accuracy and value of
his own work most regrettably. With his learning and
mental acuteness he would surely have seen that savage
ways and the conduct of the civilized spring from the
same fundamental human tendencies, if only he had kept
abreast of the progress of psychology. As it is, he dis-
regards the subjective factor in conduct, with the natural
result that he is mystified and bewildered by the variety
of the objective facts.

CHAPTER XII

FEAR CONSOLIDATES THE GROUP

IT is difficult to over-emphasize the importance of gregariousness in the symbiotic form that it manifests in man. In fact it would seem that this deserves to be rated as the instinct *primus inter pares*, in that the rise of man to his position of supremacy among the animals is directly due to his power of co-operating with his fellows, and, indeed, his innate psychic necessity to do so. This is the theme of this book, upon which I would string details as beads upon a cord.

Now, in the setting forth of characteristics of primitive psychology, we come to certain phenomena that can be conveniently classified under a general rule, which I should formulate thus :

Any society that feels itself in danger instinctively tends to enforce conformity in thought and conduct upon its members, and to suppress all thought and conduct that might disturb the internal harmony of the group.

The two chief means of obtaining tribal harmony are education and the ritualizing of actions which, if left to the sphere of individual desire, might provoke quarrels among members of the group. The sanction that lies behind the group's insistence upon conformity and peace within the tribe resides objectively in the power and willingness of the tribe to punish offenders ; but there is besides a subjective sanction of enormous potency : the transgressor feels himself damned, lost, an outcast from his group. Among primitives, it is to be remembered, the unity of the group is primarily and almost exclusively an unconscious value, just as the herd-unity is a concern

of unconscious animals.   There is no scintilla of evidence,
so far as I am aware, that peoples on the cultural level
of the Australians or the Hottentots, or the Todas or
Veddas, ever consciously devise means for insuring the
unity of their groups, or even that they are conscious that
such harmony is desirable.   To have one's place in human
society is one of the fundamental demands of the depths
of the unconscious common to all mankind, and the
sacrifices and compromises necessary to satisfy this basic
craving are made instinctively by each adult member of
the really primitive group.   In so far as the savage is
conscious, he may weigh matters, as Malinowski has shown
in respect to the natives of the Trobriand Islands [1] and
take a chance of punishment for the sake of satisfying his
personal desires.   But the less conscious the members of
the group are, the more absolute and unconscious is their
conformity to the inherited customs.   The less culture a
society possesses the more is it exposed to real and
imaginary perils, and the more therefore is it necessary
to present a united front to these.

The primitive society always and invariably feels itself
to be in danger.   The peril of witchcraft, of taboos broken
by oneself or by another that result in bringing disaster
upon the whole group, the were-animals that penetrate
even into stockaded villages,[2] and legions of ghosts, half-
men, demons, and all manner of dark powers, can hardly
be over-emphasized.   The savage is like a child who has
been fed from infancy upon ghost-stories, and who knows
that he lives in a haunted house.   The world of the savage
is really haunted in solemn fact ;   for he has not lost
contact with his unconscious to anything like the extent
that civilized man has lost it.   Hence when he meditates
intently upon his dead mother he is likely to see her
memory-image so vividly that it appears before him as an
illusion of vision, a ghost.   It may be that this is a form
of *l'image eidetique* that has recently engaged the attention

---

[1] Malinowski, *Sex and Repression in Savage Society*.
[2] Talbot, *In the Shadow of the Bush*.

of psychologists. Concerning the eidetic image the description of Dr Urbantschitsch of Vienna may be given :

' Among visual memory-images it is necessary to distinguish the simple representation (*einfache Vorstellung*) of what one has seen from the concrete images (*anschaulichen Gedächnisbildern*). In the one case the object previously seen is simply represented (by memory) ; in the other case it is seen anew subjectively. One can remember clearly what one has previously seen and describe its details, even make a drawing of it, without having of necessity a concrete subjective vision ; while on the contrary the *anschaulich Gedächnisbild* when one closes the eyes, when one is in the dark, sometimes even when the eyes remain open, reproduces the impression with the exactness of a hallucination.' [1]

' To produce an eidetic image,' writes E. Tripp, ' there is presented to the subject, on a dark grey background, an object about the size of a postcard, an object of a nature that will arouse his interest. The subject is allowed to observe the object in all its details for about fifteen to thirty seconds. Then one takes away the object, and asks the subject to look at the place where the object was. If the subject has the faculty of producing distinct eidetic images he will have one of the object thereupon ; that is to say, he will *see* it in reality upon the grey background.' This faculty occurs so frequently among children that it is considered normal. In adults, however, there is a gulf between perception and representation. The eidetic image is considered to be a half-way phenomenon, standing between perception and representation and partaking of the nature of both. The duration of the eidetic image varies ; but Tripp says that there are cases in which the subject can reproduce the eidetic image of the object some weeks after having seen it. ' One is amazed how precise the description is, even in these cases.' Frequently

[1] E. Tripp, *l'Image Eidetique, Archives de Psychologie* for May, 1926, 53–54, quoting from V. Urbantschitsch, *Ueber subjective optische Anschauungsbilder*.

no screen or background is needed to project the eidetic image upon, which then is seen standing in space. The size of the image increases with the distance at which it appears.

Tripp is of the opinion that, as the faculty of seeing these images is common in childhood (ranging from 15 to 61 per cent. of the children examined) and decidedly rare in adults, the complete loss of the faculty and the entire separation of perception and memory-image in the adult is the result of psychic development. The eidetic image is regarded as a *primitive* phenomenon by E. R. Jaensch, of Marburg.[1] ' In support of this manner of looking at it, he invokes certain facts relating to primitive peoples, facts which allow it to be supposed that among these peoples the differentiation between perceptions and memory-images has not yet been accomplished and that, for them, the eidetic image is a current phenomenon, seemingly normal.

Among the arguments advanced in support of this view, let us cite the following : Some authors, as Livingstone, Spencer and Gillen, von den Steinen, have often noted the power of memory of the primitives and the facts reported make one think of eidetic phenomena. Their supernatural beliefs depend, perhaps, also upon eidetic projection. A body seen in the past can reappear before the person present, and give rise to a belief in an astral body, a sacred aureole. It may be that the eidetic disposition is exercised to a certain degree by the medicine-men and shamans, who undergo a long preparation for their functions. Without doubt this disposition is exercised in the sense of " collective representations " of the tribe, in order to put the supernatural powers in harmony with them.

The " mystic participation " of Lévy-Bruhl also leads us to an interior eidetic phenomenon (*inneres Anschaungsbild*), a phenomenon described by Krellenberg, observed among the subjects of Jaensch, which consists in the fact that while the eidetic image appears, the subject has a

[1] E. Tripp, *loc. cit.*

sense of participating affectively, by a sort of intropathy, with the nature of the projected object. In this state the subject and the object interpenetrate one another. If there be added to this fact the further fact that in the undifferentiated world the eidetic image, the dream, and the reality are mingled, one can account for the mystic participations of the primitive.' [1]

Let us then admit the eidetic image as a factor in the seeing of spooks among not only primitives and children, but also among the ignorant and the insane and spiritualists. The darkened room of the spiristic *séance* affords almost ideal conditions for the projection of these ' concrete visions.' The eidetic image serves to throw light also upon the religious visions of mystics. In more ways than one the deeply religious person is as a little child. What could be more natural than that a mystic who has gazed adoringly hour after hour for months or years upon a picture or statue of Christ or of the Virgin Mother should at length be vouchsafed an eidetic image of the much studied, treasured features ? In support of this idea, let me point out that statues and pictures of Christ and of the Virgin Mother are abundant, while such representations of God himself are comparatively rare. So, too, is it with the miraculous visions : God very seldom appears, but Mary and Jesus are seen rather frequently. It is noteworthy also that the religious mystic generally sees his or her favourite saint, not other saints.

The eidetic image, however, does not amount to a complete explanation of all the mystic illusions and hallucinations of the primitive—or of the modern either. Some of these present monsters that the eye of man has never beheld in the flesh. Fantasy is not limited to the reproduction of what has actually been seen as a whole : it can cull its details from memory of the seen, as the head, neck, and breasts of a woman, the body of a lion, and the wings of a bird, and unite them into one creature. This is not eidetic. Moreover, there are many situations that

[1] E. Tripp, *loc. cit.*

have arisen so often in the experience of the race that the race has acquired a hereditary memory-image connected with each such situation. The study of instinct reveals multitudes of such inherited memory-images, in man and in beast, bird, and insect. Even myths repeat themselves in widely sundered parts of the world, without any inter-communication between the peoples who dream them. Jung has found a whole series of hallucinations among insane American negroes which closely parallel Greek myths.

Since hallucinations and myths are products of the subconscious (myths, of course, are often consciously elaborated), the similarity of these products the world over and among people of the most diverse cultures is further evidence that below a certain depth, below mere personal experience, the fundamental psyche is the same in all mankind, just as much the same as are the bodies of all mankind. The eidetic phenomena indicate a primordial stage far less evolved than any savagery now existing, when our ancestors had not yet become able to discriminate the actually seen from the well-remembered. It can hardly be doubted that belief in supernatural beings would be powerfully reinforced by the sight of even one ghost, or eidetic image of a dead person.

The primitive has more to fear from the uncanny powers than direct harm. There is always, except in very favour-able localities, a danger that the food-supply will fail. Since natural phenomena, to the primitive mentality, depend upon the will of mysterious beings, it is always necessary to earn the goodwill of these powers by observing the established taboos, and by performing rites that long usage has proved to be efficacious, rites which always contain a notion of self-sacrifice however hidden this notion may be. The performance of these rites among primitives means always the doing of *creative work for the common good*. The interest, the psychic energy, is trans-ferred by the ritual to something beyond mere personal concerns. Group-solidarity is here achieved by ritual work.

So it is also with the presence of enemies, animal and human. There are other tribes in neighbouring territory who are always at least potentially dangerous. It is characteristic of the primitive view that members of another community are natural enemies, only awaiting their chance to do harm to your own group. Civilization tends to increase the sympathetic rapport between neighbouring groups and to substitute humanity at large for the racial or national group ; but we have seen to our cost and sorrow how superficial our idealistic humanitarianism is, even among the most cultured, in the demoniacal fury of the last war. Modern warfare is a highly intellectual game, played by modern science gone insane. The primitive group has what may be called its delusions of persecution : someone in one group dies, and it is natural to suppose that the enemy who bewitched and ' doomed ' him is a member of another group ; for death is never natural to the savage. But only in civilization do the delusions of persecution rise to national paranoia. Warfare among primitives is an affair of punitive expeditions, of raids and skirmishes which the savage dreads to undertake : it looks almost harmless to our modern eyes.

For although existing savages tend to regard all persons outside their own groups as potential enemies, the danger apprehended from them is mostly the peril of their sorcery, and war, as we have come to know it, is rare among them. Havelock Ellis, in an interesting essay on *The Origin of War*,[1] points out that the old assumption of the ' universal belligerency of primitive mankind ' has been disproved by recent investigations. Ellis notes that ' It is not now uncommon to date the time when species that could fairly be called human first began to appear at about a million years back, of which the brief period of less than three thousand years we call historical is but an insignificant fraction. . . . We mean by war an organized attack by the whole community on another community

---

[1] Havelock Ellis, *The Philosophy of Conflict*, 42 *et seq.*

of the same species. The combats of animals—even apart from the fact that when with members of their own species they are rarely fatal and often approximate to play—cannot be said even remotely to resemble war. There are two notable exceptions—though even here fighting scarcely attains the exact definition of warfare—among the ants and the bees, the only creatures that have attained a kind of culture comparable to man's. They may also be said to be the only two groups, outside men, combining density of population with the ownership of property. . . .

'Man of the early Stone Age' (to condense Ellis' text) 'was always primarily a hunter. His weapons were for use against animals, not against himself. A hunting population is always thinly spread over a large area. There was but little accumulated property. There were boundaries between the hunting-grounds of different communities, but these boundaries were sacred, and as no one would think of violating them they could not form a cause of war.' Wars for conquest are not to be found among true savages ; for, as Lévy-Bruhl has pointed out, the territory peopled by a neighbouring group is also inhabited by mystic powers that are allied with the human inhabitants, which would bring so many evils upon the invaders that it would be impossible for them to survive there.[1]

'What appears to us as " war " among the Australians,' continues Ellis, ' is simply either the carefully regulated punishment of an offender, without bloodshed if the offence is not serious, or it is revenge in which a band of kinsmen of the dead man, and any others who choose to join, set out to take blood vengeance on another tribe. Primitive " war " is mainly juridical, and always regulated, like a duel.' The reason for warfare came in Neolithic times when people began to live in cities and to acquire property. The dwellers in the great lake-cities of central Europe ' were indeed preparing the reasons for war, but

[1] Lévy-Bruhl, *Primitive Mentality*, 446.

they had not yet developed the methods of war. That came when they had discovered the metals and found ways of smelting ores. Then were brought into the world war's "two main nerves, Iron and Gold," as Milton called them.'

'Savages are on the whole not warlike, although they often try to make out that they are terribly bloodthirsty fellows ; it is only with difficulty that they work themselves up to fighting pitch and even then all sorts of religious beliefs and magical practices restrain warfare and limit its effects. Even among the fiercest peoples of East Africa the bloodshed is usually small. Speke mentions a war that lasted three years ; the total losses were three men on each side. In all parts of the world there are peoples who rarely or never fight ; and if the old notion that primitive peoples are in chronic warfare of the most ferocious character were really correct, humanity could not have survived. Primitive man had far more formidable enemies than his own species to fight against, and it was in protection against these, and not against his fellows, that the beginnings of co-operation and the foundations of the State were laid.'

Ellis draws his conclusions from archæological and anthropological sources. It is interesting to find that these two sciences confirm the ideas derived from other considerations, such as the law of recapitulation which has been formulated by certain psychologists, and which states that the individual recapitulates the psychic as well as the physical development of the race. The psychic traits manifested up to the age of five months by a white infant are all literally sympathetic in character and potentially useful to the group ; while it is only after the child is about eight months old that characteristics begin to appear which are ego-centric, anti-social, and indicative of the fact that the baby has now reached a degree of self-consciousness which leads it to set its desires in opposition to those of the household environing it. If then this mirrors the course of evolution of the race also, the ferocious primordial man, alone with his women, who killed or drove away his sons when they approached puberty, remains a Freudian myth. All the evidence unites, from whatever source or science it may be drawn, in showing that the instinct of co-operation, of mutual defence and burden-bearing, reigned supreme among our primitive and primordial ancestors, and most likely even among their animal progenitors after they ceased to live in the branches of trees. It is obvious that the deepest, oldest layers of the human psyche are co-operative and symbiotic—not bloodthirsty and selfish. It is not sexuality or will to power that is repressed among us today, and crying for liberation : it is this instinct of co-operation, to which all other instincts are subordinate in the healthy character.

In passing we may note that savages are afraid of the dark, for it is then that all manner of supernatural beings are abroad. Strong bands of warriors may march to the point of attack, but the attack itself is usually made at dawn. Unless the first rush is successful the raiders take themselves off as rapidly as possible. This they do in any event as soon as one or two of their number have been wounded. This is an evil omen, showing that the mystic powers are not favourable to the enterprise ; and, such being the case, persistence would be sure to end in disaster.

Probably the supreme terror among primitives is the *horror novi*, the sheer panic of the new and unfamiliar, which will be mentioned later. But enough has been said to show that fear is always present and operative within savage groups, tending always to consolidate them more firmly.

A little reflection will suffice to show that our modern societies find objects of collective fear, and that this fear binds the social groups more firmly together. War always supplies examples of such objects of collective fear, and the last war was no exception. The fantastically terrible pictures of the Germans, as a people and as individuals, drawn in all the allied countries and of the Allies as depicted by the Germans show the same psychic tendencies and mechanisms as we have just seen in the savage. The bogey of Bolshevism is an even more recent example.

The truth is that fear—especially irrational fear—is necessary to hold even the most civilized together in patriotic unity. A politician would be indeed unskilful in leading the people to take the first and indispensable step in saving the nation (*i.e.*, putting him into a public office), who pointed out a real and reasonable object of fear to those whose votes he seeks. What really grips a mob is fear that conscious reason cannot reach, fear arising from the subconscious, fear of some *mystic* peril.

CHAPTER XIII

RITUAL SHARING OF DESIRABLE THINGS

WE have seen that the group to which he belongs is the supreme value in the life of the primitive, and that he subordinates all his other interests to his interest in the group. Let us examine some aspects of savage life in the light of this. Some forms of savage behaviour can be summed up in sociological generalisations, other forms are more directly dependent on subjective factors, and can be understood only in relation to the psychological tendencies involved.

A minor example of the first class is found in the fact that a hunter's kill does not, in many tribes, belong exclusively to him. Various other persons are entitled to share it with him, as for instance his wife or wives, his mother or other kin, and in those groups which have a definite headman or chief he often comes in for a portion. The custom is not at all indefinite : It is not merely that the chief, for instance, must have some of the animal. He is entitled to a definite part, as a shoulder or the neck, and the same is true with respect to the other beneficiaries. Here we have an early kind of taxation. But the value of the custom in promoting social solidarity is obvious. In time of want if there were no such obligation the successful hunter would either hide the slain animal so as to keep it for himself, or if he brought it into camp the result might be fighting within the group—the coherent unit of the group would disintegrate into a mob of struggling persons. Modern parallels are the state's powers of taxation and of eminent domain, and the legal obligation to provide for one's family and near kin : no man's earnings, in modern society, are his alone, any more than they are among savages.

Again, rights in property are universally recognized among savages. With some exceptions, the more primitive a group is, the more sacred is the right of property. As has been mentioned before, a man's belongings may even be considered part of his person. An Eskimo can safely leave food or other personal property in a *cache* with perfect confidence that no other Eskimo will steal it. Naturally this is a matter of vital importance in case the *cache* is in a locality where it is difficult to find food. It is easy to see that where weapons or tools are essential to keeping alive no group could hold together if the right of owning such property were not generally acquiesced in and respected. Among the Tiquié Indians of the headwaters of the Amazon, who in most respects are communists, each man owns his weapons.[1]

There is perhaps only one thing in the world over which men are more ready to fight than food and property, and that is woman.

Innumerable books and treatises have been written about the origin of marriage : but in spite of this, the institution has never been satisfactorily accounted for. Given plenty of food, there is probably nothing that human beings, both male and female, desire more ardently than an abundance and variety of sexual intercourse.

Yet in spite of a universal and seemingly ineradicable desire for abundance and variety in sexual relations, and in spite of the fact that obedience to this urge seems to be rewarded both physically and psychologically, our own ancestors and those of most other races passed at some stage in their development from promiscuity to some sort of restriction upon intercourse. Westermarck thinks this occurred in a pre-human stage.

There seems to be reason to think that the earliest restriction was simply against having intercourse with a member of one's own group or sub-group. According

---

[1] Gordon MacCreagh, *White Waters and Black*.

to Crawley [1] and other students, primitive man moved about in small bands hunting for food—small food-groups, as they are termed. Doubtless there were associations, more or less permanent, between a man and a woman in these groups, rudimentary marriages not requiring much sexual exclusiveness on the part of either the man or the woman : such ' marriages ' and such ' families ' are found among the Australian natives today. The simplest form of restriction upon promiscuity would be to prohibit a youth from having intercourse with a woman of the narrow circle in which he was brought up, thus forcing him into exogamy, which is the taking of a mate outside one's own birth-group. But what beneficial results could be achieved by this ?

We need not linger over Frazer's fantastic notion that primitive man feared the evil effects of inbreeding, and so put a taboo upon sexual intercourse between blood-relatives.[2] The most careful observations of modern scientists have failed to discover any such evil effects. And primitive man, it should be remembered, did not know that pregnancy is caused by sexual intercourse : many existing savages, such as the Australians [3] and the Trobriand Islanders [4] still deny that copulation has anything to do with conception.[5]

What is at once evident is that quarrels among the fighting-men of a group could not fail to be lessened by requiring a man who desired a woman to go and get her outside the group.

Another beneficial result of exogamy is this : the strange woman, captured, bought, or lured from a neighbouring group, is not a part of the warrior's home-and-mother complex. His sister (and generally speaking, any girl with whom he was brought up is a quasi-sister to

[1] Crawley, *The Idea of the Soul.*
[2] Frazer, *Totemism and Exogamy.*
[3] Spencer & Gillen, *The Northern Tribes of Central Australia.*
[4] Malinowski, *Sex and Repression in Savage Society.*
[5] Cf. also Sidney Hartland, *Primitive Paternity.*

him) is a portion of his childhood, and her psychological effect is to make him forget that he is no longer a child. She tempts him to regress towards childishness and to lose his hard-won consciousness of manhood—and this danger savages dread with an intensity of superstitious horror such as we can scarcely imagine. The taboo against allowing one's interest to flow back to childhood is the famous taboo against the mother, the incest-taboo, which we shall discuss later. The strange woman has no mystic participation with the memory-images of infancy. Rather, she is a badge of manhood, a token that her possessor is a fully-grown warrior.

Two or more food-groups whose hunting grounds were contiguous might become friendly and consolidate to some extent : one would suspect that such a process had taken place where a tribe is found which comprises several distinct groups each with a different totemic emblem. Such tribes exist in Australia and in other localities. Here something is added to the rule of exogamy, which is a prohibition of sexual intercourse between persons born in the same group : an affirmative right appears for a man of Group A to have lawful intercouse with any woman of Group B. The matter becomes so complicated in cases where the tribe consists of several exogamic groups that the superior intelligence of the civilized investigator frequently must strive diligently in order to understand the complexities of the savage customary law. But one result is always clear : regarding woman as a desired object over which warriors might quarrel, a great step forward in minimizing the danger of civil strife is taken when the permissible female mates are ritually apportioned among the men. This is accomplished by any form of marriage.

Group-marriage, in cases where the groups are comparatively large, is almost as good as promiscuity ; but the historical tendency has always been to decrease the number of mates that are ritually allowed. The Mohammedan law allows a maximum of four wives to one husband,

and in Christian lands monogamy is the rule. But why, if our ancestors were already in a stage of development that accorded with the purely biological demands of Nature, and that gave them every opportunity to satisfy their inborn desire for unlimited promiscuous sexual intercourse, did they ever abandon their paradisiacal state and fetter themselves with any kind of marriage, even group-marriage ?

Here again I think that the answer must be that the solidarity of the group is more important than the desires of any member of it. The only way to prevent men from fighting for possession of women is to apportion the women ritually among the men.

This is not so difficult among savages as it would be among moderns : for as self-consciousness and individuality increase the element of individual preference enters into the matter. But to the primitive every woman is about the same as every other woman, provided she is not too old : a woman is a woman, and that is all that is required. And to the woman a man is simply a man. Love, as moderns know it, the passionate preference of one woman to all others, or of one man to all other men, is not known to the primitive.

Among savages sexual intercourse between men and women who are ritually prohibited to each other is deemed incest, even though there is no blood kinship between them. The usual penalty for breaking primitive customs is avoidance—that is, the offender becomes taboo. A dreadful influence inheres in him which makes the other members of the group afraid to touch him or to associate with him. But the penalty for incest is usually death. The savage gives as a reason for this severity that the mystic powers are especially outraged by incest, and that there is no limit to the calamities that they will bring upon the group unless it effectually purifies itself ; to their minds the very *existence of the group* is endangered by one incestuous act. They themselves give this explanation. This makes it clear that the ritual apportionment of women among the men is felt to be of supreme importance in keeping the group together.

Although we have narrowed down the definition of incest until it now means sexual intercourse with one of near blood-kin, the primitive horror of the act is with us still. Curiously enough, primitive peoples sometimes relaxed the prohibition, or—to speak more accurately— there were occasions when the incestuous act became a religious duty. Thus among some tribes a young man at the time that he passed into the warrior status was obliged to have sexual intercourse with his own mother : the psychological result apparently being that by so doing he ceased to be her child. Frequently, after the manhood initiation he might not look at his mother or speak to her ; and this prohibition often included his sisters as well. But there were periodical religious festivals, or orgies, during which the taboos were replaced by the religious duty to have intercourse with ordinarily pro- hibited persons. This curious custom is very interesting psychologically : it shows that the consciousness of being a disciplined adult, subject to duties and to restrictions of liberty, is onerous ; that the will to be a social man is opposed by a will to kick over the traces and to violate the taboos ; that the libido flowing in consciousness toward being a warrior is opposed by a stream of libido, not so conscious, directed toward childish irresponsibility. It indicates that these anti-cultural impulses could not be wholly suppressed or eradicated, but had to be given periodical expression, and that it is safer to licence such expressions in a strictly ritualized form than to refuse to recognize them. It proves that being conscious is burden- some, as is even a rudimentary individuality ; and that a temporary return to animality is a relief. And in this temporary casting off of individual responsibility and return to childlike irresponsibility—to the collective unconscious—is one of the deepest roots of religion.

As civilizations grew up the religious duty became a mere licence to indulge in all sorts of sexual irregularities,

H

such as took place during the Roman saturnalia at the middle of December. All over continental Europe today, carnival is a time of sexual licence and toleration ; and no religious commandment is needed to induce the people to enjoy themselves. The universal tendency toward promiscuity, usually restrained by stronger interests, suffices. Since human society has been made possible by ritualizing actions and situations that contain the seeds of danger, it is probably advantageous to ritualize the promiscuous tendency in fixed festivals of this character ; for it is probably safer and less wasteful of energy to have a public orgy at stated intervals than to replace this by a more or less continuous private orgy such as goes on in the upper strata of American and European society. It should be noted that alcohol plays the same dual rôle of excitant and remover of inhibitions in the informal orgies of America and the conventionalized orgies of Europe that it does in the religious orgies of the savage. But while drunkenness is usually regarded by the primitive as a holy state, it has come to be looked upon by civilized persons as merely pleasant and desirable during an orgy. The orgy itself has the same function with us as with the primitive. Each conventional restriction upon conduct (as well as each self-imposed one) has the effect of bottling up psychic energy and increasing the internal pressure of the libido. Part of this energy is thereby rendered available for useful work which would not be possible if the libido were being continually dissipated. Part, but not all ; for no established and hereditary libido-outlet can be completely closed by the individual will, and the attempt to do so is invariably dangerous. It results in an accumulation of libido at an explosive pressure. The orgy is a safety-valve for this libido. In civilized life a person meets obstacles at every stage, especially in the transition from childhood to adulthood, in finding sex-objects, in winning the object of one's love, in earning one's livelihood, and in accomplishing the work which one wishes to accomplish, or even the work that is required of one. Normally each serious obstacle calls a halt to progress, during which imagination works upon the problem, and energy is gathered to attack the difficulty. If morale fails, and the problem is avoided, the stored-up energy may burst in the form of a neurosis. Or a substitute outlet may be found. This is usually sexuality or alcohol, or both ; in short, it is the orgy.

The orgy is also a relief from the monotony of work and of our self-imposed respectability. Monotony is simply the objective side of what, psychologically considered, is subjective onesidedness—a condition that lies at the root of neuroses and of many cases of insanity. The physical lives of primitives are dull and uninteresting in the extreme, consisting mainly in a perpetual search for something to eat and in continuous physical discomfort. As a set-off to this the primitive has art, especially in the fashioning of his weapons and implements but, above all, in his rites and ceremonies and myth-making. As soon as he has peopled the world with demons and ghosts it becomes less dull. And if the scattered small groups that are out hunting food come together to perform ceremonies of dancing and drinking and worship they are seized by what Durkheim has called ' the religious thrill.' [1] That is, they are back in the paradise of the unconscious. Their limited consciousness, that has been attained by so much effort and privation, disappears ; and all the old hereditary desires that have been so painfully suppressed are allowed full expression. In fact the opinion is widely held that one of the main roots of religion is this need to escape from the monotony of life.

So far as simple sexuality is concerned, the primitive readiness to enjoy promiscuous relations is certainly with us still. Why, then, do we limit ourselves—seeing that we are no longer living in weak armed bands ? Often in contrasting times that are past with the present, it is said that women of a generation or two or three generations ago were more ' virtuous ' than the woman of today ;

[1] Durkheim, *Formes élémentaires de la vie religieuse*.

but we should remember that the woman of the past did not have much chance to show whether she was virtuous or not. As a child she was closely guarded; she was frightened by the horrible examples of misconduct cited to her; she was taught that the sexual act was of the devil until a certain ceremony had been performed, whereupon it immediately became a holy rite; and while she was still a child she was handed over in marriage to some man who was thenceforth responsible for her and whose control of her every act was sanctioned by law and social usage. She was, in fact, a prisoner within the walls of an intolerant society. If she made even one slip, her only recourse was to die.

When one dares not do an act there is no moral credit in abstaining from it. My personal belief is that our grandmothers and great-grandmothers, if in their youth they had been set down in a society as tolerant as our own, would have exercised far less self-restraint than do the women we know. Many of the old sexual taboos have disappeared and many more are going. Today when a girl is found to have a lover and her father turns her out of his home we are filled with moral indignation, as of old. But now our wrath is not against the girl, but against her self-righteous father. Stories such as *Pamela* and *Clarissa Harlowe* would shock the moral sense of moderns, if they were not too long to read, with their portrayal of the then conventional sport suitable to gentlemen of seducing innocent girls, and their revelation of the accepted convention that a woman who had yielded to nature was damned and lost and should be treated as an outcast from society. Among many highly intelligent people no stigma whatever now attaches to being born out of wedlock, or to an unmarried woman who brings forth a baby; and these look upon persons who adhere to the old collective opinions simply as interesting survivals of recent antiquity. In America and England the form of repressing knowledge concerning birth-control is still gone through with—with precisely the same results as have always attended the attempt to prevent by law the spread of ideas. In Zurich (as in practically all of Europe that is not ' black Catholic ') contraceptives are sold entirely openly.

So that, so far as external restrictions upon the individual are concerned, we might expect to find an absolute sexual promiscuity in continental Europe, and nearly the same condition in England and America. But such is not the case. There may perhaps be more sexual intercourse outside of marriage than there used to be in the good old days, but there is nothing even remotely resembling promiscuity. For in proportion as woman has been freed from social penalties and put upon her own responsibility she—and man also—has developed a greater consciousness in regard to sexual matters. This is especially true of the better-class woman of continental Europe. However much she may be physically tempted, she looks with clear eyes upon all the possible consequences to herself, asking herself, What would be the results to me, socially, financially, and as regards health ? And what would this do to the relations which I really cherish ? How would this affect my home, my husband, and his career, if it should become known ? Except, perhaps, among some of the primitive peasantry, the day has gone by when the European woman yielded herself in a daze of cow-like unconsciousness.

So much for the real promiscuity, so cherished in fantasy. When it comes to a relation that is meant to endure the same difficulty arises. The more individual— the more conscious, that is—a person becomes the less can that person endure a continued relation with just this or that person of the opposite sex. To a real individual there are few other persons who, as friends or lovers, actually fit his developed and specific character. All the rest are psychological misfits, who may arouse a passing interest but with whom a permanent intimacy would be intolerable. When a conscious man or woman has found one of the few persons who can be a real friend or a real lover, the relation is too rare and too precious to be lightly given up. Not one offence against conventional notions, but many, will be either forgiven or treated as mere passing adventures of little importance so far as the realities of life are concerned. When love and sexuality come into apparent conflict, as they often do, it is usually love that finally wins, the errant one returning willingly to the more cherished relation.

CHAPTER XIV

PRIMITIVE SOCIALISM

IT has been pointed out that the primitive ritualizes all tendencies and situations which might be dangerous. He makes a ceremony out of nearly all actions that involve strong emotions, so that there shall be some one correct way of doing them which will obviate misunderstandings and possible conflict, not with conscious purpose, as modern laws are enacted, but instinctively. The ritual apportionment of food and of women have been mentioned. But any meeting between men is inherently perilous, especially if they are armed. At the time when our west was really wild it used to be said that God had made some men big and some little, but that Colt had made them all equal; and it is generally held that politeness reached its zenith during the days when every man carried a six-shooter on his thigh.

It is sometimes assumed that good manners are an artificial invention and that they are the mark of decadent societies. Nothing could be further from the truth. Even animals have their ritual ways of approaching each other. This is very obvious in the case of dogs. The wagging tail and lifted leg disarm suspicion and are an assurance of friendly intentions. When two savages belonging to different African groups draw near to each other each stops, lays his weapons on the ground, and squats. After a few minutes both advance a short distance and squat again. This is repeated until they are close to one another, when conversation is opened by the exchange of formal greetings. Savage salutations are very courteous. 'Are you at peace ? ' one may ask. ' I have only peace,' the other replies.[1]

Just as the dog ritualizes an action that contains the seeds of combat and danger so does the partly conscious savage. The intuition that wariness is needed in approaching another member of the same species and the tendency to ritualize such an approach are unconscious processes ; and this tendency is simply confirmed when there is added a conscious belief or creed that the formality is correct. Among ourselves the neglect of another to perform the customary rites almost invariably stirs within us the quick distrust and latent hostility of the savage. Our irritation when an acquaintance neglects to raise his hat when we are with a lady or when he offers the left hand in salutation instead of the right is not accounted for by rationalizing the situation and saying that he wished to depreciate us. Our resentment comes up from primitive psychic strata. This is what makes it vivid ; for we might not care the proverbial brass farthing about the other fellow's intentions.

It is important to note that good form is primarily a religious duty. Even among highly cultured races it still has something of the mystic sanction behind it, as witness the Chinese who have made the teachings of Confucius their chief rule of conduct for two and a half thousand years. These teachings can hardly be said to be moral guides, in the sense that the teachings of the New Testament are such, but rather constitute a code of behaviour designed to apply to various situations that are likely to occur in the life of a superior or scholarly man. By obeying these precepts the superior man is able to avoid arousing irritation and opposition in others ; and this is always the part of wisdom, inasmuch as life usually presents enough difficulties to satisfy even the most energetic without one's inviting opposition needlessly. Psychologically considered, this is a saving of libido ; and, since politeness not only obviates friction in social inter-

[1] J. and J. Tharaud, *La randonnée de Samba Diouf.*

course but also invites friendship and friendly co-operation it frequently results in an increase of available energy. The penalty for failure to observe what has been established as orthodox manners is the ancient religious punishment of taboo. Each society from the Australian up to the most cultured and most powerful says in effect, If you behave as we behave you are at one with us ; you are welcome, and we shall co-operate ; but if you do not observe our conventions you are not of us, and we shall avoid you. Even the primitive notion of the contagiousness of the tabooed conditions is clear in such modern sayings as that " evil communications corrupt good manners," and mothers instinctively try to keep their children away from the children of classes lower than their own for fear that they may learn manners that will cause them to be excluded from desirable circles. Moreover there is another religious element contained in these notions, although it is disguised : to the primitive psyche the social group is not so much a political organization as a brotherhood, a communion, composed of initiates. From other members of the same communion no danger is to be feared, but friendliness and helpfulness are to be expected ; while with the outsider the conditions are reversed. The weaker a society is the more it tends to consolidate itself ; and I remember that years ago in the financially impotent circles of the old families of Washington all these primitive views used to be summed up in the damning phrase, ' Senator Blank does not belong.'

Another detail in which society enforces conformity is in clothing and personal decoration. The soldier's uniform is a visible proclamation that he belongs to a certain social unit, and the silk hat and the gloves, spats and stick of the gentleman are a similar proclamation. Psychologically clothing is an extension of the personality : it is part of the *persona* or mask with which one impresses others. The high bearskin hat formerly worn by soldiers and the towering plumes of the savage warrior are meant to frighten the enemy : they make the wearer look taller.

Tattooing is another method of indicating at first sight to what group a savage belongs, so that another savage will know what to expect from him. In our modern armies the uniform brings to the fore another primitive trait : in order that a fighting force shall be as efficient as possible it is necessary that the human units composing it shall be as much alike as possible. Homogeneity, uniformity, and the absolute interchangeability of each man with every other are extremely desirable, while variations in character, training, or even in appearance are to be avoided. It should be remarked in passing that trim clothing is recognized by military writers as an important factor in maintaining morale. Emerson said that good clothes were a consolation that religion was powerless to convey.

Sometimes we are admonished that clothes do not make the man, and that the externals of appearance are not important. The *persona* is not the man ; that is true. But the *persona* reveals the attitude of the man. It is safe to assume that the man who dresses freakishly, or who shows his disregard of social conventions by boorish manners, is psychologically unbalanced and is a social misfit. Such people are signalizing a futile revolt against society due, usually, to their own inferiority feelings. Revolt is useful and even necessary to the evolution of society ; but there is a vast difference between the character of a man who revolts against some social injustice and the man who tries to advertise himself by declaring that he has never worn socks and never will. Eccentricities of dress and manners are often manifestations of sexual exhibitionism. The intuition of a society which declares that such people 'do not belong' is correct, and society saves itself trouble by tabooing them.

Among the external factors that produce homogeneity in a savage group, and consequently enhance its power to present a united front to whatever dangers other groups or the mystic powers may threaten, is the fact that the life-experience of all the members is roughly the same.

All live in the same physical environment, and so the factors that might induce individual variation of character are limited to various phases of experience, such as education, hunting for food, marriage, the performance of religious ceremonials, and so forth. In primitive societies there is very little specialization in labour : every man makes his own tools and weapons, catches fish and kills wild animals ; each carries out various rites, works himself into excitement and experiences the religious thrill at religious dances and during sacred orgies. Marriage, as has been mentioned, has nothing individual about it : the savage is simply permitted to have intercourse with the woman or women ritually allotted to him, and all the other men are allowed the same physical pleasure. The first division of labour is the difference in social function between the sexes. Woman bears children, and takes care of them up to a certain age. When agriculture comes in the cultivation of the fields is usually assigned to the women on the principle of sympathetic magic ; for woman is the fertile one, the bringer-forth, and her example teaches the fields to bring forth crops. For this reason a sterile wife is divorced among many tribes : her example would teach the fields to be barren. In general women do most of the work that requires a comparatively low output of strength over a long number of hours, while man reserves to himself the tasks that require much strength to be exerted during comparatively brief periods— fighting, hunting dangerous beasts, and the like.[1] Man's other physical occupations seem to be those which afford amusement, such as making things with his hands and decorating them—weapons and the like. (Weapons would of course be infected with womanishness if women made them.) It is impossible not to see that a very great element of amusement enters into many savage religious ceremonies ; and these are chiefly in the hands of men, though often the women have their own cults in addition.

[1] Havelock Ellis, *Man and Woman*.

Two of the earliest specialists are the witch-doctor or shaman or medicine-man, and the artisan. Vulcan, it will be remembered, was the god of smiths and artificers, and he was lame. It seems quite likely that the peculiar habit of humanity of protecting the old, infirm and incapacitated members of the group was responsible for the first professional weapon-makers, wood-carvers, smiths and boat-builders. A lame man is no good as a warrior ; but the fact that he is sedentary may make him all the more skilful as a weapon-maker : his interest is more restricted to such work. The shaman may have originated in nervous or mental abnormality. To the primitive mind epilepsy, fits, convulsions, insanity, dementia, and even drunkenness are sacred, filled with the fascination of mana ; and the ravings of a person in one of these abnormal conditions are listened to with awe and reverence. The use of intoxicants to produce states of trance, during which the mystic powers speak through the medium, is practically universal in all stages of culture. The savage knows that alcohol or other drugs free him from his limitations to such an extent that he feels himself possessed by a divine power ; and he seems to assume that delirium in anyone else means a like possession. Medicine-men usually go through ceremonies that involve a sort of self-hypnosis, even when they do not have recourse to drugs. It seems likely that the permanently abnormal, as well as the individual whose consciousness is unusually permeable to images arising from the unconscious (people with exceptional imaginations, that is, and people in whom consciousness has been destroyed so as to leave unconscious processes on top) are those who are accepted as seers by the primitive mind, both in savage groups and in modern societies. Such persons would usually be little value as warriors and providers of meat, but they would fascinate the attention of normal savages with much the same wonder and dread that an insane person exercises upon ourselves. The medicine-man, believing in the mystic virtues of various plants and rites, is the psychic ancestor of the modern physician on the one hand and of the clergyman on the other.

How closely knit the bonds which bind a savage community together may be is well illustrated by the communal mode of life of the Tiquié Indians. It is worth our while to notice some of the details of their social organization, as they have been described by Gordon MacCreagh.[1]

' They live, then, twenty or thirty families in a moloca, which is nothing other than a lofty empty barrack of split palm-trunks and palm-leaf thatch, almost invariably a hundred feet in length, with a frontage of eighty. To each family in the moloca is assigned an eight or ten-foot space along the wall—separated from the next, very often, by no more than a low rail as a line of demarcation. Privacy is unknown. The space acts as hammock-room for the family ; that is all. Cooking is done at the communal fireplaces between the central roof-supports ; and *not* by each individual wife, but by the women who have been told off to that job.'

The work of the community is allocated to the men and women, each being given the kind of work he or she is best fitted for.

' All labour is for the community. There is no private property, although a man retains for his personal use the tool or weapon or whatever it is to which his hand has become accustomed. But here again these people draw a curious distinction. It seems that certain duties are necessary for the benefit of the community. But when a man has done his allotted stint, if he cares to make for himself or to earn some article, that article may belong to him as an individual.'

The men, when they had earned a reward from the explorers, would almost always ask for cloth or beads or some other frippery desired by their wives, even when they themselves earnestly desired a knife or some other masculine implement.

' All the more extraordinary is this henpecking because the women are only temporary burdens. In this perfect

[1] MacCreagh, *White Waters and Black.*

commune there is no permanent marriage. A man and a woman live together for just as long as they are individually so inclined. Either one may at any time change to another moloca, or perhaps just sling the hammock across the hall. There seems to be no jealousy or quarrelling about such a transfer of affections—if the crude instinct of mating may be so termed. The necessity for jealousy has not been evolved.

' The children are the children of the tribe. And, as a matter of practice, the children, as soon as they are old enough to toddle, eat at the communal cooking-pots with the other children and are cared for by the women who have been assigned to that job, while their own mothers go out to work perhaps in the *mandioca* fields.'

This is an extreme example ; yet in general primitive society is socialistic. Every sound and healthy man has precisely the same tasks and obligations to perform as every other man of like age, and receives the same compensations and benefits. At first only those who are physically or mentally unfit for the standard life are allowed to become specialists. As soon as we have specialized occupations, such as the artisan and the shaman, we have the beginnings of special types of man and of individuality ; for the life-experience of the priest and the lame weapon-maker is not the same as that of the ordinary healthy hunter. At the middle period of life each will have different memories, different psychic contents, and consequently a different *Weltanschauung* or view of life. The primitive society tolerates these variations from the norm because their peculiarities are made to serve collective ends : these also are doers of creative work for the common good, though their duties are not those of the ordinary man. The savage who is a variant from the standard of his fellows is fortunate if his peculiarity places him thus in a recognized special class ; for otherwise he is likely to pay with his life for his inability to conform. Even when culture has progressed to the degree that iron is smelted and worked, the fundamental fear of the new and strange and of the innovator

still reigns.   There is an orthodox way of making knives
from iron, for example ; and if some psychic variant of
a smith, with a tendency to become an individual, makes
knives that are much superior to the old and familiar
article he meets with punishment instead of reward.   The
' flight of creative genius ' upon which the validity of a
patent is made to depend among us is an offence to the
primitive mind.   By breaking the accustomed order, the
malignant mystic powers will be aroused, precisely as
Christian clergymen prophesied that the wrath of God
would descend upon the world when it was discovered
that chloroform could be used to relieve the pains of a
woman in childbirth.   There are great numbers of instances
in anthropological literature of useful inventions being
suppressed because of the *horror novi*.

Parenthetically we should note that special tools and
specialized occupations develop together.   Consequently
we can attribute a very important part to the tool in
breaking the magic circle of primitive socialism, and in
making human variation and the growth of self-consciousness and individuality possible.   It is the fashion to deplore
the modern use of machinery, and to say that it stunts
individual development.   At the present time it does often
have a very deadening effect, because too often it results
in a brutalizing monotony of labour for such long hours
that there is neither time nor energy left for avocations
that would correct the resulting psychic onesidedness.
But already many factory-owners are finding that it is
economical to keep the machinery which never becomes
tired and in which much capital is invested, running more
continuously, and to use more shifts of operatives, each
shift working shorter hours.   Miners, in the good old
days of hard work, used to work twelve hours ; now there
are often, even usually, three shifts of men working for
eight hours each.   In some factories there are four shifts
of labour, each working six hours, and the machinery is in
continuous operation.   When a man needs to work only
six hours out of the twenty-four he has ample time and

energy left for study and recreation : it is his own fault if
he does not make himself a whole man, a well-rounded
individual.

This is a transition period in labour questions, just as it
is with sexual morals ; but personally I believe that
machinery is going to give man a power over nature, a
freedom from physical necessities, that will make possible
a more happy and beautiful world than has been known
heretofore—a world in which there will be leisure for
developing human individuality and consciousness on a
scale surpassing anything that has yet been seen.

It seems to me that specialization in labour—due more
to machinery than to anything else—is already bringing
great gains in consciousness. I refer, of course, to the
class-consciousness of different kinds of workers. A man
who finds himself in a class which is overworked or under-
paid has the facts brought home to him vividly in their
relations to himself ; and this is what consciousness
means—the relating of psychic contents to the ego. That
is one psychic gain, and there is another. Such a man has
his choice between getting out of his subterranean class
(if he can) or of joining with his fellows to better their
lot. The latter means that he is now one of a definite
social group, with a definite place in human society, and
with creative work to do for the benefit of his comrades.
In other words, he has found an outlet for the symbiotic
instinct, without which he could not be psychically whole.
Society at large is benefited also. One more discontented
man is prevented from becoming a social misfit, potentially
an enemy of organized society. He helps to raise a buried
class to its rightful place in the sun. Considering the
dynamite that human nature contains, both of these
results are socially valuable : they are bio-moral.

CHAPTER XV

EDUCATION, AND SOME ORTHODOX VIEWS

IN modern societies there are two methods of making good citizens, as those who conform to the collective standards of conduct are termed. One of these is a system of rewards and punishments : conform to the rules of the game as it is played in the society where you happen to find yourself and you are welcome, you belong, and the gates of opportunity stand open before you ; violate the rules and you are put out of the game, you are an outsider, and perhaps the only doors that open to receive you are those of the prison or the asylum. Many of the rules are extremely unjust to the individual and needless or even harmful to society, and many thoughtful and earnest people work for their abolition. But meanwhile the rules are here, whether we like them or not ; and organized society seldom errs on the side of mercy. The other method of making good, orthodox citizens is education— which Bertrand Russell says with a good deal of justice, consists in training the youth not to think. Certainly a very large part of education results in planting firmly in the youth's mind ' correct ' collective views that enable him to mingle freely in society without having to think (which is a great convenience) and which discourage him from trying to think for himself (which is a risky thing to do).

We have noted some of the primitive's rules of conduct that are analogous to our own system of rewards and punishments, and now we come to his system of education. It is astonishingly like our own, as Bertrand Russell describes the latter.

Among primitive peoples education has two main results, one of which has mostly dropped out of view in advanced modern societies. The formal education of an Australian boy or girl consists of special rites of initiation, in which torture and mutilation play a large part. The effect of this cruelty is to relegate childhood definitely and unforgettably to the past, so that the way back to home-and-mother is barred. The girl becomes at once a woman, and the boy a warrior. There is no more childhood or *childishness* for either. Thereafter their lives must be devoted to the service of the group. For the boy especially the rite of initiation is important ; for Australian boys run with the women and girls until the time of initiation approaches, and the primitive (who, in practical matters at least, lives in what Dr Radin has called ' a blaze of reality ') instinctively recognizes that for a boy to be brought up by and among women makes him a psychical weakling, makes him effeminate. This is confirmed by the fact that among races such as our American Indians, where the boys associate with the men from an early age, the initiation-rite is not marked by such brutality as the knocking out of teeth or circumcision and ripping up the urethra with a jagged stone, all of which the Australian candidate for manhood-status must endure.[1] It is just this making of an adult, conscious of responsibility to the group, and aware that childishness is henceforth taboo, that seems to have dropped out of sight among the varied decorative aims of modern education.

The initiation is the great event in the education of the Australian, but it is by no means the end. His life falls into three main divisions : he is first the irresponsible child, then the warrior, and at last, when his fighting days are over, he becomes a member of the group of wise old men who are the repositories of tribal lore and who determine in council the affairs of the tribe. That this division is natural and fitting is obvious : we see it among civilized races also, as an ideal that circumstances often do not

[1] Spencer and Gillen, *The Northern Tribes of Central Australia*.

make possible of attainment. First comes childhood, with
its light tasks, then the period when the man makes his
place in society. During both these periods the interest
turns outward to external things. Then, as Jung has
pointed out in his lectures, there comes a day when for
the first time he feels ' the cooler airs of afternoon ' and
begins to go down the declining slopes of life. Until this
day there has been psychic growth and expansion ; after
it comes the period of concentration, of ever-narrowing
values so far as the outer world is concerned, when the
interest turns more to mental and spiritual values and to
the search for wisdom. The natural rôle of the old man—
if circumstances permit—is to be a guide, a tempering
influence, to those who are still in the heat of the battle
of life, a teacher and counsellor. And it is surely significant
that man, who cherishes and supports the aged members
of his species, has risen to supremacy among the animals.
Old people are the natural oracles of orthodoxy, conventionality and respectability of every kind.

Formal education is continued after the initiation among
many peoples of lower culture by means of the ' age-
classes.' The savage rarely knows exactly how old he is ;
but he knows to what age-class he belongs. These age-
classes are like the degrees of Masonry : they result in a
progressive, step-by-step revelation of tribal wisdom. This
continuous education of the adult has also disappeared
from modern educational systems : when a youth has
taken a degree at his university courses or finished his
course at a professional school we say that his education
is completed, and the young man himself is quite sure
that such is the case. The formal education of the primitive, although it is almost a life-long process, is entirely
standardized : there are no elective courses. More, even,
than our modern universities, the process is one that
grinds down all human material to one standard, correct
size and pattern, and ruthlessly polishes off any budding
tendency to individuality.

Along with the formal education there runs, precisely

as with us, an informal and mostly unconscious education, by which many of the collective representations (as orthodox views are technically called) are implanted. Jung has insisted, especially in a series of lectures that he delivered in London in 1924,[1] that the psychic life of the infant is practically a continuation of that of the parents— at first a continuation of the psychic life of the mother, and later also of the father and other members of the household. That is, the infant starts life with certain tendencies and powers that are a common heritage of the human race ; but the *contents* of its psychic life are derived at first from other members of the family. As the infant grows its psychic powers develop, its interest expands beyond the family group, and it begins to absorb ideas and points of view from playmates and other persons. Except as an intuitive judge of character, the child is decidedly uncritical and undiscriminating : not only are the most fantastic tales and explanations of natural phenomena swallowed whole, but the child actually prefers a mythical explanation to a scientific one. Thus Jung relates an example : a normal child three years of age who was perplexed as to the origin of babies was given the correct explanation by her father. This she followed with great interest. She was apparently completely satisfied by learning that her baby brother had grown within the body of her mother from seed planted by her father, just as the flowers grew in their beds from seed that had been planted by the gardener. But the very next day she had reverted to the much more mysterious and artistically satisfying myth that it was the stork that brought babies.[2] Primitives, children, and the mystically-inclined civilized adult are alike in this : the processes of Nature, as such, seem to them cold and lifeless, they have no warmth and glow, no artistry, such as myth provides ; and consequently the myth is welcomed and believed.

---

[1] Jung, *Three Lectures upon Psychology and Education*, in *Contributions to Analytical Psychology*.

[2] Jung, *Collected Papers on Analytical Psychology*, 132–152.

Thus it comes about that the more imaginative and fantastic are the explanations and the points of view that are presented to the child, the mystic, or the savage, the more eagerly does the primitive mind accept them. This love of the strange, the dramatic, and the fantastic powerfully reinforces the fear that always accompanies a collective representation—the fear of being punished by the mystic powers if one should dare to disbelieve, of becoming taboo if one should dare to act upon a secret doubt, of being avoided by one's fellows, killed as a heretic and an enemy of the group, or, worst of all, of being expelled from the brotherhood of the group and forced off alone to meet the horrors of the unknown.

The collective representations mentioned by Lévy-Bruhl sound mad enough to us—this being a characteristic of all the creeds and points of view that prevail in any group to which one does not oneself belong.

One of the most curious articles of belief among primitives, which is often cited as an example of the incomprehensibility of savage thought, is the collective representation that unites misfortune with moral delin-quency and the disfavour of the higher powers. In Lévy-Bruhl's *Primitive Mentality* the reader comes across many interesting examples. ' In the primitive's eyes misfortune is a disqualification, and he who has been attacked by it has at the same time suffered moral degeneration. As an object of wrath of the unseen powers he becomes a danger to his friends and to the social group, and they avoid his presence.' [1] ' *Res est sacra miser.*' Here *sacra* means ' in a special condition which does not allow of its being approached or touched ' : taboo, that is.[2] In the Basuto language innocent and joyous are synonymous, and so are impure and unhappy. ' They consider sufferings and accidents of all kinds as an impurity, a stain.' [2] Among the savages of the Orinoco nobody troubles about the sick or dying—' Nobody cares

[1] Lévy-Bruhl, *Primitive Mentality*, 290.
[2] Lévy-Bruhl, *loc. cit.*, 291.

whether he eats or drinks. From the attitude of these people, one would imagine that they have no feelings, or else that they are anxious for his death. When the hours for the repast have arrived, they place by the hammock where the invalid is lying the same food as is given to everybody else. If he eats it, it is well ; but if he does not taste it, that is also all right.'[1] It might be that the sick man thrives as well under these conditions as he would if he were tenderly stuffed with food ; but the kindness is inadvertent.

In Kamschatka it is a great sin to help one who has fallen into the water. He should, in fact, be made to drown. If he does escape he must be treated as dead— not spoken to, not allowed to enter a dwelling, given no food. No woman would have him. The Eskimos and Greenlanders do not dare to help one who falls into the water.[2] So is it with the Kafirs, who also abandon the dying.[3] In the Solomon Islands a man who has escaped from sharks is thrown back to them. Among the Fiji Islanders a man who has been shipwrecked but has succeeded in getting ashore must be eaten.[4]

Is there nothing of this sort among us ? Civilized people often manifest uneasiness over associating with persons who seem to be pursued by hard luck. Such a one is a ' Jonah ' in popular parlance. Gamblers (who are usually superstitious) always avoid Jonahs. Many prominent operators in the stock market refuse to have associated with them in business deals anyone who has a record of misfortune, and it is difficult for a person who is known to be unlucky to find employment in Wall Street. In general, there are probably few of us who do not prefer to be associated with a person who has a reputation for success than one who is dogged by failure. This is good sense : there is something wrong with a man all of whose projects go astray. Often one can point out his defect, and say that he has poor judgment, that he jumps at

[1] Lévy-Bruhl, *loc. cit.*, 292.　　[2] Lévy-Bruhl, *loc. cit.*, 280.

[3]　　　Do.　　282.　　[4]　　Do.　　283–5.

conclusions, that he is too optimistic, too easily discouraged, that he is lazy or has some other vice. Often the practical psychologist can detect a psychic split in the victim of ' accident.' Freud has dealt admirably with such cases in his *Psychopathology of Everyday Life*. The difference between ourselves and savages in regard to Jonahs is simply one of degree : we are sorry for them, and piously hope that someone else will help them, and we hasten to increase the distance between them and ourselves ; but the primitive is not even sorry for them, he fears to oppose the will of the Power that is afflicting them, and he either leaves the Jonahs without pity to their merited fate or helps that fate along.

The most interesting of primitive collective representations is that which is known to anthropologists as *mana*. This is the Melansian name for a mysterious power, comparable with static electricity. Other savages of course use other words for it, but the underlying idea is the same and in all cases classifies a wide variety of objects, persons and phenomena on the basis of a common quality and to some extent even abstracts this quality.

The primitive, however, is not inclined to think conceptually. The languages he uses are marked by the poorness of generic words, even when highly developed in other respects. In Zulu ' my father,' and ' his-or-her father ' are distinct words without any element in common. The natives of Tierra del Fuego have a single word, *mamihlapinatapai*, which is said to mean ' to look at each other hoping that either will offer to do something which both parties desire but are unwilling to do.' In the old Huron-Iroquois language there are separate words for ' I have been to the water,' for ' go to the water,' for ' there is water in the bucket,' and for ' there is water in the pot,' and these lack any common element meaning ' water.' These holophrases are called portmanteau words by Marett, who adds, ' in many other cases the difficulty of isolating the common meaning, and fixing it by a common term, has proved altogether too much for a primitive language.' [1]

Thus among primitives generally a manifestation of any kind is not detached from the thing or the situation that manifests it : the quality of *thing-ness*, concreteness, adheres to the idea ; and we might find powerfulman, powerfulwoman, and powerfulbeast in some primitive language that lacked the conceptual noun, power. A step, in progress, both in thinking and in language, is made when the word ' power ' is coined. But even yet the idea of power may not be completely discriminated in the operations of reason from those things that manifest power. This is indeed what we find among primitives : their thinking and other psychic processes are concretistic. ' The good, the beautiful, and the true,' seem to us actual enough without attaching any manifesting object to them ; but the savage would think of ' the good man,' ' the beautiful woman,' ' the true legend.' The idea of mana has reached this stage : it is almost a concept, but not quite. Many savage peoples have their different names for this mystic power, but they think of it always in connection with some objects that manifest it.

Many terms have been used to translate mana. Marett says, ' Mana, or grace, is that within a man which inspires him, raises him to a higher power, endows him with such virtue as passes the ordinary.' ' It is true that the savage is apt to say that mana resides in the ceremony ; but this is hardly more than a way of putting the fact that the ceremony is a means of grace.' [2] The savage attributes mana to the symbol used in his rites : if the Australian diligently rubs his *churinga* (which is a piece of wood or stone that participates mystically with himself) in order to work himself up to the point of doing something, he imagines that he derives energy, mana, from the churinga. His sense of mounting power and courage seems to him to come from the churinga ; for he has not arrived at a

---

[1] Marett, *Anthropology*, 140.
[2] Marett, *Psychology and the Sciences*, 48.

degree of consciousness that would enable him to see that energy and courage are potentialities already latent within himself which are summoned into consciousness and rendered kinetic by the ritual and the symbol with which he works himself up. Unconscious psychic contents, when perceived at all, are always projected upon some object as upon a screen, and appear as qualities of the object.

' This tendency to objectify his feelings,' says Marett, ' is, moreover, greatly strengthened by the fact that they are almost wholly group-feelings. The mana sought and obtained by way of the public ceremony is a grace for all ; so that the means of grace, the grace-imparting symbol, must necessarily consist in something external to which all can look at once. Meanwhile there is good evidence that the savage, even while he tends to place the mana in the symbol, does not on that account regard it as a permanent property of the thing. Much has been written about the primitive doctrine of the transmissibility of mana, the contagion of holiness. It is a balm that can be transferred from one vessel to another. Moreover, all sorts of vessels may be used together, their size and shape being indifferent so long as they yield their quota of the precious medicine. " The more forms, the more mana " would seem to be the primitive creed ; and the inference is that however obscurely, the mana is perceived to be independent of the particular nature of its vehicle.' [1]

Mana, from the objective and concrete point of view of the savage, is simply ' That which acts,' or ' That which is potent.' Regarded from the point of view of psychology, one can say that mana is fascination : it is that power in any object that rivets the conscious attention or stirs up activity in the unconscious. Carrying the analysis further, we can trace the fascination of conscious attention —often it is an unwilling attention—that an object exercises to the unconscious. There is always fascination where an instinct is involved, for example. An instinct is an inherited tendency to perceive and pay attention to

[1] Marett, *loc. cit.*, 48–9.

objects of a particular class, and to react to them in a definite manner, or, at least, to experience an impulse to do so; and each instinct is usually accompanied by a specific emotional excitement—if I may be permitted again to paraphrase McDougall's definition.[1] That is to say, each animal has a memory-image of the definite objective situation or subjective need appropriate for the functioning of a given instinct; and this image does not depend upon individual experience or even upon consciousness. It is part of the hereditary psychic equipment, or structure of the unconscious, of the collective unconscious because it is common to all individuals of the same species and sex. Thus food fascinates the attention of the hungry man. When a man needs sexual intercourse he finds (if he is healthy) that woman is very fascinating : she is full of mana for him. Whether this mana is regarded as natural and desirable, or whether it is considered evil, depends upon one's point of view. Marett, in speaking of mana as ' grace ' and a kind of contagious holiness, omits to mention that the primitive usually ascribes more evil mana than good mana to surrounding objects. In fact, all mana is dangerous. The chief has good mana ; the more potent he is the better for the tribe ; yet the Maori held that a commoner who touched him would surely die. Whatever is sacred or unclean carries with it a taboo ; and in primitive and early historical usage the unclean and the sacred are synonymous. An example of this is seen in the prohibition of incest, in the concrete physical sense : the woman of the group into which an Australian man is born is taboo to him, she is at once sacred and unclean so far as he is concerned. With us the taboo extends only to near kin by blood, whom we feel to be in some mystic way sacred, and with whom sexual intercourse would be mystically defiling. Another civilized example is the sexual organs : most of us, as children, have been informed that these are unclean and, in the next breath, sacred. When I write of ' mystic ' elements

1 McDougall, *An Introduction to Social Psychology*, 29.

in the modern psyche, my readers will, I hope, bear it in mind that I mean psychic actualities arising from the unconscious, or motivated by the unconscious, and nothing more.

It has been mentioned that a very slight resemblance or analogy between objects suffices to link them up in the unconscious in a mystic participation that the limited consciousness of the primitive is incapable of dissolving. It is noteworthy that, to the primitive, it is often the similar *activity* of two or more objects that results in a mystic participation : it would seem that mere visual resemblance was of less importance. In fact, the total visual dissimilarity of objects is often disregarded. The primitive seems to say, ' Tell me what you do, and I shall tell you what you are.' With all his mysticism, the savage is intensely practical ; he cares for results. If two objects act upon the subject identically, they are identical, no matter how different they may look to the ignorant white man. Hence many mystic participations are doubtless due to the fact that the objects manifest mana of the same degree or quality. In many localities where the spirits of the dead are feared the dead man's personal belongings are buried with him or destroyed. Partly this may be due to the pious notion that he will need them in spirit-land ; partly to the idea that his ghost lurks about the place where his property is located (and the company of ghosts is regarded with disfavour) ; but often it seems that through mystic participation the man's property is the man himself, now a dead man, whom nobody wants about the place. The participation is through the deceased's mana. One can almost say that the actuality of a man, living or dead, is his mana or libido ; so that the idea of mana is closely connected with the idea of the actual essence of the man, with his non-physical existence —it is related to the idea of the soul, though it is not the same as the soul.

Lévy-Bruhl points out that certain distinct objects which evoke ' the same collective emotions ' are taken to be identical [1] and this is from the point of view of analytical psychology an absolutely correct explanation of why savages do not distinguish these objects from each other. He cites the beliefs of the Huichol Indians, to whom ' corn, deer, and hikuli are, in a way, one and the same thing.' ' The hikuli is a sacred plant which men (destined and prepared for this end by a series of very complicated rites) gather every year with great ceremonial, in a remote district, and at the cost of much fatigue and personal privation : the existence and well-being of the Huichols are mystically connected with the harvesting of this plant. If the hikuli were to fail, or were not gathered according to the obligatory rites, the cornfields would not yield their usual crops. . . . The welfare and preservation of the Huichols depend (also) on the number of deer killed ; and the chase is accompanied by the same ceremonial practices and evokes the same collective emotions as the search for the sacred plant. Hence results the identification of the hikuli, deer, and corn. The hikuli, deer, and corn participate in mystic qualities of the highest importance to the tribe, and, for this reason, are considered as " the same thing." This participation, *which is felt* by them ' (the italics are Lévy-Bruhl's) ' does not present the same confusion which we, despite all our efforts, see in it.'

Let me observe, by way of parenthesis, that the customary use of the copula *is* may be the cause of our seeing confusion in savages' thoughts about mystic participations. We might better, I think, use some form of the word ' act.' Then the Huichol Indian would be reported as saying, ' Corn, deer, and hikuli have the same action ; we see the same mystic power, the same mana, in all three.' For it is as subjective actualities that they are identical, not as objective realities : no Huichol, surely, would ever dream of shooting an arrow at either of the two plants, nor would he try to garner a deer with his hands like a vegetable. I wish to emphasize this distinction because so many civilized persons have diffi-

[1] Lévy-Bruhl, *How Natives Think*, 123.

culty in discriminating between what is *actual* in the psychic processes, and what is objectively *real*. God is an indisputable actuality in the psychic life of many people, but whether there is an objective reality corresponding to the concept God is questioned by many. To the psychologist these two are completely distinct. Whether God exists does not come within the field of psychology at all ; but the effects upon the subject of a *belief* in God has been the object of much psychological research. The ' actual ' is a far more inclusive term than the ' real.'

But let us return to our Huichols. Not only hikuli, corn and deer are important to them and associated with the same psychic activity in them. Certain insects are also identical with corn. The white tail of a deer is the same actuality as a plume ; so are the deer's antlers ; so is the deer itself. Clouds and cotton wool are actually plumes. All serpents are believed to have plumes. Mystic power—in this case good mana—resides in plumes : they are health, life, and luck-giving symbols to the Huichols. By the help of feathers the shamans ' are capable of hearing everything that is said to them from below the earth and from all points of the world, and perform magic feats.' This is because birds, especially eagles and hawks, hear everything. Perhaps their organs of hearing are their plumes—Lévy-Bruhl's quotation from Lumholz' *Symbolism of the Huichol Indians* leaves us in the dark as to this. One can hardly fail to note almost universal associations in these and related participations : the bird is a spiritual messenger from above ; it is itself a spiritual symbol ; the Power above is very wise ; he hears and knows everything ; the serpent is a symbol of wisdom, though generally of a dangerous wisdom ; the serpent is a symbol of danger and death ; the god is dangerous, charged with terrible mana ; the god is a spiritual being ; he can fly through the air like a bird ; there are winged serpents (dragons) ; wings are made of feathers. These are just such connotations as the dream brings to our dim sleeping consciousness ; and a myth is like a dream that all the group believes.

There is neither rime nor reason in such associations, whether they occur in dreams or in collective representations or myths. They cannot be analysed satisfactorily as logical products, but must be taken in the way Tylor advised, as poetry is appreciated, or music. The imagination must be allowed to play about such images according to its own laws, with as little interference as possible from the reasoning function. By so doing ideas are permitted to happen to one, ideas that may lead to an understanding of these products of the unconscious which reason could not attain.

What do these strange, irrational collective representations accomplish ? Since those who think alike will tend to act alike, it is clear that the group's solidarity is promoted by them. What the belief is, or what it is about, is of no importance. All that is needed is that there shall be a belief which all firmly hold. Orthodoxy prevents individuality and cements the group together.

CHAPTER XVI

MANA AND SACRED THINGS

CONSERVATISM is pre-eminently a primitive characteristic. Custom, according with savage orthodoxy and tradition, governs every situation and every piece of conduct which people of simple cultures deem important—and they regard as vital a host of details which to us seem of no weight at all. Only neurotics among us attach so much importance to trifles as do savages. Custom, to the primitive mind, embraces all that we know as good manners, good morals, law, duty, and religion. When we refer to primitive religion we include, as a matter of course, all of these aspects of conduct ; for not only are they all enforced by the same social sanctions, they also spring from the same psychological roots. Custom itself is sacred : that is, it is untouchable—not to be questioned, and not to be modified. If the laws of the Medes and the Persians never changed, this shows that they were primitive laws involving religious emotions and fears. Custom fascinates the primitive mind and evokes admiration, reverence, awe and fear in it ; these emotions arise from the collective unconscious, which holds people true to the hereditary pattern ; and religion evokes the same emotional responses. On the savage theory that objects which arouse the same emotion in the subject are in mystic participation with each other, are ' identical ' as Lévy-Bruhl expresses it, custom is religion. Both have the same action upon the subject ; or rather, the subject acts the same in respect to both.

As culture increases, the conscious superstitious reverence and unconscious awe for precedent decreases.

Malinowski has shown that the Trobriand Islanders, who are decidedly primitive as existing races go, frequently violate sexual taboos when they do not expect to be caught although the theoretical sanctity of the customary prohibition remains unimpaired.[1]

So far as the origin of religion is concerned, it has already been noted that it could hardly have come out of metaphysical speculation ; for the simpler the culture of a people the less do they indulge in abstract reasoning, and the fewer conceptual nouns have they at their disposition with which to reason abstractly. Besides, the savage finds it boring and distasteful to follow logical chains of thought. If existing savages employ directed thinking less than we do, the inference is that really primitive man employed it practically not at all. Instead of religion arising from philosophy, it is the other way around. Dewey has pointed out that classical Greek philosophy arose when belief in religion weakened : when the supernatural authority for customary morality was doubted, the philosophers went to work to find logical reasons for being moral.[2]

It would also be incorrect to say that religion arises from myth. Myth enriches and profoundly modifies religion, without a doubt : when some natural agency, as the fertilizing wind, or some subjective urge, as the longing to overcome weakness and death, is represented as a person (the Holy Spirit or the Redeemer), appropriate legends are likely to gather about that person and to be regarded as an integral part of the religion in which he figures. Herakles, for example, was a pagan Christ ; and we have an excellent example how myth grows around the personification of a subjective longing in the tale of his twelve labours. So we must reject both metaphysics and myth as the original sources of religion.

To the analytical-psychologist it seems that religion is something immediate, something inherent in human

---

[1] Malinowski, *Sex and Repression in Savage Society.*
[2] Dewey, *Reconstruction in Philosophy.*

nature ; not a by-product, derived from something else, not simply handed to us by our elders or society or by any power exterior to ourselves except, of course, as to its particular form. If it seems to come to us from without, this indicates only that it comes from subconscious sources —from the collective unconscious, since it is universal. If this view is correct, it is as futile to try to get rid of the religious urge as it is to try to abolish our natural needs for food, sex, or human companionship. Such an attempt is also unhealthful.

Some results of primitive religion have been noted : the collective ceremonies of religion cement together the human brotherhood in the totemic communion ; they let joy and gladness into the toneless monotony of daily life ; they afford relief from the repressions of culture and allow the individual to lay aside for a time the burdens of individual responsibility ; and they relieve the strain of consciousness, letting each man lose himself by merging into the mystic brotherhood of the common faith. In other words, in religion the regressive longing for the mother (for childlike joy and freedom from care) is agreeably canalized and directed to a socially serviceable end, the consolidation of the group.

Yet behind these factors (which may be regarded either as results of religion if one looks at what they effect, or as causes of religion if one considers the innate needs which they satisfy) lies something further : the compulsive, inescapable fascination of certain objects for mankind ; or, putting it subjectively, the inescapable compulsion to pay attention to certain objects and to be powerfully stirred by them. This, I think, is psychologically the essence of religion : a definite, serious, subconsciously-compelled attitude with regard to something, this attitude being deeply felt emotionally. This ' something ' has to do, directly or indirectly, with the welfare of the human brotherhood. In expressing the primitive religious urge there is a marked change of attitude from that of daily life : individual burdens are forgotten, or perhaps cast

K

upon a scapegoat or something fulfilling the same function ;
ennui disappears ; there is a sense of loss of individuality
through submersion in the mystic group ; and there is a
joyful exhilaration and sense of increased power (also
found in other types of group-action). Finally, all things
are lawful for the participants : all taboos may be broken.
And the breakable taboos naturally include the sexual
taboos. Here is one connection between sexuality and
religion.

Religion does not necessarily include the worship of a
god. Confucianism, Taoism, Shintoism, and Buddhism,
as well as many of the beliefs of savages, do not. Yet it
is doubtful whether there is any race or tribe which does
not regard certain objects as sacred, as being charged with
mysterious power. Among these there are some objects
which fascinate the subject's attention to a supreme
degree. They manifest mana of such high voltage and
great amperage that the imagination can picture nothing of
intenser interest. Such objects are the sexual organs, the
sun and moon, the earth, the sea, the social group, the
ruler, and the god or gods. All these objects are bound
together in a mystic participation because of the quality
and quantity of the interest they excite : they are all
divine.

Phallic worship is one of the oldest forms of religion—
perhaps it is the very oldest. It includes the worship of
the external generative organs of both the female and the
male. In its simplest form phallic worship consists in a
compulsive fascination, accompanied by the thrill that
Durkheim [1] wrote of as characteristic of primitive religion.
These emotions arise from the collective unconscious.
Because of this, they appear to consciousness as qualities
of the object : that is, it seems to the subject that phallus
and yoni are themselves fascinating and thrilling. This
sense of being compelled to pay attention to an external
object always has something mysterious about it ; and,
as the response to sex-objects or their symbols is peculiarly

---

[1] Durkheim, *Les formes élémentaires de la vie religieuse*.

potent, the subject usually has a feeling of awe in respect
to them. One has only to consider that the sexual organs
are almost universally regarded among ourselves as being
' sacred '—so holy and so taboo that an undue part of our
conventional morality concerns them, and that they
cannot even be named without confusion (the name, to
the primitive in us, being in mystic participation with the
object)—to realize that we still respond psychologically to
phallus and yoni as did the ancient primitive who openly
worshipped them.

There cannot be any doubt that some forms of sexual
activity which we consciously regard as abnormal and
immoral are religious to the primitive layers of the psyche.
Freud, who seldom sits in judgment upon any human
tendency, drops into a moralizing vein concerning one of
these which is so common that I incline to believe it to
be statistically normal.[1] This is the practice symbolically
performed by the faithful when they kiss the great toe
of a priestly king. This is a symbolic assimilation of the
divine man, whose mana thereby passes into the worshipper : it is a primitive act of communion and atonement,
totemic in character. A highly cultured American once
showed me some paintings she had made, which were of
such a fantastic character that it was clear that they were
products of the subconscious : in fact, when she made
these pictures she had simply sat down with her materials,
and had begun to draw without having any notion as to
what the drawing would turn out to be—which is an
excellent method of bringing unconscious material to light.
One of her pictures arrested my attention strongly. It
represented an ancient altar, or perhaps a throne, roughly
hewn from great blocks of stone. On this stood a male
figure, nude, rigidly poised as the figures of gods often are
in very ancient sculptures. In the foreground a naked
woman knelt, adoring the god. But the detail of most
interest was a great serpent which coiled around the waist
of the god and extended himself ten feet or more to the

---

[1] Freud, *Leonardo da Vinci.*

worshipper, who was kissing his head. The colouring was as if the scene were enacted deep down in a cavern or in a subterranean temple : it was unreal and mysterious, and very effective. The light came from behind the god—or rather, it seemed as if a light was about to arise behind him to illuminate both god and worshipper. The woman's attitude expressed both absolute humility and passionate devotion.

This picture needs no explaining to the psychologist : the form of its religious meaning is clear, but what I was especially interested in was the fact that it was created *through* (I intentionally put it thus) a modern, very highly civilized woman, who, so far as I could detect, had no religious beliefs of any kind. If a primitive, or even an ancient Indian or Egyptian had been the artist, there would have been nothing remarkable about the composition.

A curious form of the phallic religious impulse is found in exhibitionism. Just as gazing upon phallic objects, whether natural or in some conventionalized symbolic form, and surrendering oneself to the potent awed thrill which rushes up from ancient strata of the collective unconscious constitutes the basis of phallic worship, so there seems to be an equally potent primitive urge to expose oneself. That this is a primitive religious manifestation it seems difficult to doubt. It is the desire to be worshipped, involving, of course, an escape from the restrictions and limitations imposed by social usages. The exhibitionist plays the rôle of a god or a goddess. Various drugs, notably alcohol, have the power to produce an illusion of escape from one's limitations and unimportance ; and this temporary illusion of boundless power and happiness would in itself be enough to account for the universal use of them. Man undoubtedly needs to escape from the truth about himself occasionally, by some means ; and the only objection I can see to the process is that the escape is so often sought (or allowed to overtake one) just at the moments when one should be most keenly alive to every fact entering into an existing situation—of which facts the real extent of one's powers and limitations is perhaps the most important. The savage's magic rituals allow him to escape from his own limitations, even to the extent of becoming the master of the multiplication of wild animals and the growth of vegetation; but the fact that he ritualizes nearly every method of arriving at an elated psychic state is evidence of his unreasoning wisdom. The modern exhibitionist seems to secure the same divine inflation as the more statistically normal man derives from alcohol, or an Indian devotee gets from hashish or the opium-smoker derives from his pipe — the use of drugs to obtain religious mystical experiences being well known.[1]

Exhibitionism does not seem to me to be derived from sexual desire, though this may also be present. I have had opportunity to study a number of exhibitionists carefully, and they have all assured me that the sexual impulse, when it arrives, is stronger than the desire to be seen and admired. On the other hand, one woman ex-hibitionist among these cases was something more than frigid: she had an aversion to being touched at all, though she was eager to pose or to move about the room naked for hours at a time. She possessed a good deal of insight into her own inner processes, and her explanation seemed to me illuminating. ' I have to be so dreadfully respectable,' she told me, ' and to show myself naked seems to set me free. Besides, it seems to change me somehow. With my clothes on I am only myself, only a woman ; but with them off I am more than a woman, I am Woman Herself.' That is, psychologically speaking, the boundaries of her personality disappeared and what the German psychiatrists term *Gottähnlichkeit* (literally ' god-almighty-ness ') appeared. This condition, first described by Adler, means that consciousness is flooded by collective, mostly unconscious, images and tendencies.

[1] Spencer and Gillen, *The Northern Tribes of Central Australia.*

In such a case as this young woman's there is nothing dangerous in the condition ; but when too many of these elements come up the subject is liable to identify himself with them, and then the conscious personality is lost, and the subject is insane. Such subjects have become as gods.

Many modern systems of autosuggestion, such as Coué's, ' new thought,' ' faith cure,' and Christian Science, deliberately aim at inducing a partial *Gottähnlichkeit*. In fact, all European religions do this to some extent with their teachings that the believer is the child of God, under special protection, and that whatsoever he shall ask believing that he will receive it will be granted to him. Every close observer must have seen cases of deeply religious persons whose characters have undergone a subtle change, in which the clear outlines of the former personality have become blurred and indefinite—a change which makes the primitive in us uneasy, as if in the presence of a being at once more than human and less. Such super- and sub-human beings—shamans, priestly kings, the insane, and persons in states of contagious psychic excitement—are dreaded by savages.

But to continue with phallic worship, let me point out a particularly objectionable survival of it which is widespread among us. I refer to the pernicious books upon sex, mostly addressed to children and youths, in which it is argued that God created human beings, that this is a divine power and prerogative, and that since the sexual organs and the sexual instinct are the instruments of the divine purpose and power they are themselves sacred. In true primitive style any misuse of sexuality—the authors of these books, who frequently are clergymen, of course assuming authority to define use and misuse in these matters—is threatened with mystic penalties, especially with demoniacal possession, now called insanity. Psychiatrists do not know of any mental disorder that can be laid to any form of sexuality ; but they all recognize the evil that is done by arousing these mystic terrors in unstable

minds. Our asylums are full of people who, having
satisfied autoerotic impulses in the same way that all
normal men and women do when intercourse is denied
them, now are preyed upon by a fixed idea that they are
and must remain insane as a punishment. Dr William A.
White has told me that it is usually impossible to cure
patients so long as this delusion persists, and that un-
happily it is extremely difficult to eradicate the idea once
it has been admitted to consciousness. The idea itself is
primitive : If I violate a sexual taboo, I am lost ; all
manner of mystic evils will descend upon me ; demons
will carry me off. This way of thinking is always latent
in our hereditary psychic equipment. It is easily put in
motion, for hereditary paths are always paths of least
resistance. And once conscious reason and morale have
been shaken it is very difficult to restore authority to
them. It is nothing short of criminal for a parent or
teacher ever, upon any ground whatever, to arouse in the
sensitive mind of a child the terror of insanity.

The topic of phallic worship in the psychology of the
individual is one of great interest, and much exploration
remains to be done in the rich fields into which it leads.
The hypothesis that all religion springs from sexuality
and is nothing but a modification or ' sublimation ' of it
seems to be erroneous, and to be based on an incomplete
survey of the facts. The fascinated attention which the
subject, by reason of his hereditary psychic structure,
finds himself compelled to pay to certain objects would
seem to be a surer basis for the psychological origin of
religion. Powerful emotional responses arise in connection with this fascination : fear and desire, awe, and a
mysterious sense of being controlled by the object. These,
especially the feeling of being in the power of something
outside oneself, are of the essence of religion. If the
sexual organs alone were capable of exciting the religious
response we might perhaps correctly say that religion is
sublimated sexuality only. Certainly some libido pressure
may be withdrawn from the sexual instinct by religion, but

at the same time it is as well to realize that religion may also stimulate sexuality and apparently give the sexual urge more energy than it had before. We shall presently consider other objects of worship which are so remote from being biologically connected with sexuality that it would be absurd, in the absence of convincing evidence, to suppose that they could arouse the sexual impulse : trees and rivers may be worshipped, for instance, but how could they excite the desire for detumescence ?

Quite aside from attributing the worship of the sexual organs to the mana which the primitive finds in them, as I have done, there is still another factor which must not be overlooked. This is the indisputable fact that sexuality may serve as a surrogate for any positive libido pressure. Through sexuality as through a safety-valve anger and vengefulness may be drained off, a fact of which some savages take advantage as a practical matter.[1] Excessive ambition can be handled in the same way, history being full of examples of this. The maniacal instinctively lessen their unbearable nervous excitement by seemingly superhuman sexual activity—a fact which has doubtless contributed to the myth that masturbation causes insanity. Even great fear when it mounts to panic in the group finds an emotional relief in sexuality. Save for hunger and the desire for sleep, there seem to be few if any strong emotions which cannot be relieved through the sexual safety-valve. But the fact that any particular emotion, as the exaltation of religion, may be drawn off sexually does not entitle us to say that the original emotion itself is nothing but sexuality.

Inman considers the use of the phallic symbolism employed in modern Christian public worship a degrading survival of primitive superstition and obscenity, and thinks that such symbols should be discarded.[2] I believe that it would be a mistake, from the believer's point of view, to do so. Public worship is intended to put the

---

[1] Spencer and Gillen, *The Northern Tribes of Central Australia.*
[2] Inman, *Ancient Pagan and Modern Christian Symbolism.*

worshippers into a definite psychic state, into a religious mood ; and there can be no doubt that the rich display of phallic symbols in the church acts upon the unconscious of the congregation and powerfully incites the religious response. Few, if any of the symbols used are so realistic as to lead the conscious mind to recognize what they represent ; even the sistrum, emblem of virginity, with its shape of an oval or loop with bars across its opening, is not unduly suggestive of the yoni. Far franker representations used to be common during the Middle Ages, and in some places wax images of the sexual organs were employed as votive offerings by persons seeking to be cured of some ailment as late as the eighteenth century ; but these have mostly disappeared.[1] Those phallic symbols which are still employed suggest nothing sexual to the consciousness of one who has not studied their history and meaning. But that they work (through unconscious channels) is evidenced by the fact that the Church has continued to use them. Probably the fathers of the Church were fully aware of the sexual significance of most of the ancient symbols which they took over from pagan religious ceremonials and they must have believed in their efficacy, or have felt their power themselves, or they would not have adopted them. It would be hard to explain otherwise how a church whose ideal was asceticism and the denial of the demands of the flesh, above all the denial of the sexual urge, could have taken over conventionalized representations of the sexual organs as symbols of its deepest faiths and most sacred divinities.

In the foregoing pages I have tried to show, primarily, that the phallic religious tendency is alive in the modern and the civilized. To most people, phallic worship seems a strange aberration of antiquity, wellnigh incomprehensible, and dead as the civilization of Babylon or Egypt. There is hardly any primitive phenomenon which one could select off-hand as better evidence for the theory that the primitive mentality is different in kind from the modern.

[1] Payne Knight, *Phallic Worship*.

If, then, phallic religious processes are found to be living and working elements in the modern psyche, a further case has been made out against Lévy-Bruhl's hypothesis, and in favour of the theory that the whole primitive psyche lives and works in civilized mankind. Such a case would *prima facie* be established, in my opinion, by a study of collective religious phenomena alone. In order to clinch the argument, however, I have gone beyond these collective manifestations, and have endeavoured to show that the phallic religious elements can be found operating in the individual psyche.

This method of presentation by treating individual and collective psychic phenomena separately does not imply the existence of a ' group mind ' or ' collective soul.' These are misleading terms which have brought much confusion into scientific discussion. The fundamental similarity between individual psyches and individual modes of conduct is an objective reality ; but apart from this there is no reality in group mind or collective soul. In a situation where all the individual minds in the group act the same, they act as one, unitedly ; but that does not mean that the sum of one hundred minds is one hundred and one minds. The mythical hundred-and-first mind, called the group mind, is nothing more (speaking scientifically and not metaphysically, of course) than a convenient metaphor for a real similarity between the individual minds in the group. It is, therefore, a mistake to speak of the group mind working thus or so ; for a similarity does not think. What thinking is done, is invariably done by individual minds.

The reader will have noticed that in writing of phallic worship I have throughout referred to the sexual organs and not to the generative organs. This is because the generative aspect of the sexual function is of secondary importance, or of no immediate importance at all, in evoking the primitive religious response to phallic objects. Since there are savages today who refuse to admit that there is any causal connection between the sexual act and pregnancy [1]—the Trobriand Islanders and the Australians, for example—we must suppose that really primitive man was always ignorant of the physiological truth. When one comes to think of it, the discovery that no woman gives birth to a child except when she has been impregnated by a man is truly a triumph of scientific observation. Nine lunar months separate the effect from the cause ; and there is, moreover, no regularity in the sequence—for only in a fraction of the cases of sexual intercourse does a child result. In addition, the scientific truth has had to fight against all manner of accepted orthodox views concerning the cause of pregnancy : it was not a truth launched *in vacuo*, but a truth contradicting religious doctrines. To the primitive mind, children are the results of mystic causes, such as the eating of certain fruit or the seed of this fruit ; or ancestral spirits congregate in certain spots, awaiting a chance to be reborn, and enter the bodies of passing women through their navels. Impregnation through the ear is held possible—the word becomes flesh. The wind also may be held responsible : about two hundred years ago a French court held that a lady had not been unfaithful to her lord, but that she had carelessly slept by an open window and had been fertilized by the night air.

The primitive sees in sex an immediate personal satisfaction and an immediate matter of religious importance. When the remote biological product in the form of a child is also recognized, the religious connotations of sexuality are naturally enlarged and enriched : phallus and yoni are associated with divine creative beings who were assumed to exist before the physiological truth about pregnancy was known. Very primitive monotheistic Creators usually begin creating either by dividing themselves or by burying themselves—sometimes actually in the earth, and sometimes figuratively in meditation or

[1] Cf. Malinowski, *The Father in Primitive Psychology* ; and Spencer and Gillen, *The Northern Tribes of Central Australia*. See also Sidney Hartland, *Primitive Paternity*.

brooding—a fact of extraordinary psychological interest, into which it is impossible to delve here. Or else the creator is conceived as being androgynous, both male and female : this primordial image has been revived by the most successful of modern mystics, Mary Baker Eddy, who in giving a ' spiritual interpretation ' of the Lord's Prayer, adds to the words, ' Our Father which art in heaven,' the explanation that this being is really ' Our Father-Mother God.' [1] Or, in a third form, the creator consists of two persons, male and female : sometimes these two are united in a perpetual sexual embrace.

After the fact of human paternity is recognized the way is clear to imagine father-gods and mother-goddesses, with sexual attributes, of whom phallus and yoni naturally become the symbols. Myths arise about these beings, stories of creation ; and the original fascination of phallic objects is fortified by the support of an orthodox creed, or collective representation explaining them as divine symbols. But savage tales of creation do not explain phallic worship itself ; for the religious interest in sexual organs and representations of them was present before the cosmogonies were invented.

[1] Mary Baker Eddy, *Science and Health*, 16.

CHAPTER XVII

SOME MORE DIVINE OBJECTS

CONSIDERATION of mana-charged objects which fascinate man's attention superlatively, and awaken in him the religious thrill, brings us to the worship of the sun and other non-human natural objects.

Primitive man fears night and the darkness, not only because predatory beasts prowl then, seeing clearly when man is blind, but also because wizards, were-animal and dark powers are abroad upon their evil business. Ghosts seldom walk by day : in fact, they must take themselves off when the cock crows. The fearful spirit had power over Peter, it will be remembered, until the cock crew. It is only at night that vampires can leave their undecaying bodies in the grave and slip forth to suck blood from sleeping men and women. When the days shorten and the light of the sun begins to fail the primitive in us is melancholy, just as our ancestors used to be. For them winter meant cold, suffering, lack of food, as well as longer hours of darkness. Probably man had progressed far from his primeval condition before he realized that winter and summer invariably succeed each other : he was in the same condition of dread that we now observe among pious people who believe that each diminution of moral convention will be followed by total and permanent moral darkness ; and each autumn he feared that the sun god was about to die. Later he observed that the divine power always came back, and learned at last to have faith that it always would ; and then primitive man welcomed the triumph of the sun with a holy festival and orgy. This is our modern Christmas, which the early church took

over from paganism in the same way that it adopted pagan
sex-symbolism in its ceremonies. The moon is also divine,
and is sometimes regarded as being more friendly than the
sun. The sun is dangerous in some latitudes, it is true ;
but perhaps the theory is that whereas the sun shines only
by day the moon kindly provides light in the night, when
it is needed. But usually the sun and the moon are
opposites, opposite subjective tendencies being projected
onto them ; and the sun reflects the sane, intelligent,
constructive tendencies, while the moon reflects madness,
mystic (that is, unconscious) impulses, and tendencies
destructive of the values of the day.

The earth is a divinity with double aspect. On the one
hand, she is the nourishing mother. All plants and animals
spring from her womb and are nourished by her breast.
Man is formed from earth, from dust or clay, or from
stones that one of the divine heroes threw over his shoulder
after an angry god or goddess had destroyed the human
race. In other accounts, Heaven rested upon earth in an
unending embrace, until their child, Man, came between
them. It is healing to touch the earth, for all our strength
comes from her. Even Herakles could not conquer
Antæus so long as this giant could touch his mother,
Earth. We have the same idea in our expression that
Jones is up in the air, while Smith is a solid chap with
his feet on the ground. It crops up also in modern cults
of going barefoot : Father Kneipp's ' reasoning' about
the advantage of doing this is simply the highly rationalized
intrusion into his consciousness of the primeval image of
touching Mother Earth, and of receiving some of her
mana through the contact.

But the earth is also the Terrible Mother, in which
aspect she is the devourer of her children. ' Earth, that
nourished thee, shall claim thy dust to be resolved to earth
again ' ; as Bryant put it. The fact that each must die
has usually been deplored ; for death, even when he comes
as a friend to one who is tired, seems an enemy to those
who are left behind. As a matter of fact, the will to die

always coexists with the will to live ; but normally the will to live is conscious up to a certain age, when it begins to fade away leaving the field to the conscious or subconscious will to die. When the time has come death is usually not fought against, or even dreaded, provided that a person is not a prey to superstitions, and provided also that one knows that one has really lived and has accomplished one's work. On the other hand, people who have not enjoyed the full richness of life dread leaving it.

It has been mentioned that after the meridian of life has been passed the interest is gradually withdrawn from the outer world, and turned to inner values : the extraverted attitude is replaced by introversion. Curiosity as to the things of the world is strong in childhood and youth and up to a certain age ; than it fades naturally away, and meditation and memory-dreams take the place of it. A number of years ago I questioned fourteen men of various ages to whom the approach of death had been announced as to their escapades during the years of their vigour— particularly concerning their adventures with women. I was considerably astonished to find that not one of them felt any regret or fear of future punishment on this score, but that on the contrary they loved to let their imaginations play with these memories. One of them said to me, ' When you come to die, you will compare the shortness of youth with the length and sadness of the years that come after, and you will be thankful if you enjoyed the years that were open to you to enjoy. If you have really lived, you will not mind dying.' Some day, perhaps, we shall have some honest autobiographies, writter by ordinary men and women who did not feel called upon to moralize, and who did not care to keep up the pose of respectability after their escape from this world of conventionality. And then we shall find out whether this is not the usual attitude of those who await death. I believe it is : the banquet of life is left without regret by those who have feasted and drunk deeply, while the procrastinators and nibblers dread being torn away from the table.

Nevertheless, man has always dreamed about conquering the grave in the Terrible Mother. In myths the hero triumphs over death. That is, he triumphs over his mother—over softness, unmanliness, childishness, and the temptation to retreat from conflict, danger and suffering. The mother stands for all these infantile urges, which persist in the psyche of the adult. She does not wish her son to adventure and to go into danger : she would have him remain the irresponsible child, and she tries to lure him back to her, to shelter and safety. In so doing she tries to kill the hero in him, and to destroy his manhood. In myths the hero is apparently conquered by the mother ; he descends into the womb of earth, the grave ; but the proof that he is a hero is the fact that he is reborn. When this final and supreme test has been passed the hero is divested of all human weaknesses, and becomes a god. All the evil mana of the human mother and of man's longing to flee back to childhood is symbolized in these myths of Earth the Terrible Mother, and of the demigod who conquers her. The descent into the grave is pictured symbolically as incestuous intercourse with the mother, fatal for the ordinary man. Only the hero dares to long for his mother ; if the ordinary man lets this desire for childhood become strong in his consciousness he is done for. In this connection it may be noted that in many myths the hero, when he is ill or has some particularly hard task ahead of him, hides himself among women and even wears women's clothes and practises the arts of distaff and loom. In other words, a regression toward effeminacy marks the period of hesitation when he is gathering energy to attack a great obstacle.

It is interesting to note that the primordial image of the earth as a divinity has its modern defenders. Fechner holds that the earth has its own collective consciousness, as has each of the heavenly bodies, each astral system, and the whole universe. One sees in Fechner's theory a very clear example of how a primitive psychic content—here the perception that the earth is powerfully fascinating—

comes in time to be dressed in rational terms, so that at first glance one takes the primitive psychic content as the result of reasoning, whereas usually it is the rational explanation which follows the pre-existing primitive view. Primitive man feels that the earth is divine ; and Fechner reasons that the spiritual is the rule and not the exception in Nature. To think otherwise he holds is the original sin in both popular and scientific mental processes. Our lives are sustained by some greater life, and our individuality by some greater individuality. To believe that there is a bodiless divinity on the one hand, and a soulless nature on the other, is a cold and comfortless doctrine. Mind is always found in connection with body, not necessarily a human body, but still some body. Our bodies move at the command of our minds. It is fair to suppose that any body that moves does so at the command of some mind that inhabits it. The earth moves. . . . And so we are brought, by Fechner's process of reasoning, back to what the primitive believed before he was able to reason abstractly and before his language contained the abstract terms that might have enabled him to reason. This is the way in which philosophies are mostly made, and theologies as well.

The sea is also divine to the primitive mind. Frazer tells of savages living some hundreds of miles from the coast who have never seen the ocean ; but if by any chance one of them is brought within sight of it he immediately makes a propitiatory sacrifice. The sight of the ocean was dreaded by some Central American Indians, who believed that to look upon it brought sickness.[1] This is an interesting example of how the collective representations of primitives often contain the seeds of scientific truths ; for these particular Indians lived in the mountains and seeing the ocean involved descending into the fever-haunted coastal jungles, where they did in fact sicken.

Besides these natural objects, in which the inherent mana is divinely potent, there are a host of lesser things

[1] Frazer, *Taboo and the Perils of the Soul.*

L

containing enough mana to make them semi-divine at the very least. Such was Jerusalem to the Jews, and such is Mecca to the followers of Mohammed, Paris to the Frenchman, and London to the Englishman. A city can so fascinate the attention that one instinctively personifies it, and speaks of it as a loved or hated or puzzling woman. Among the ancient Greeks almost every little streamlet, pool, and grove had its local spirit. By personification an indefinite something that is felt, perhaps very vaguely even when strongly, is made representable to consciousness. It can then be thought about more easily, and can be spoken of to another person without circumlocution and tiresome description. Whenever an object is personified we know that it contains mana. To the Greeks even a tree was often the home of a dryad ; and a Negro of British Nigeria may hear the mystic voice of the individual tree with which his life is bound up calling him to come many miles to her in the dead of night through jungles filled with dangerous beasts and demons. And he obeys, unless forcibly held back by other men.[1] We must all feel, it seems to me, that in losing this intimate emotional relation with Nature something rich and vital has gone out of our lives. The æsthetic admiration of Nature (which is the modern substitute for the mystic participation with Nature in which the classic ancients lived, and that still acts powerfully upon the savage) is a poor wishy-washy thing : the blood of the world does not pound in the veins of one who sees in Nature merely something pretty or something scientifically interesting. Our modern view of Nature, including man and the other animals, is anæmic. And bloodless views make bloodless characters.

In losing our heart-and-soul relation with Nature we have almost blocked a libido-outlet that functioned freely through many thousands of years, right down to the coming of Christianity at least. Among the ignorant, whose conventional religion is only superficial, it functions still. A thin trickle still comes through in the form of

[1] Talbott, *In the Shadow of the Bush.*

scientific curiosity and æstheticism ; but Christianity succeeded in diverting the main stream of interest to the bodiless God of whom Fechner speaks. By doing this, God was made to appear as an opposite of Nature, and Nature took on an evil aspect. To show that one loves God, it became necessary (in ascetic theory and practice) to hate what he was supposed to have created. The Christian Science doctrine that all matter is an evil illusion is in line with this theory. As a reaction against the extreme sensuality of Roman times asceticism was badly needed. But asceticism is not called for except to emancipate persons who are onesided : it is one exaggeration to correct another ; and Nature is wise enough to see to it that most people who set out to be ascetics become backsliders after a while. The balanced, full life calls for self-control, but not for asceticism and the denial of Nature. Those people are lucky who, like John Burroughs, Jack London, Stewart Edward White and White of Selbourne, Walt Whitman, Fabre, and W. H. Hudson (to name a few of them) feel deeply and strongly that they are at one with Nature. To them the men and women and all the living things that inhabit the broad bosom of our mother are brothers and sisters : like the Ancient Mariner they bless these unaware, as well as consciously. The bush soul ' did not desert these men ; and every primitive knows that it makes a man ill to lose any of his souls. This is another way of saying that it makes a man ill to lose any of the hereditary values of the race, so that he fails to express race-habitual interests. Let me repeat : no individual can successfully change, in his short lifetime, the hereditary habits of the race ; and if he wishes to remain sound in body and psyche he had better not try. An emotional relation with Nature is one of these habits.

The primitive's strong emotional relation with his group and his totem reappears constantly in history whenever an old group is endangered or a new group is in process of formation. This was the case when Christianity was struggling for existence. In Christian theory all men are brothers in Christ, and all achieve the uniformity of primitive socialism in the eyes of God : one soul is as precious as another. There have been many to whom this was more than a mere intellectual hypothesis ; instead, it has been a fact, an actuality pulsating with meaning and life. Among some of the Gnostics the doctrine found acceptance that Humanity is God, and God is Humanity. It was pointed out that Jesus did not call himself the Son of God, but the Son of Man. At the same time, he referred to God as his father. This was taken to mean that God and Mankind are one. The totemic quality of these ideas is obvious. The Church, which had set itself up as the mediator between God and man, naturally showed no enthusiasm for this heresy, which would have made the love and service of humanity the natural method of demonstrating one's devotion to God, and would have rendered an official mediator unnecessary. So the intellectual theory was suppressed without much difficulty. But it is interesting to observe that though the conscious theory of the identity of God and Humanity is so rare nowadays that it may be called extinct, the intuition that the best way to serve God is to serve humanity is not rare at all. I have spoken of man's social instinct, gregariousness plus co-operation, as the basis of bio-morality, and have shown that it is so powerful an urge that it easily subordinates such important impulses as hunger and sexuality. When this social instinct is blocked or atrophied we have on our hands an individual who subjectively is deformed and ill, and who objectively is a social misfit—an idler, a neurotic, a lunatic, or a criminal, social waste that the community excretes in one way or another. In contradistinction to these crippled characters we have relatively many healthy souls who, without bothering their heads about theology, philosophy, or psychology, instinctively like other people and enjoy doing what they can for them. For them, the ancient mystic participation with their fellows has not been dissolved by consciousness : it is natural for them to form warm human relations, and to put into these relations the libido that race-habit has earmarked for such spending. Further along in the process of the evolution of consciousness we find a good many individuals who consciously do creative work that they believe will be useful in the world. People of both these classes have found an indispensable libido-outlet. And there are also the altruists, people who try to benefit others because it is their melancholy duty to do so. Perhaps they better their condition in the next world thereby, but they get no rich human satisfaction in this, or health either. For the social instinct demands that love be poured out freely and happily. It is impossible to overestimate the value of the primitive attitude toward Nature and man as a psychic medicine.

The reader may wonder why I have given so much space to the subject of mana (and am about to give more), and why mana is looked upon as an idea tending to secure the unity of the group. The reason is a double one : it is impossible to gain an insight into primitive psychology without understanding this curious idea of mana, which is a forerunner of so many modern concepts—divine power, energy, and libido, for example. Moreover, mana is a collective representation, an orthodox conventional point of view ; and it needs no argument to prove that men who believe alike will generally tend to act alike in the same situation. This really is one of the main objects of all education : to prevent psychic variation that might imperil the homogeneity of the group. So far we have discussed rather the positive side of these matters, the group benefits and individual satisfactions, the rewards, that collective representations afford. Now it is time to take up the other side of the picture, and examine taboo and its workings.

CHAPTER XVIII

MANA AND TABOO

TABOO is a collective representation intimately bound up with the idea of mana. When a primitive fears an object because of the mana in it, he naturally avoids it. If a member of his group does something unusual, whether this consists in inventing an improved knife or a new implement, or in escaping from sharks or from drowning if he chances to fall into the water, or in transgressing some orthodox custom, it becomes at once clear that this strange person contains dangerous mana ; and the rest of the group avoid him. Either partially or wholly, he ceases to belong to the communion and becomes an outcast heretic. The tabooed person cannot be restored to his former status in the group until the pernicious mana has been sterilized by fitting rites ; and if his novel conduct was extremely shocking the whole group must be disinfected ritually. The analogy between a tabooed person and a modern who is suffering from a contagious disease is too marked to escape attention : indeed, savages often establish rigid quarantine against another village where an epidemic is raging. In so doing they have no idea of the transmissibility of disease, as we understand it : they know that such sicknesses are unusual, and that they are proof that the inhabitants of the afflicted village have violated some important prohibition or failed to perform some important duty toward the mystic powers ; and the illness shows that they are being visited by divine wrath. They are, in short, taboo ; and therefore paths must be blocked with thorns between the two villages, and no one living in the stricken village must be

permitted to approach. Primitive religion often reaches
the same results in practice as modern science, the
difference lying merely in the reasons that are assigned
for the act. Taboo is a tendency of the collective unconscious : it is even found among animals. Köhler
notes that a group of chimpanzees will refuse to associate
with another chimpanzee which is especially stupid : they
taboo the dullard by common consent.[1]

This fact disposes of the notion that taboo was originally
a form of criminal penalty. Among comparatively advanced races, as in Tahiti for example, taboo is used as a
penalty ; but among really primitive peoples the idea of
punishment seems to be limited to the feud. Even when
a sorcerer is found and killed the purpose is not punishment but the destruction of the dangerous power that acts
through him. Primeval man, if we may judge from the
apes, probably was capable of furious bursts of rage ; but
it is unlikely that he indulged in deferred vengeance to
any great extent—the further back we look the more do
we find all animals, including man, living exclusively for
the affair of the moment. Taboo, in its simplest form, is
instinctive avoidance of the unfamiliar, from which a
mystic danger is apprehended. It is the response to the
horror novi.

Frazer has collected a great number of cases of taboo,
and has arranged them according to classes,[2] which it
will be convenient to follow here. I omit the positive
duties regulating the life of kings, and other persons, the
failure to perform which would result in taboo (or something more violent) for the taboo itself is clearly distinguishable from the duty, just as in modern civilization
the failure to perform an obligation is distinguishable
from being fined for not having performed it.

' In primitive society the rules of ceremonial purity
observed by divine kings, chiefs, and priests agree in
many respects with the rules observed by homicides,

---

[1] Köhler, *The Mentality of Apes.*
[2] Frazer, *Taboo, and the Perils of the Soul.*

mourners, women in childbed, girls at puberty, hunters and fishermen, and so on.' The savage, according to Frazer, does not differentiate between these various people on moral grounds but classes them together, because ' To him the common feature of all these persons is that they are dangerous and in danger, and the danger in which they stand and to which they expose others is what we should call spiritual or ghostly, and therefore imaginary. The danger, however, is not less real because it is imaginary ; imagination acts upon a man as really as does gravitation, and may kill him as certainly as prussic acid. To seclude these persons from the rest of the world so that the dreaded spiritual danger shall neither reach them ' (here Frazer is speaking of kings and other important persons) ' nor spread from them, is the object of the taboos which they have to observe. These taboos act, so to say, as electrical insulators to preserve the spiritual force with which these persons are charged from suffering or in- flicting harm by contact with the outer world.' [1] Taboos may attach to persons, things, or words.

Strangers are very frequently the objects of taboo. Savages say that they bring disease : that is, either the fact that the stranger has a disease shows that he has violated some custom, incurred the anger of the mystic powers, and is therefore already taboo, or, if the stranger does not show any disease but still brings it (is a ' carrier ' we should say) this is proof of his dangerous mana. In addition, he is unfamiliar ; he speaks and acts differently from the native ; perhaps he is practising sorcery upon the group or some member of it. In any event, he awakens the *horror novi*. And since a foreigner always fascinates the attention it is obvious that he is charged with mana. ' The men of a certain district in Borneo, fearing to look upon a European traveller lest he should make them ill, warned their wives and children not to go near him. Those who could not restrain their curiosity killed fowls to appease the evil spirits and smeared themselves with

[1] Frazer, *loc. cit.*, 224.

the blood.'[1] Some form of ceremony to guard against the magic powers of strangers or to remove or counteract their evil influence is very frequently found among savage peoples. It is as if strangers must be depotentialized of their dangerous mana, just as a Leyden jar must be discharged before it is handled. In this connection it is interesting to remember our own instinctive distrust of aliens, Russians, Chinese and Turks for example.

There are mystic dangers attending upon the acts of eating and drinking that are difficult to explain psychologically, unless upon the ground that when you do either of these things you are likely to be quite intent upon them, and so off guard. Also, the natural orifices of the body have a special importance analogous to the gates in a fortification : the soul may escape from one of them, and evil powers may enter thereby. The mouth, naturally, is the most likely opening for anything to enter the body, whether it be food, a spirit, or a magic animal. The teaching that it is not what goes into the mouth but what comes out of it which defiles a man, must have seemed revolutionary indeed some nineteen hundred years ago.

' The Thompson Indians of British Columbia thought that a shaman could bewitch them most easily when they were eating, drinking, or smoking ; hence they avoided doing any of these things in the presence of an unknown shaman.'[2] Here all the conditions for becoming a victim of evil mana are fulfilled : the Indian is in the presence of a shaman, a person who is known to be full of potent mana, and of whom it is not known whether his intentions are evil or not. Under such conditions it certainly is necessary for him to remain alert and upon guard : it would not do for him to let his attention wander to his food, his drink, or his pipe in such a dangerous situation.

If the matter were as simple as Frazer seems to think it is—if the danger consisted simply in opening the mouth—it is clear that the savage would not dare to

[1] Frazer, *loc. cit.*, 103.   [2] Frazer, *loc. cit.*, 116, 117.

speak to the strange doctor ; and in that case we should find all over the world where this superstition prevails customs of communicating with dangerous persons by gesture or sign language. But this, so far as I know, is never the case. The rule of conduct seems to be this : In the presence of mana, be watchful ; do not do anything that will take your attention off the source of danger.

The savage's own explanation of his fear to eat in the presence of others, lest a wandering soul should enter his body or his own soul should be lured away, does not really conflict with this theory. For what is a ' soul ' ? As this is one of the most difficult and disputed points of psychology and anthropology, it requires careful consideration.

In analytical psychology the soul, *anima*, is regarded as the subject's relation to the unconscious. It corresponds to that relation to external objects and situations which we term the *persona* or pose. Every man manifests more than one pose or *persona* in different situations : he acts differently, and regards himself differently, when he is wooing a woman and when he is among roughs in a bar, for instance. The two distinct poses that are most in evidence in the lives of most of us are the *persona* used in the business or professional environment and the *persona* used in the environment of the home : we all know that the servile, cringing employee is often a tyrant in his home, and that the efficient and ruthless man of business enjoys being babied by the members of his family. There is frequently a pious Sunday *persona* also, especially among people who are not noticeably merciful and loving during the week. No one of these *personæ* is the real individual, of course, though long continued habit often leads a man to identify himself with one or more of them, the most common identification being with one's position or profession—the subject coming to regard himself as solely a lawyer, soldier or priest, and forgetting that he is also a human being. As this occurs in perfectly healthy people (albeit not in those who have reached a very advanced psychological development) we are justified in saying that such people exhibit split personalities : the interest, the libido, devoted to business forms one person, while the psychic energy devoted to the home and the members of the home circle forms another.

But everyone also takes a certain attitude, varying from contemptuous disregard to superstitious sensitiveness, toward his dreams and waking fantasies and the vaguer stirrings of the unconscious. In so doing, he is taking this ' inner ' part of himself (the unconscious) as an object distinct from the conscious subject or ego. To this inner object he devotes some attention, some interest, be it little or much. This relation of consciousness to the unconscious—or, to speak more exactly—the libido that is devoted to this relation, becomes personified ; and this is a convenience, in that it makes the relation between consciousness and unconsciousness more representable— and therefore easier to grasp and deal with. This per- sonification of the energy that goes into one's attitude toward the processes and demands of one's unconscious is what, in psychology, we term the soul or *anima*. In dreams it appears to a man as a woman : the reader may remember the wild, free girl who recurrently appeared in the dreams of convention-bound dull Babbitt and tempted him to escape with her over great moors and along the shore of gleaming seas. This girl is Babbitt's *anima*. Sinclair Lewis, with the unerring intuition of the true artist, has made this dream figure stand in antithesis to the conventional *persona* with which Babbitt identifies himself and, in so doing, becomes mildly neurotic. The exaggerations and the inhibitions of the conscious *persona* are balanced by the soul. Or to put the matter more accurately, one of the most important functions of the unconscious is to balance and compensate the onesidedness, the deficiencies and exaggerations, of consciousness, and to protest against them in the interests of the sanity and balance of the entire self. The visible messenger of the unconscious in these matters is the *anima*.

About the only novelty in these theories is the psychological language in which they are couched. Everyone, I think, is aware of a certain duality in his nature. St Paul complained that he did not do what he would, and did that which he would not. In this he has never lacked company, and never will, presumably. Let us return again to the case of Babbitt, for the sake of fixing our points : Babbitt was a ' good fellow,' a ' realtor ' (he could not have found this word in the dictionary, but he knew he was one anyhow), an Elk, and a Presbyterian : these were various *personæ* of his, or rather they were aspects of his general *persona* of a good, law-abiding, convention-ridden citizen. He was completely identified with his *persona* : when he was asked a somewhat unusual question he was caught off guard, hesitated, and did not know what to say because he did not know what a good fellow, a realtor, an Elk, a Presbyterian, or a good citizen *ought* to say. His unconscious protested against his mistaking his dismally restricted *persona* for his whole self : the reader will remember that, *in spite of himself, and in spite of his ' ideals '* (for Babbitt, like most crippled souls, was a great idealist), he could not avoid being interested in the socialist reformer and demagogue ; he could not help timidly expressing his feeling that the strikers might have some justice on their side (with the result that he was tabooed until purified) ; and he could not help feebly seeking a little romance with Ida and Tanith. Neither could he avoid occasional drunkenness, or a debauch with prostitutes when he attended the convention of ' realtors ' in another city. These are all manifestations of the efforts of his unconscious to force or tempt him directly out of his hidebound, paralysing enslavement to convention and to his identification with his *persona*. But the whole purpose of the unconscious is also expressed by the dream-girl, who lures him toward freedom.

It depends only partly upon the direction in which the *anima* invites one whether she is regarded as beneficent or evil. The modern religious conception of the soul seems to have been developed quite early in the Christian epoch, when such brutality and sensuality as we can hardly imagine were very prevalent ; and it is natural that the unconscious protest against these should be carried by a messenger of ethereal beauty. The soul personifies the longing of the unconscious. Conversely, the lady who appeared to ascetics (to the first St Anthony, for instance) was a person of voluptuous enticement—as may easily be understood. The ascetics regarded such tempting *animæ* as being either messengers of the devil or the devil himself. At one time the Catholic Church instituted a special inquisition against dream-women and dream-men : great numbers of persons confessed under torture that they had had sexual intercourse with a succuba or succubus, and were either purified by exorcism or put to death.[1] On the other hand, the Hausas of Northern Africa welcome these nocturnal spirit mistresses, and have special rites for the purpose of securing one for any man who finds himself neglected.[2]

Light is thrown upon the nature of the soul by the fact that among many primitive races each member of the group has several, the number sometimes running as high as six. In British Nigeria there is what is known as the bush-soul.[3] These Negroes now live in villages and cultivate plantations outside the village stockades ; but there is every reason to suppose that this mode of life is comparatively recent, and that for a very long period they lived in the wild jungle, the bush. Their primitive civilization rests but lightly upon these people, and the British authorities are forced to be vigilant in order to prevent them from reverting to human sacrifice and other manifestations of savagery, the longing for which is still with them. Here clearly the bush-soul corresponds to the longing to escape into the woods and wild places that

[1] Tylor's *Primitive Culture*, Frazer's *The Golden Bough*, and *The Romance of Sorcery* by Sax Rohmer.
[2] Tremearne, *The Ban of the Bori*.
[3] Talbott, *In the Shadow of the Bush*.

periodically assails Americans whose forefathers were pioneers, the longing that has been made representable by the phrase, ' the call of the wild.' City life becomes tiresome to us now and then ; it irks us ; we become periodically restless, without consciously knowing why. Unbidden fantasies arise from the unconscious of canoes, trout-streams, camp fires, and beds of balsam. This is the protest of the unconscious against too much city life, the lure which it offers to tempt us away, the call of the wild. It is the stirring of the American's bush-soul.

Psychologically this means that, whether through heredity, tradition, or personal experience, we have a certain amount of interest invested in camping out. This forms what is called a complex. When we have plodded long enough at the routine of our daily work, and have toiled long enough at the routine of our artificial pleasures, there comes a time of fatigue and staleness when city life seems flat and unprofitable and ceases to hold our interest. To continue is up-hill work, for there is no spring, no enthusiasm, any more ; and to continue long enough would result in onesidedness, a psychic deformity, or in illness. The call of the wild is the voice of the bush-soul, bidding us to take steps to restore our psychic balance.

It is probable that careful investigations would demonstrate that all plural souls are personifications in the same way of libido-complexes which are unconscious most of the time. When there is only one soul it is a personification of what is going on in the unconscious at the time being and of the energy invested in these unconscious processes. When (as with Babbitt) the same outer attitude is maintained over a long period the *anima* takes on a very definite appearance and character with men—even to the point that a man knows the colour of his dream-woman's eyes.

Any kind of soul, then, is a definitely organized libido-charge, personified. But this living, acting psychic energy that we call libido the primitive would call mana. Hence it is perfectly comprehensible why the primitive fears losing his soul, and rates the loss of a soul as a dangerous sickness. So it is, too ; for to lose a soul is to lose a very considerable amount of vital energy, a very definite amount of mana, of grace, spiritual power, virtue—using this last word in its antique true sense. Loss of interest often precedes death.

Since the function of the unconscious is to balance the conscious (in addition to furnishing libido to the latter) it follows that the loss of the principal soul means a break in the normal means of communication between the conscious and unconscious sides of the psyche, with the result that the psyche is stretched, so to speak, between the opposite goals or strivings of consciousness and the unconscious. This condition is found in neurotic patients : an extreme attitude in consciousness, which is balanced only with difficulty and by using up of a great part of all the available libido, by the antithetical attitude of the unconscious. Since the unconscious plays a far greater rôle in the life of the primitive than it does with us—for his consciousness is applied to an extremely small field, and is usually of low voltage and intermittent in operation—he pays more attention to the whisperings of his inner monitor than we do, and (within the limits of custom) tends to carry out the impulses arising from his unconscious. For him to lose his soul, or the principal soul if he has several, means at least as much to him as it would have meant to Socrates if he had lost his *dæmon*. Without his soul, the savage is like one of the half-men of his own myths.[1] These half-men are *split personalities*, in a literal sense : they are men with only one eye, ear, arm, and leg, and with only one-half of the organs such as the nose that lie in the middle of the body.

After making this somewhat lengthy detour to investigate the psychological meaning of soul, we can return to the taboo upon eating and drinking in the presence of strangers, which I should interpret as follows :

[1] Talbott, *In the Shadow of the Bush.*

Here is a fascinating stranger—fascinating because he is a stranger, and full of mana because one can feel his fascination. His mana is dangerous and evil, for he is not one of us. He does strange things and speaks strange sounds : these are probably spells he is working against me. I know my soul can escape through my mouth. Perhaps he will try to charm it out of me if I am not on my guard. Moreover he can cast his sorcery upon me if I am not alert. I had better not get interested in eating or drinking while this fellow is in sight. If he charms my soul away he may put another in that will do me harm : it might devour my life, my kidney-fat, from within. We moderns are full of prejudice about eating with strangers.

Related to the custom of not letting a stranger see one eating or drinking is the widespread fear of being seen with the face unveiled, which probably arises from the same subjective tendencies. 'The men of the Touaregs wear a veil over the lower part of the face constantly. Other peoples cover the mouth when speaking or performing certain actions lest a demon or other dangerous object should enter the body through the mouth and harm the soul.'[1] Clearly the mouth is regarded as being especially liable to mystic invasions, though savages assign various, and sometimes mutually contradictory, reasons for this fear. One wonders whether there may not be a dim perception here of the dangers of rash or needless speech. Many savages are extremely economical of words (words, especially names, are themselves sacred and full of mana) except among trusted members of their own group. It has been noted that two savages belonging to different groups frequently squat and keep silent for a considerable time before addressing each other in the courteous terms prescribed by custom. We moderns have sayings warning against foolish talking and too much speech : speech is silvern, but silence is golden ; when angry count ten before you speak, and so forth. Whatever you say will be taken down, and may be used

---

[1] Frazer, *Taboo and Perils of the Soul*, 122.

against you. Part of the danger instinctively felt in not keeping one's mouth shut or covered might be due to an instinctive fear of conflict among men.

The fourth taboo discussed by Frazer is against quitting the house. ' The king of Onitsha, on the Niger, " does not step out of his house into the town unless a human sacrifice is made to propitiate the gods : on this account he never goes out beyond the precincts of his premises." . . . Yet once a year at the Feast of Yams, the king . . . is required by custom to dance before his people outside the high mud wall of his palace. In dancing he carries a great weight, generally a sack of earth, on his back to prove that he is still able to support the burdens and cares of state. Were he unable to discharge this duty, he would be immediately deposed and perhaps stoned.' [1] Such restrictions are usually imposed upon a priestly king, who is regarded as divine, or—where the kingship has split into the two offices of high priest and temporal ruler—the chief priest is put under some such taboo. The explanation generally given is that the rainfall, the health of the people, and the whole welfare of the kingdom (or even of the entire earth) depend upon the divine man scrupulously obeying the customs ; and, as he is so precious to his subjects, he must be kept indoors in the utmost safety. No doubt there is some truth in this. But there is also the fact that he is charged with divine mana, so that it would be most perilous to his subjects to approach too near him, or (sometimes) even to see him. We moderns like the titular chief of our nations to appear in pomp and circumstance ; and we are interested beyond reason in his health.

It is taboo to leave remains of one's meal about. Food is often held to be sacred. Besides, ' On the principles of sympathetic magic a real connection ' (a mystic participation) ' subsists between the food a man has in his stomach and the refuse of it he has left untouched, and hence, by injuring the refuse you can simultaneously

[1] Frazer, loc. cit., 123.

M

injure the eater.' Bones that have been left over are especially good objects to use in witchcraft.[1]

Psychologically, these spells—like all sympathetic magic —depend upon mystic participation : what you eat becomes yourself, and what you leave is not distinguished from what you have eaten.

Carrying the same notion a step further, the dish from which a man has eaten can also be used to bewitch him. I do not know whether the custom still prevails ; but there was a time when the Emperor of Japan never ate or drank except from a new vessel, which was broken as soon as he had used it. Frazer ends his chapter upon tabooed things with some reflections that come curiously close to the theory which has been insisted upon in this present work—the theory that all is subordinated to maintaining harmony in the group :

After pointing out that the taboo on food leavings has had a beneficial effect in the destruction of much refuse which might otherwise have been a source of disease, he adds : ' Nor is it only the sanitary condition of a tribe which has benefited by this superstition ; curiously enough the same baseless dread, the same false notion of causation, has indirectly strengthened the moral bonds of hospitality, honour, and good faith among men who entertain it. For it is obvious that no one who intends to harm a man by working magic on the refuse of his food will himself partake of that food, because if he did so he would, on the principles of sympathetic magic, suffer equally with his enemy from any injury done to the refuse. This is the idea ' (Frazer would have come nearer to the truth if he had said this is one of the ideas) ' which in primitive society lends sanctity to the bond produced by eating together.' [2]

Eating is the satisfaction of one of the basic instincts : like the satisfaction of the other instincts, it leaves a man in a condition of lazy gratification. Most animals are peaceful after a good meal. Among some of the

[1] Frazer, *loc. cit.*, 126 *et seq.*   [2] Frazer, *loc. cit.*, 130.

Australian tribes, when a party approaches to demand vengeance for some injury, the matter is formally discussed. If the visitors show moderation, one of the natives calls his wife, and offers her to one of the visitors ; and if the pair go off into the bush together the danger that a fight will develop is realized to be past. Sexual desire, hunger, thirst, lack of sleep, make men tense and irritable ; their satisfaction incline men to feel at peace with the world. Danger to the group is minimized by hospitality which includes some or all of these satisfactions.

CHAPTER XIX

TABOOED PERSONS

' SUPPOSE,' a civilized reader might ask, ' that a savage touched a high priest or a great chief by accident— would not this experience teach him that this whole fear of mana is an absurd superstition ? Would he not learn that priests and kings are simply ordinary mortals, like himself except for the fact that they by chance occupy rather important offices, and that there is no mystic danger in touching one of them ? '

Lévy-Bruhl and his school would answer, No : for the primitive is incapable of learning by experience : his mind is impervious to it. Frazer, and a host of reputable observers, would also answer in the negative though on somewhat different grounds, for they are more concerned with facts than with theories. They would say that he does not learn from experience, partly because the effects of a breach of taboo is to produce experiences which corroborate the savage's belief.

' In Fiji there is a special name for the disease supposed to be caused by eating out of a chief's dishes or wearing his clothes. The throat and body swell, and the impious person dies.' The same thing used to be true of the Mikado : eat from a dish he had used, and your mouth and throat became inflamed ; and if you put on a garment he had worn swellings and pains over the entire body would result. This is the other side of the god-man's character : ' The divine person is a source of danger as well as of blessing ; he must not only be guarded, he must also be guarded against. His sacred organism, so delicate that a touch may disorganize it, is also, as it

180

were, electrically charged with a powerful magical or spiritual force which may discharge itself with fatal effect on whatever comes in contact with it. . . . His magical virtue is in the strictest sense of the word contagious.' [1]

There are ritual ways of drawing off the deadly force from one who has come in contact with it. ' A commoner who had incurred this danger would disinfect himself by performing a certain ceremony, which consisted in touching the sole of the chief's foot and afterwards rinsing his hands in water. After that he was free to feed himself with his own hands without danger of being attacked by the malady which would otherwise follow from eating with tabooed or sanctified hands.' [2]

There are some familiar psychological elements in such a system. A chief, even when he has no priestly function, is an important personage. When danger comes, the group has a recognized head and commander. This makes for more efficient fighting than the Australian system of deciding measures in committee—the council of old men. The fact that there is a chief also helps to make the unity of the group more representable and definite in the minds of the members : it is a gain in group-consciousness. The group itself is the supreme value ; and the chief, as the symbol of the group, is himself a great value, full of mana, and not to be treated with levity or indifference. In conforming to these customs a good beginning has been made toward conscious self-abnegation and drill on the part of the commoners, and also toward that standardization which is one of the prime necessities among fighting folk and one of the chief aims of all education—modern as well as savage. In the eyes of the chief, all these savages may be supposed to be equal, just as we think we are before the law and God. This all makes for group-solidarity.

One reason why criminal law, and its penalties, are not needed among primitives is the psychological effect upon

---

[1] Frazer, *Taboo and the Perils of the Soul*, 131, 132.
[2] Frazer, *loc. cit.*, 133.

the subject himself if he breaks a custom. ' For instance, it once happened that a New Zealand chief of high rank and great sanctity had left the remains of his dinner by the wayside. A slave, a stout, hungry fellow, saw the unfinished dinner, and ate it up without asking questions. Hardly had he finished when he was informed by a horror-stricken spectator that the food of which he had eaten was the chief's. " I knew the unfortunate delinquent well. He was remarkable for courage, and had signalized himself in the wars of the tribe," but " no sooner did he hear the fatal news than he was seized by the most extra-ordinary convulsions and cramp in the stomach, which never ceased till he died, about sundown the same day. He was a strong man, in the prime of life, and if any pakeha (European) freethinker should have said that he was not killed by the tapu' (*i.e.*, mana) ' of the chief, which had been communicated to the food by contact, he would have been listened to with feelings of contempt for his ignorance and inability to understand plain and direct evidence." ' [1] Had we space scores of similar examples of people dying as a result of breaking some taboo, could be quoted from anthropological literature. Frazer has collected a great many in his *Taboo and the Perils of the Soul*, to which book the interested reader may turn.

It is not difficult to understand the nature of the mystic energy which is involved in these taboos. On the one hand, mana behaves much as does static electricity, as has been noted : it flows from the higher potential to the lower, from the higher social rank to the lower. The fact that the highest caste may receive evil mana from a member of an ' untouchable ' caste is an only apparent exception ; for untouchables generally have a sacred office, as scaveng-ing or attending to the removal of corpses, to perform : they are, therefore, in a sense more-and-less than human. On the other hand, mana (especially when it is due to an abnormal psychic state of its possessor) is dangerous

---

[1] Frazer, *loc. cit.*, 133–138.

without actual contact. It is then imagined as an aura surrounding the dangerous person. This aura is visible, like light, under some conditions by those who have the gift to see ; and under other conditions the aura is more like a cloud of vapour—a poisonous odour, likely to infect anyone.

So far we have been discussing persons who are permanently taboo because of their rank, priests, kings, and chiefs, who are, in Frazer's apt words, ' at once more and less than human.' But commoners also may become taboo because they themselves have violated a sacred custom, or (as we have seen) may from their misfortunes be presumed to have violated one. In addition there are a number of temporary conditions into which the commoner may pass which cause him to become taboo until he has been ritually purified, and so made once more a member of the communion. These taboos are of peculiar interest, in that no plausible explanation has ever been advanced to account for them, even the leading anthropologists frequently stating either that they are incapable of being understood rationally or even going so far as to pronounce them definitely irrational and opposed to commonsense. Psychology, however, offers an explanation of them : Primitive societies taboo a person who is in a state of excitement or depression which might be communicated to other members of the group, with resultant interference with the inner tranquility of the group. So regarded, these taboos fall in line with the ritual apportionment of women and other objects likely to cause quarrels among the fighting males, with the stern suppression of unorthodox conduct and views, and with all the other phenomena which in actual practice result in the group retaining its coherence and solidarity. There are psychic states which are infectious, regardless of the degree of culture, such as panic and blood-lust to take extreme examples, which temporarily disrupt the social organism entirely ; and there are other conditions, such as insanity or an epileptic seizure, the sight of which makes most normal civilized persons profoundly uncomfortable. The savage's instinct is to quarantine any member of the group whose condition is such that it might disturb the tranquility of the others. We know that even among the civilized, when a number of people are gathered together almost any action by one that is conspicuous—as gazing up toward the sky, yawning, laughing, fanning oneself with one's hat, mopping one's forehead with a handkerchief, applauding in a theatre or making a sudden run for an exit—is likely to be imitated by the whole crowd. These phenomena have been partially explained ; but we are far from knowing all about them as yet. Naturally, the more potent the emotion that is aroused the more easily it is communicated ; and the more instinctive or reflex an action is the more likely it is to be imitated—one has only to think of how even the supposedly sane behave in a theatre panic. It is characteristic of the primitive psyche that strong emotions are communicated from one person to another with lightning rapidity, and take irresistible hold of all the members of a crowd.

Thus mourners are tabooed, and so are persons who have touched a corpse, among very many tribes. This is understandable on several grounds. All misfortune is due to the wrath of the mystic powers, and indicates that the sufferer has offended these beings or forces. Misfortune and sorrow connote moral delinquency. Death is never due to natural causes. Not only are the souls of the dead dangerous, but the body which has suffered is either full of evil witchcraft or at least is tainted with the unorthodox conduct that resulted in death. Hands that have touched a corpse are therefore taboo, and the person whose hands they are cannot feed himself with them. All who suffer in heart from the death are themselves tainted, and sometimes persons who have stood in a particularly close relation to the deceased are taboo because of mystic participation. This is especially true of widows though sometimes the taboo extends to widowers. 'Among the Agutainos, who inhabit Palawan, one of the Philippine Islands, a widow may not leave her hut for seven or eight days after the death ; and even then she may only go out at an hour when she is not likely to meet anybody, for whoever looks upon her dies a sudden death. To prevent this fatal catastrophe, the widow knocks with a wooden peg on the trees as she goes along, thus warning people of her dangerous proximity ; and the very trees on which she knocks soon die. So poisonous is the atmosphere of death that surrounds those to whom the ghost of the departed may be thought to cleave. In the Mekeo district of British New Guinea a widower loses all his civil rights and becomes a social outcast, an object of fear and horror, shunned by all.' [1]

Such examples might be multiplied indefinitely. I am far from denying that the reasons given by the natives themselves for these customs play their part : there can be no doubt that consciously the savages believe them. But there is a fact that lies back of them, which the savages themselves do not know because it is unconscious : just as association with the happy and confident buoys one up and heightens one's courage, so does association with the suffering and sorrowful depress one and rob one of one's morale. A man feels his mana, his libido, his enthusiasm being drained away by contact with the unfortunate. These are Jonahs. Christian Scientists consciously make a special point of avoiding persons who talk of their ills or misfortune : this is the primitive taboo against mourners in its modernized guise. Instinctively we all do more or less the same thing, and it is wise. Mourning is a definite psychological condition ; it deprives the mourner of the psychic energy that normally would be devoted to carrying on the affairs of life ;

[1] Frazer, *Taboo and the Perils of the Soul*, 148.

and persons who associate with mourners are infected thereby, and lose their own energy and morale.

We have seen that women are always regarded as potential menaces to the solidarity of the group by savages, and have ascribed exogamy and marriage itself to the necessity of apportioning them ritually among the adult males. The quarrels of friends and comrades-in-arms over women, from the time that Agamemnon took Briseis from Achilles and the latter quit their common enterprise of war, is a favourite theme in the literature of the civilized ; and it may be that there was a stirring of the primitive fear of similar disharmony and lack of co-operation in the minds of the Russian communists when they practically abolished marriage : for the desirable objects, women, are least likely to cause trouble when they are either theoretically free to all or else when they are irrevocably apportioned. The topic of temporary taboos brings us back once more to woman as a source of danger to the group's solidarity ; for most savages impose rigid taboos upon women during the menstrual period, taboos that can be explained only by remembering that at this time natural woman is often dominated completely by the sexual instinct and, unless quarantined, likely to disregard the conventional restrictions upon her conduct. She is in a state of excitement which is very infectious to the males of manhood status, a powerful incentive to what is perhaps the gravest transgression known to peoples of really low cultures, incest. Consequently among various tribes we find the menstruating woman compelled to live alone in a secluded place, to refrain from touching even her husband or the food or weapons of any man, to confess her dangerous condition by word of mouth or by wearing a distinctive garment, to avoid meeting a man on a trail, or to avoid speaking to a man or even looking at one.

Definite psychological conditions that are infectious are also found among lads at the time of initiation, warriors who have killed an enemy, murderers, and persons who have eaten human flesh as a religious ceremony. Taboos attach to all of these persons, and they must remain in quarantine for a prescribed period and then undergo purification before they may mingle with other members of the group. We ourselves feel a sense of horror toward murderers and the insane : there is something uncanny about such persons, who compel an unwilling fascination on our part, and who cause our psychic processes to deviate from their daily commonplaces. Consider the multitudes of ill-balanced women who write love-letters to murderers in prison and often offer them marriage. This is no charity on their part, no desire to reform the victim of society, though they rationalize their conduct thus—it is the lure of the murderer, who attracts them just because he is a murderer ; they are thrown off their precarious balance because they feel his mana. The insane are also psychically infectious ; many attendants upon the insane themselves become mad, and so do many students of mental diseases. An eminent psychiatrist told me that he believed that no one became an alienist unless he had a little streak of madness, or at least a predisposition to it, in himself. We are always fascinated by something which is in ourselves, particularly if we are unconscious of it. Even neuroses are infectious : the children of neurotic parents almost always become neurotic.

Among primitives the insane are regarded as holy, inspired, there are demons in possession of them : and consequently they are looked upon with awe—to a certain extent tabooed. Murder is a direct blow to the social fabric ; and this alone would suffice to make the transgressor taboo. In addition, he has the fascination that envelops all shedders of blood. Moreover, he may be assumed to be in a highly emotional condition, at least during and for some time after his crime. So is the youth during the season of his initiation : we ourselves, under the pretext that we are bored, exhibit an instinctive tendency to shun the recent convert to religion, who is a close analogue to the youth just initiated. But why should the fighting-man, returning from an expedition in which he has risked his life for his people, be isolated and purified, and shunned by those for whom he fought? One would expect him to be received with open arms and showered with honours and gratitude.

CHAPTER XX

Continued

ALTHOUGH the savage warrior is exceedingly glad to leave territory inhabited by human enemies, and by mystic beings allied with these enemies, and to find himself once more among familiar occult powers and people, the members of his own group do not act enthusiastic about his safe return. If he has been successful on the war-path and has killed someone, his comrades evince a positive aversion from his company. Let us look at a few of the many examples given by Frazer.

' Warriors are conceived by the savage to move, so to say, in an atmosphere of spiritual danger which constrains them to practise a variety of superstitious observances quite different in their nature from those rational precautions which, as a matter of course, they adopt against foes of flesh and blood. The general effect of these observances is to place the warrior, both before and after victory, in the same state of seclusion or spiritual quarantine in which, for his own safety, primitive man puts his human gods and other dangerous characters. Thus when the Maoris went out on the war-path they were sacred or taboo in the highest degree, and they and their friends at home had to observe strictly many curious customs over and above the numerous taboos of ordinary life. They became, in the irreverent language of Europeans who knew them in the old fighting days, " tabooed an inch thick " ; and as for the leader of the expedition, he was quite unapproachable. Similarly when the Israelites marched forth to war they were bound by certain rules of ceremonial purity identical with the rules observed by Maoris and Australian black-fellows on the war-path. The vessels they used were sacred, and they had to practise continence and a custom of personal cleanliness of which the original motive, if we may judge from the avowed motive of savages who conform to like customs, was a fear lest the enemy should obtain the refuse of their persons, and thus be enabled to work their destruction by magic.' In a note on the same page Frazer refers to Deuteronomy xxiii. 9–14, and Samuel xxi. 5, adding, ' The rule laid down in Deuteronomy xxiii. 10, 11, suffices to prove that the custom of continence observed in time of war by the Israelites, as by a multitude of savage and barbarous peoples, was based on a superstitious, not on a rational motive. To convince us of this it is enough to observe that the rule is often observed by warriors for some time after their victorious return, and also by persons left at home during the absence of the fighting men. In these cases the rule evidently *does not admit of a rational explanation.* . . .' [1]

The italics here are mine. I shall endeavour later on to show that while anthropology does not, as Frazer says, offer any explanation that can be called rational for this custom, there is a psychological explanation which is rational enough. But for the moment we shall pass over the rule of continence, which does not come within the psychological class we are discussing. Frazer's theory of the reason for the rule of cleanliness is clearly correct. We shall also postpone consideration of the taboos imposed before victory.

' In Logea, an island off the south-eastern extremity of New Guinea, men who have killed or assisted in killing enemies shut themselves up for about a week in their houses. They must avoid all intercourse with their wives and friends, and they may not touch food with their hands. They may eat vegetable food only. . . . The intention of

[1] Frazer, *Taboo and the Perils of the Soul*, 158, 199.

these restrictions is to guard the (other) men against the
smell of the blood of the slain ; for it is believed that if
they smelt the blood they would fall ill and die.' [1] The
reader will recall that Apollonius of Tyana and numerous
other wise men, mystics and saints who desired to attain
philosophic calm, became vegetarians ; and though the
natives of Logea rationalize their taboo of victorious
warriors and attach to it the sanction of a mystic danger,
the result in practice of this quarantine and slender diet
is to quiet the infectious excitement of the man-killer.

' In the island of Timor, when a warlike expedition has
returned in triumph bringing the heads of the vanquished
foe, the leader of the expedition is forbidden by religion
and custom to return at once to his own house. A special
hut is prepared for him, in which he has to reside for two
months, undergoing bodily and spiritual purification.
During this time he may not go to his wife nor feed
himself ; the food must be put into his mouth by another
person.' [2]

Frazer again gives the fear of the ghost of the slain
enemy as the reason for this quarantine and ritual of
purification. But this fear is sometimes taken care of by
a special ceremony, which Frazer describes at length :
' A part of the ceremony consists of a dance accompanied
by a song, in which the death of the slain man is lamented
and his forgiveness entreated.' Let me point out that if
the victor, after the manner of primitives, was inclined
to be arrogant and boastful on account of his exploit,
there is scarcely any procedure imaginable that would so
tend to lessen his sinful pride and to reduce him to his
ordinary workaday dimensions than two months of solitary
confinement, followed by publicly deploring what he had
done and asking forgiveness therefor.

The taboo upon successful warriors is connected in
some way with the men who have never as yet proved
their valour. Among the tribes at the mouth of the

---

[1] Frazer, *loc. cit.*, 167.   [2] Frazer, *loc. cit.*, 165, 186.

Wanigela River, in New Guinea, the hero must undergo a short seclusion, followed by elaborate rites of purification. One feature of these rites is that ' He then walks solemnly down to the nearest river, and standing straddle-legs in it washes himself. All the young untried warriors swim between his legs. This is supposed to impart courage and strength to them.' [1] That is to say, the first intercourse between the great man and the ambitious neophytes must be a *ritual* intercourse. Clearly some danger is intuitively recognized here.

One factor that may have contributed to making the man-killer taboo among some tribes lies in the mystic participation between the slayer and the slain. The Koita of British New Guinea suppose that the victor grows ' thin and emaciated, because he had been splashed with the blood of his victim, and as the corpse rotted he wasted away. . . .' This naturally requires ceremonies that will result in dissolving the participation. Apparently this reason for the taboo is rare : I do not recall that it has been noted in any other tribe. But that it is sound psychology is hardly to be doubted : many a civilized person who has killed another has found himself psychologically bound to his victim, and has so felt the need of expiation and purification that he has confessed and paid the penalty for his act   This phenomenon recalls Emerson's line, ' I am the slayer and the slain.' The mystic compulsion arising from the unconscious to wipe out and efface the deed no doubt is partly due to the fact that war is not a primary tendency in man, but only a secondary result of the acquisitive instinct and of fear. The urge to form societies and to be peaceful and friendly with other men is primary ; and when this instinct is forcibly suppressed by fear or by the property-owning tendency the unconscious registers a strong protest : the killer has violated himself, in the deepest and most potent layers of his nature. In a sense, he has removed himself from human society, and is no longer a human being but a

[1] Frazer, *loc. cit.*, 187–8.

strange creature mystically different from men, unclean, sacred, dangerous. A purification from his evil mana, equivalent to rebirth, must usher him back into human society.

Perhaps we can gain some insight into the workings of this strange taboo that requires penance and purification after victory by trying to imagine what conditions would result if no such taboo existed. Suppose that the victors marched home and at once mingled with the other members of the group. They would certainly not come calmly, as though from a fishing-party, but in a state of acute nervous excitement. How much the savage dreads going on the war-path may be judged by the extent of the ceremonies with which he finds it necessary to work himself up to the pitch where he can force himself to go. Even civilized people have to excite themselves through mass-meetings, with flags and martial music and oratory, and all the apparatus that can be gathered and put in motion by expert advertising specialists, before they can still their doubts and fears and suppress their fundamental love of peace and awaken enthusiasm for war. The savage also must be harangued. He must dance until he is intoxicated with the monotonous rhythm of the dance and with the beating of the drums. He must go through the motions of killing an enemy, feeling the while the adulation of the women and the envy of the youths ; he knows they look upon him as a hero, and he tries to believe he really is one. In order that he may not be diverted from his brave purpose he must shun women, even his wife, and the ordinary affairs of every day. By rites and taboos he must devote himself to the war-path before the eyes of all, so that for shame's sake he dares not change his mind. When he has committed himself to this business of being a hero to such an extent that he is more scared not to be one than to go out and try it, he is ready for the war-path.

So he with the rest of the party set forth, with the most dismal fears for his own hide temporarily suppressed

N

by a stronger fear and by the excitement induced by the ceremonies. The raid, let us say, is successful. Creeping up on an enemy village they rush in at dawn, and by good luck manage to spear two or three of the enemy. Seeing this proof that the occult powers are against them, the other defenders take to the jungle. Then nothing remains to the invaders but to slaughter the old men and such of the women and children as they do not care to take away as slaves, and to set fire to the village. The victory and the subsequent butchery and destruction are accomplished as mobs always act, with a furious feeling of unlimited power, of 'God-Almightiness,' and with ordinary self-consciousness completely in abeyance.[1] The march home is probably not long, for the primitive penetrates no further into the territory of another tribe and its local spirits than he must, and once in he does not tarry. He does not feel safe until he is back with his group.

One can imagine that these victorious warriors are in anything but a dispassionate and equable frame of mind when they find themselves with their trophies and captives (if any have been taken) among their own people. They have suffered hardship and intense nervous strain and an excitement comparable with mania, then a nervous let-down and a flight to safety. Some time must pass before they can quiet down and be once more ordinary, un-excited members of the community. So long as the excitement is upon them it is doubtful if they would observe the customs upon which the welfare of the group depends : fighting men are usually ripe for orgies and every sort of deviltry when they reach home. And women are naturally hero-worshippers ; here taboos may be broken, resulting in jealousy among men and anger among the mystic powers. Moreover, by his boasting and arrogance the hero is likely to infect other fighting men

[1] Gustave Le Bon, *La Foule* (14th English translation, *The Crowd*, 35 *et seq.*) ; Freud, *Group Psychology and the Analysis of the Ego*, 17 ; Trotter, *Instincts of the Herd in Peace and War*.

and youths, so that even if no fights take place within
the group itself others are liable to be seized with the
desire to win similar glory, and to do things that may
result in further conflict with neighbouring tribes. All in
all, the returned hero is likely to be a disturbing influence
to the inner harmony of the group and to its external
peace, at least until his infectious excitement has worn
off. All the various evil results that might ensue can be
effectually guarded against by putting him in quarantine
for a sufficient period for him to come back to psychic
normality ; while his own subjective needs are further
relieved by the ceremonial of purification.

This does not mean that the primitive reasons all
these things out, and then acts upon his rational processes :
I have simply stated some of the obvious benefits of the
taboo against victorious warriors—emphasizing the results.
After the custom has become firmly established the savage
is sure to invent some reason for it ; and, with his strong
preference for a dramatic and mystical explanation he
may be relied upon to furnish a colourful account of
why the taboo is imposed. The more dramatic and
colourful it is the further it will probably be from the
truth.

Ask any veteran of the latest war whether something
analogous to this takes place in civilized societies. The
newspapers were full of exhortations to give preference
in employment to ex-service men, and everyone agreed
that their plight was pitiable and that, really, something
should be done about it. Employers subscribed money
generously for homes and hospitals for ex-soldiers, and
whole communities taxed themselves to give them bonuses.
Everybody recognized that their service had been in-
valuable and their self-sacrifice had been noble. But few
employers cared to have a hero in their business organizations, loafing on the job, unable to settle down to work,
feeling that what he had done for his country made him
a privileged character for life, boasting, infecting the men
with unrest and the girls with excitement, and upsetting

the whole workaday atmosphere of shop or office. Of course, it is cruelly unfair to the returned successful warrior to treat him thus; but, after all, the first duty of society is to protect itself. The modern taboo upon soldiers of the Great War was wise.

It would seem clear that murderers and persons who have indulged in eating human flesh as a religious rite are also in an abnormal psychic state, that might prove infectious. It is interesting to note that one of the surest artists of our day, Joseph Conrad, depicted a European as feeling that he must be taboo because he had been forced to partake of human flesh when shipwrecked. The hero of Conrad's story is a straightforward, likeable English sailor. Of course he falls in love; but he is held back from proposing marriage by the overpowering intuition that the girl would shun him if she knew the truth. The primitive in him comes into consciousness, forcing him to know that he is apart from human society.

But why impose taboos upon a warrior before he goes out upon the war-path? Havelock Ellis has pointed out that many knights and soldiers famous for their valour have been markedly indifferent to the charms of women [1] and some of them have even been virgin. *Magis in armis et militaribus equis libidinem habebant* [2] than in sexuality. The virgin knight is a favourite theme of romance. Conversely, when the hero is defeated at last it is often through the wiles of a woman, or because he was caught with his armour off in a lady's bower, or because giving himself over to the strange delights of love he has lost his interest in war. The same idea of the danger inherent in woman appears in many myths: over against the constructive or beneficent male valour and strength of the divinity appear the female destructive or evil qualities of treachery and maliciousness—opposites indissolubly associated, not because evil is feminine of

[1] Havelock Ellis, *Studies in the Psychology of Sex.*
[2] Sallust, quoted by Jung, *Collected Papers on Analytical Psychology,* 231.

itself (the devil is male) but because if you begin to arrange the opposites in pairs you must find a negative for each positive : for good, evil ; for male, female ; and so forth.

The primitive feels the antithesis between martial ardour and uxorious softness, between having man's work to do and setting about it with a whole heart, and dallying with sensual pleasures at home. It may be that this insight comes from the fact that the consciousness of the savage is childlike in its vagueness, diffuseness, and low intensity : a trained civilized mind focuses with so much energy upon one of the opposites—duty, for instance —that the other opposite remains unconscious. It has been amply demonstrated that all emotions in civilized people exhibit this ambitendency (or ambivalence, as it is often called) and that where only one of the pair appears in consciousness the other opposite is sure to be found in the unconscious : this is part of the unconscious process of maintaining the psychic balance. The civilized man or woman can be extremely onesided upon occasion (in fact, the capacity to be onesided when onesidedness is needed is a mark of high culture) and so can put all the energy available for conscious disposal into the chosen task. But the savage can do this only when worked up to it ; ordinarily both opposites, desire to do and desire not to do (or to do something incompatible with the task, which amounts to the same thing), are present to his diffuse consciousness. If he ought to go off hunting, or fishing, or on the war-path, all of which are fatiguing and may be dangerous, he is too conscious of desiring at the same time to do something else to be able to focus his interest exclusively upon the task. He is like the ass which starved to death between the two heaps of hay because he could not make up his mind which one to eat. The ' something else ' that presents itself to his mind as a desirable alternative to doing the work and undergoing the hardship is very likely to be represented by the image of a woman. In fact, we may be sure that this is the

198 PRIMITIVE MIND & MODERN CIVILIZATION

most frequent temptation that holds him in a state of indecision ; for it is just here that primitive society almost invariably imposes a taboo.

This taboo against sexual intercourse plays a very different rôle psychologically from the taboo against warriors who return victorious from the war-path, murderers, and participants in cannibal rites—taboos that result in protecting the group from psychic infection from persons in an abnormal condition. The taboo against sexual intercourse, running from the time when preparations for the war-party have been formally begun, is really a means of saving libido for the task in hand. We saw that the taboo against unfortunate persons, such as mourners, results in preventing an apparent loss of libido ; for contact with mourners infects one with melancholy and causes one's energy to sink out of consciousness. But the taboo against sexual intercourse when a difficult task confronts him is a way of preventing a real loss of libido. The custom requires that the man who has announced that he is going on the war-path may not have intercourse with a woman until he returns from the expedition. What, then, would be the use of thinking of his wife until the expedition has taken place ? The possibility of this alternative of conduct is wiped out : in fact, the quickest way to get to his wife is to finish the expedition in the least possible time. In other words, the same interest in sex which would have kept him in a state of indecision and have made it difficult for him to give his whole attention to the expedition, is now added to the interest he has in the expedition. If his will was split and balanced between the woman and the raid, the taboo diverts to the expedition the libido directed to the woman, thus making the total of his interest available for the task. The matter can even be stated mathematically. If the libido directed to the woman and the libido directed to the task are exactly equal, the man is in a state of equilibrium and indecision, and cannot move until some interest is added or lost upon one side

or the other.   If his interest in the task is twice as strong
as his interest in the woman, he will go on the expedition ;
but now his interest in the woman will cancel one-half
of his interest in the task—so that only one-third of his
total psychic energy can be devoted to the task.   He has
a ' libido-fixation ' that theoretically reduces his efficiency
to one-third of normal.   It does not reduce it so much in
actual practice for the simple reason that once he nears
the enemy he tends to forget the woman : the pull back
toward her becomes unconscious, still potent to hinder
him and to cause him to make errors, and to suffer
' inexplicable ' accidents, but not dividing his conscious
will.

In passing, the element of formal commitment to the
task which such a custom brings should not be overlooked.
The hunter's announcement that he is resolved to go out
on a hunt is equivalent to a military enlistment, or a
convert's public declaration of faith ; to recant would
bring shame and humiliation upon him.   And the primitive,
according to Dr Radin, values his prestige more highly
than anything else in his life.

The men of the Hidatsa tribe have elaborate ceremonies
and taboos when they are trapping eagles, which include
fasting and going with little or no sleep (both of which
are admirable methods of stilling sexual desire) and the
complete avoidance of woman, and of their friends—who
also might divert their interest from the task.   Frazer
remarks that ' It is obvious that the severe fasting coupled
with short sleep, or even with total sleeplessness, of these
eagle-hunters can only impair their physical vigour and
so far tend to incapacitate them for capturing eagles.
The motive of their behaviour in these respects is purely
superstitious, not rational, and so, we safely conclude, is
the custom which simultaneously cuts them off from all
intercourse with their wives and families.'

Naturally, the physical vigour of the hunters is lessened
by such self-discipline.   But their realization of the
importance of the task can only be heightened by it ;

and their determination to get the work done, so that they can go back to a more pleasant way of living, must be enormously enhanced. Hardly any custom could be invented that would chain the libido to the work in hand more effectually. True, Frazer tells us that the whole custom is superstitious and non-rational; but this is only another way of saying that the motivation is unconscious, or that Frazer himself sees no useful result from the custom.

The imposition of taboos is by no means confined to war and hunting. An enormous number of other activities are surrounded by these mystic rules. We are told that the mere presence of a woman when a Wandorobo is making poison would destroy the virtue of the poison, as would also adultery on the part of the poison-maker's wife. This on the surface would appear to be irrational, but the explanation is not far to seek. The poison-maker must devote his libido exclusively to his task, and not allow it to be diverted to sexual desires ; and, by mystic participation, the husband and wife are one.

The extraction of cocoa-nut oil is in Indonesia likewise encompassed by taboos. In some cases the oil must be made only by unmarried girls when it is to be used as a protection against demons. In another case, as an antidote to poison it is only effective if the cocoa-nuts ' have been gathered on Friday by a youth who has never known a woman, and if the oil has been extracted by a pure maiden, while a priest recited the appropriate spells.' [1]

All these taboos result in concentrating the attention upon the task, and in putting the person who does the work in a special psychological state. Probably most of these tasks are regarded as being of more than personal concern to the worker ; they are matters in which the group itself has an interest. That is to say, they have a religious significance. Such being the case, we might expect the persons engaged in them to feel the religious thrill and to arrive at an infectious state of exaltation

[1] Frazer, *loc. cit.*, 197–201.

that would lead to their being quarantined for a while
after the task was finished. Such is in fact the case.
But now let us return to the taboo against persons excited
by success.

Frazer rejects the hypothesis that taboos on hunters
and warriors are imposed as precautionary measures to
maintain the health and strength of the men on the
grounds that in that case they would cease on the successful
termination of the operations. He contends that they are
based on superstition and that this accords with the
stringency of the taboos on the successful warrior or
hunter. ' The rationalistic theory of them therefore breaks
down entirely ; the hypothesis of superstition is clearly
the only one open to us.' [1]

It would be erroneous to exclude the motive of fear
of the shades of slaughtered animals from our explanation
of the taboos upon killers of game, just as it would be to
disregard the fears of a dead man's ghost in accounting
for the taboo laid upon a murderer or a victorious warrior.
These fears are certainly present in the consciousness of
the savage, and have a great effect upon him. But to
call such fears superstition amounts only to attaching a
label to them, a sort of moral judgment as to the religious
opinions of the people who hold them ; and this label
gives us no inkling of the psychic processes that originate
the fear or the taboo. If there were nothing to the
matter beyond the fear of a spirit, it would seem much
more suitable for the killer to seek the closest possible
contact with his fellows at once for protection, just
as he would do if pursued by a wild animal or any
other tangible danger. Moreover, the primitive knows all
about ghosts ; he employs specialists to deal with them—
shamans and witch-doctors ; and he has ceremonies which
experience has proved will infallibly lay unquiet spirits.
Why does he not employ these rites at once, and so rid
both the killer and the group of the troublesome occult
creature which is hanging about ? Why tolerate a spectre

[1] Frazer, *loc. cit.*, 204–5.

one moment longer than is necessary ? And why, when a man has shown himself to be a hero on the war-path or has brought to camp the meat upon which the existence of the community depends, should he be sent off to dwell alone, excommunicated, in a distant hut, where he must live upon a diet that we should describe as reducing ? In such an isolated situation, if there is an able-bodied ghost about, he seems exposed to a great and entirely avoidable danger. It seems to me that these ' superstitions ' bear every mark of being invented after the customs have become fixed in usage—that they are *ex post facto* picturesque and dramatic rationalizations of long antecedent unconscious intuitions of danger or need. To my mind, every detail of these customs points to a few simple and indisputable facts. First, in order to accomplish anything particularly arduous or dangerous, one must work oneself up to a definite psychological state by means of appropriate symbolism and rites ; the churinga ceremonies of the Australian natives are an excellent example of this calling into consciousness of the interest and energy requisite to the task. Second, one must abjure persons and actions that might divert one's energy and attention from the matter in hand—women, for instance. Third, it is well to commit oneself to one's duty in such a public manner that one would be ashamed to fail in it. Now at last one is fit to go on the hunt, the war-path, or to undertake whatever task lies before one, with one's whole energy and undivided interest, and with the consciousness that the sooner the work is ended the sooner one will be back in the arms of one's wife and enjoying the pleasures of ordinary life ; and so the task is attacked and finished successfully. No one, I think, could say that such motives would be foolish or superstitious if they were conscious : it is only when they are felt as unaccountable, mystic (*i.e.*, unconscious) compulsions that they seem irrational. They certainly are purposive and accurately adapted to reach the ends sought. Fourth, the definite psychological state mentioned above disappears only gradually : one does not pass from high nervous tension or religious exaltation to normality abruptly ; and, until isolation or restricted diet, or both, have reduced one to normal, one is likely to infect others with a like excitement. So the rest of the group feel a mystic compulsion to taboo one—to quarantine and avoid one for a time.

CHAPTER XXI

CONFESSION AND REBIRTH

THERE are many taboos besides the ones we have been considering, of which Frazer's account makes fascinating reading. But as they all fall within the psychological classes already mentioned we need not devote much time to them here. One of them allows me to draw again, somewhat fantastically, the analogy between mana (or libido) and electricity, this being the taboo upon knives and sharp-pointed instruments. An electric charge, as is well known, leaps most easily to or from a pointed body; for this reason lightning-rods have sharp tips. So it would seem to be with mana. There is a German superstition that a knife should not be left edge upwards, because God and the spirits dwell there, or because it will cut the face of God and the angels. After a death the Rumanians of Transylvania are careful not to leave a knife in this position so long as the corpse is in the house, for fear of injuring the soul of the departed. The Chinese taboo the use of knives, needles, and even chopsticks under the same circumstances and for the same reason. Among the Kayans of Borneo, when the birth-pangs begin, all men leave the room, and all cutting weapons and iron are also removed—probably in order that neither the soul of the child nor that of the mother may be injured as they fly about. In Uganda, when the hour of a woman's delivery is at hand, her husband carries all spears and weapons out of the house.[1] The soul, as has been said in an earlier chapter, is the personification of a libido-complex. It is a charge of psychic energy attached to a

[1] Frazer, *Taboo and the Perils of the Soul*, 237 *et seq.*

definite object—to the wild life, in the case of the bush-soul; to the relation between consciousness and the unconscious in the case of the general soul. It is curious that it shows this tendency to strike knives and needles (and, by analogy, all pointed or sharp objects) just as electricity would do. Similarly, evil mana may be warded off on the principle of the lightning-rod by keeping these sharp conductors, or anything made of iron, on the person or in the house : demons and evil spirits then do not dare to approach. If one meets a person who has the evil eye one should always 'make the horns.' This consists in closing the hand with the exception of the first and fourth fingers, which are then extended like two horns in the direction of the person with the evil eye.

In passing, we may note that the head is especially liable to mystic dangers, which calls forth a variety of taboos. In many parts of the world houses are built only one story high for the express reason that no one must be allowed to stand or pass over the heads of the occupants. Important personages will not pass under anything erected by the hands of men.[1] There is also the custom which required that conquered soldiers should pass under the swords or spears of the victors, under the yoke. One thinks at once of the psychology of Adler, in whose theory all human conduct springs from the will to dominate others, to be 'on top' and not 'beneath.' This idea of the sensitive sanctity of the head is also related to customs which made it shameful to shave the head or cut the beard, a punishment reserved for especially detested malefactors or enemies ; with oaths 'by my beard' ; and with such expressions as 'I would not injure a hair of your head.' The virtue or mana of a man is often thought to reside in his beard or hair, as the power of the sun is in its rays ; Samson exemplifies this ; and the glory of saints and divine personages shows in a visible halo about their heads. The importance of hair is also shown in the German saying, 'Wo Haar ist, ist Freud.'

[1] Frazer, *loc. cit.*, 252 *et seq.*

We now come to the main topic of this chapter, which has to do with what in analytical psychology is termed a change of attitude. We have seen that, through an extreme fascination felt toward an object, or by means of an interest in an object which is continued over a long period of time (as Babbitt's interest in his pose), a psychic result ensues that may be compared with the physical disproportion which would follow the habitual employment of only one set of muscles. A man whose work requires him to sit all day, moving only his hands and arms, may develop powerful muscles here, while his legs are likely to remain weak and underdeveloped. What he has to do with his hands he will do with just the right amount of force, and with precision and grace. When he walks he is likely to shamble along uncertainly, his legs giving an effect of unreliability. The same thing is often seen on the psychic side : many a person has some one function, such as thinking, developed to the point where it is swift, precise, not easily fatigued, and its operations give an observer an impression of power and grace in action. Very often this same person, when it comes to dealing with a situation that calls for the exercise of the heart rather than the head, acts so uncertainly, with so little precision and sureness, that we can almost see the tottering and stumbling of the infantile or atrophied feeling-function. To be obliged to use his feelings causes him all manner of distress and bewilderment, just as the tailor when he must walk may feel all sorts of discomforts which he labels rheumatism in his neglected legs. This contrast between developed thinking and infantile feeling is the stereotyped illustration of what is meant in analytical psychology by psychic onesidedness.

When conscious interest moves too far in one direction, or stays fixed in one attitude too long, the energy of the unconscious goes in an opposite direction. This balancing and correcting operation of the unconscious is seen very plainly sometimes in dreams. For instance, a man of forty is deeply devoted to his mother and is unwilling

to marry because no other woman bears comparison
with her. In his conscious thoughts he adores his mother
and does not wish to be separated from her even for
a few hours. In his dreams, however, the mother appears
terrible and evil, so that he tries to flee from her. Another
actual case : a young man is madly in love with a
woman whom he believes to be an angel of purity. He is
afflicted with a strange difficulty in swallowing—can eat
only liquids, a spoonful at a time. The doctors cannot
discover anything wrong with his throat. Analysis of his
dreams shows that the betrothed appears in a most
repulsive guise to his unconscious ; and investigation
then shows that she really is a prostitute in a quiet,
secret fashion. Again, a middle-aged man hates his
father with exceeding bitterness for having thwarted his
ambitions and ruined his career. But he dreams that
while he is snug in his bed at night a terrific blizzard
rages without ; and his father is somewhere in the blinding
snow-storm, lost. In his dream he realizes that he will
probably perish himself if he tries to go to his father's
assistance ; but his feeling of pity and love is so strong
that he cannot resist the desire to go. The moment the
resolve is made he wakes up, with his tears running. Such
examples might be multiplied indefinitely. In these cases
the conscious attitude is very onesided, and the allegory
brought up from the subconscious in the form of pictures
presents an antithesis to the attitude of consciousness.
' Your mother is the Terrible Mother, the emasculator
and devourer of men,' says the first dream. ' Your
betrothed is disgusting—I cannot swallow her at all,'
says the unconscious in the second dream. ' Your father
is himself lost, and very pitiable, and you love him,' the
third dream tells the dreamer. And Babbitt's soul shows
him how wild and free, a child of Nature and of beauty,
she is, and invites him to follow her. Every dream of
the kind that savages regard as important—that is, a
dream which is not forgotten upon awakening, but which
impresses and haunts the dreamer in spite of himself and

which will not let itself be forgotten—means, ' I, the other side of yourself, tell you that your conscious attitude is onesided and biologically evil, and that you should change it.'

The ' change of attitude ' means giving up existing values (against which the unconscious has been protesting in this way) and finding some new object of interest against which the unconscious does not protest. A man, let us say, is completely given up to sensuality ; at last the time comes when he feels an inner weariness and disgust (the protest of the unconscious) and would leave his manner of life if he could. But of course he is bound to his vices by the chains of habit, and cannot leave them by sheer force of will. In such cases it very often happens that he is attracted to religion, and finds in a religious symbol an object of interest upon which both consciousness and the unconscious can focus. The psychic energy devoted to the new object has to come from somewhere : it is not *new* energy that he invents ; but the more libido he gives to the religious symbol, the more, of necessity, he withdraws from his sensuality. The vices lose their attraction, sometimes as if by magic ; and often a completely new character emerges. Naturally, when the opposition between consciousness and unconscious interests ceases, so that there is no longer such a cancellation of libido as we spoke of in the case of a savage who wishes at the same time to go hunting and to stay at home with his wife, the subject has a sense of having received a vast accession of new energy : the whole world looks young and fresh to him. All these aspects of the change of attitude known as religious conversion have been admirably treated psychologically in William James' justly famous book, *The Varieties of Religious Experience*. As the impulses leading to the change of attitude arise in the unconscious, they are felt to be mystical, supernatural, and altogether above conscious reason (even when they are rationalized elaborately in a theological form) ; the unconscious spirituality within the psyche is projected, as unconscious contents always are, upon the suitable screen of a divinity; and the certainty of each convert as to the truth of his creed, though they may be in perfect opposition to other converts' beliefs, apparently surpasses any other certainty of knowledge known to man.

Of course religious conversion, in the accepted sense, is only one of the means by which a change of attitude may be brought about. James notes that exactly the same effect is sometimes reached by combating religion : ' But to find religion is only one out of many ways of reaching unity : and the process of remedying the inner discord is a general psychological process, which may take place with any sort of mental material, and need not necessarily assume religious form. In judging of the religious types of regeneration which we are about to study, it is important to recognize that they are only one species of a genus that contains other types as well. For example, the new birth may be away from religion into incredulity ; or it may be from moral scrupulosity into freedom and licence ; or it may be produced by the irruption into the individual's life of some new stimulus or passion, such as love, cupidity, ambition, revenge, or patriotic devotion. In all these instances we have precisely the same psychological form of event—a firmness, stability, and equilibrium succeeding a period of storm and stress and inconsistency.' [1]

It is, of course, as a ' general psychological process ' that we are interested in the change of attitude. If the process is really a general one, and does not arise solely from conversion to this or that religion, then we can discuss it as a matter of pure psychology without assenting to any form of religious dogma, and without dissenting therefrom. Moreover, if the process is general—that is, if it is the constitution of the human psyche itself that makes necessary an effort to correct psychic onesidedness, we may expect to find the change of attitude taking place

[1] W. James, *The Varieties of Religious Experience*, 175 *et seq.*

O

among people of lower cultures, though perhaps not among true primitives.

But first we may inquire what actions usually accompany the character-metamorphosis which we call a change of attitude. The clearest civilized examples come from the field of religion, as might be expected. The first manifestation of ripeness for character-metamorphosis is usually discontent with the present manner of life. The subject loses interest in those things which formerly exercised a strong fascination for him. Often these things have been sensual pleasures ; often it is worldly ambition to which the subject has been chained ; sometimes (as in the case of Tertullian) it is the intellectual life of which the subject wearies ; and sometimes it is just objects, the whole external world, from which the interest withdraws. The will may help this withdrawal of interest in cases where the old object of interest does not meet the approval of the subject : this frequently occurs when the subject has been given over to sensuality or ignoble ambition. But this is not always so : in many if not most cases the interest disappears without the subject willing it—indeed, very often in spite of his most earnest efforts to go on with his usual life. He feels tired ; his energy disappears ; it passes out of consciousness as though something sucked it away. This is in fact the case : the energy is sucked into the unconscious and there reinforces the processes that are to lead to a change of attitude. His self is no longer united, but is split.

In the orthodox religious programme, the next step is repentance, which is followed by confession. Then the church takes an active hand, and furnishes the would-be convert with a symbol or symbols which are to be studied and meditated upon. When it is seen that the convert's interest has turned to these symbols, he is ready to make a public declaration of faith, and to be received into the brotherhood of those who believe. It must be noted that the element of sacrifice is always present ; and what is sacrificed is the old way of life, the old way of looking

at things, the old beliefs ; in short, the old values. But
these values are the habitual psychic contents and tendencies of the subject ; they are his point of view, his
attitude toward the world, and his *persona* ; they are
part and parcel of himself. So he is really sacrificing
himself. It is always the dearest possession that must be
sacrificed.

Let me give an example from my own observation.
The subject was an American woman of good family
who had a nervous breakdown when she arrived at
puberty. From that time on, until she was about forty,
she lived in a state of invalidism, spending most of her
time in bed, attended always by at least one trained nurse.
The whole life of her family centred around her ; and
there can be no doubt that this supremacy catered to
that morbid will-to-power which often is so characteristic
of chronic invalids.

In her fortieth year she was converted to Christian
Science, and a great change in her character and behaviour
followed. All her illness disappeared ; she ate ordinary
food instead of the prepared invalid foods ; and she
travelled through the western States of America as a
Christian Science teacher, founding new branches.

It is indisputable that one reason why she turned to
Christian Science was because her father had died, and
when his estate was examined it was found that he had
spent almost everything upon her nurses and doctors,
so the rôle of the interesting, tyrannical invalid was no
longer open to her. But that does not matter. What is
important is the fact that from a death-in-life existence
her character-metamorphosis took her out into a strenuous
life of such continuous activity as few healthy men could
endure, from hopeless invalidism to robust health, and
from dependence to independence. She had more than
fifty thousand dollars in the bank when she died.

James cites at some length the case of a young man,
who wasted in three years of riotous living a large inherited
estate. When he had absolutely nothing left, the com-

panions of his revels all forsook him. In utter despair he resolved to kill himself ; but, while he was wandering about in a bewildered 'and practically unconscious condition,' he chanced to come to a place where he could look over what had lately been his own property. He sat down, and brooded over his case for several hours, at the end of which he sprang from the ground with a vehement exulting emotion. He had formed his plan to make all these estates his own again ; and at once he went about the execution of it. By taking a succession of the most menial jobs, by begging his food when he could, and by saving every penny which he was not absolutely obliged to spend, he found himself after a long time with enough money to begin small trading. 'The final result was, that he more than recovered his lost possessions, and died an inveterate miser, worth £60,000.' [1] In this case it was not religion that brought about the character-metamorphosis : it was nothing higher than bitterness toward false friends, and avarice.

Tolstoi, in *My Confession*, describes a case of counter-conversion from belief in religion to disbelief. The subject was twenty-six years old. One night, when he had been out on a hunting expedition with his brother, he knelt by his bed to say his prayers. His brother asked, ' Do you still keep up that thing ? ' From that moment the subject gave up all religion. In Tolstoi's words, ' The words spoken by his brother were like the light push of a finger against a leaning wall already about to tumble by its own weight.' James' comment is that this case ' exemplifies how small an additional stimulus will overthrow the mind into a new state of equilibrium when the process of preparation and incubation has gone far enough. It is like the proverbial last straw added to the camel's burden, or that touch of a needle which makes the salt in a supersaturated solution suddenly begin to crystallize out.'

Exactly the same processes are seen in the case of

[1] W. James, *The Varieties of Religious Experience*, 178–9.

neurotic patients : except for the comparatively rare cases in which the neurosis is due to a shock, the patient is usually found to be extremely onesided. This onesidedness has gone to such a point that there is a conflict between consciousness and the unconscious—a conflict that absorbs so much energy that little is available to meet life and its problems. The aim of analytical treatment is to bring this conflict and its cause clearly into the consciousness of the patient, so that he can decide for himself what is to be done to remedy it.   He eventually, if the treatment is successful, sets up a new goal for himself upon which both consciousness and the unconscious can focus ; and these draw together into a new equilibrium as he works toward his new goal.   Meanwhile, he has to sacrifice his old values, which had become part of himself. He confesses all his most private acts and thoughts to the analyst ; and the great advantage of analysis lies largely in the fact that he confesses things of which he himself has been entirely unconscious.   It is universally recognized that confession brings a great relief from nervous tension, and in the early days of psycho-analysis it was thought that the cure came from the confession. Hence one spoke of the ' cathartic method ' —or, as Breuer and Freud's patient put it, it was ' chimney-sweeping,' the ' talking-cure.'   But Anna, the patient in this famous case, was not cured.   Freud told Jung that after he had dropped the case all her old symptoms came back.   Nothing really cures except the change of attitude, the real character-metamorphosis, whether this comes through analysis, through conversion to religion or away from it, or the irruption of a powerful new motive such as those James lists.

The idea that the character-metamorphosis is a rebirth is not limited to the Christian theory of conversion.   It is found in many pagan religious systems, and among savages as well.   The reborn person is purified of all his sins ; he starts life anew ; the world looks fresh and new to him ; he is conscious of a vast accession of energy and power. No one could describe these effects more accurately or readably than James has done. Psychologically, as James points out, the change of attitude means that the previously split self has attained a new unity. Thus the energy that was being wasted in the conflict between consciousness and the unconscious becomes available for the tasks of life.

The rebirth is not infrequently made representable to consciousness by a special ceremony. 'Two Hindu ambassadors, who had been sent to England by a native prince and had returned to India, were considered to have so polluted themselves by contact with strangers that nothing but being born again could restore them to purity. " For the purpose of regeneration it is directed to make an image of pure gold of the female power of nature, in the shape either of a woman or of a cow. In this statue the person to be regenerated is enclosed, and dragged through the usual channel. As a statue of pure gold and of proper dimensions would be too expensive, it is sufficient to make an image of the sacred Yoni through which the person to be regenerated is to pass." Such an image of pure gold was made at the prince's command, and his ambassadors were born again by being dragged through it.' [1] The savage is often very consistent in carrying the rebirth idea to its logical consequences, even to the extent of pretending to have forgotten the ordinary ways of men and having to learn them anew as a child does. This happens among the Kwakiutl Indians to men who have eaten human flesh as a ceremonial rite and who have consequently had to undergo a long period of semi-isolation.[2]

Incidentally, it must be remarked that religious cannibalism puts the actors in the rite into a strange state of conflict between love, devotion and reverence for the dead, and horror and disgust at the rite itself. Bronislaw Malinowski writes, ' One extreme and interesting variety in which this double-edged attitude is expressed in a gruesome manner is sarco-cannibalism, a custom of

[1] Frazer, *loc. cit.*, 113.   [2] Frazer, *loc. cit.*, 189.

partaking in piety of the flesh of the dead person. It is done with extreme repugnance and dread and usually followed by a violent vomiting fit. At the same time it is felt to be a supreme act of reverence, love and devotion. In fact it is considered such a sacred duty that among the Melanesians of New Guinea, where I have studied and witnessed it, it is still performed in secret, although severely penalized by the white Government.' [1]

Now let me turn to the topic of confession. The usual result of pregnancy is that the woman gives birth to a child, head first. A child born feet first is regarded as a monstrous portent of evil, and among some races must be killed. The *horror novi* is also aroused in the hearts of many primitives by miscarriages and abortions—indeed, it is probably the unconscious primitive in ourselves which motivates our objections, theological and legal, to abortion. Miscarriages and abortions are not in the regular course of affairs: therefore they suggest taboos broken, and evil to come. This savour of sin is doubtless one reason why some races require that abortions and miscarriages must be publicly confessed. Dr Franz Boas, writing of the Eskimo of Baffin Land and Hudson Bay, says, ' Cases of premature birth require particularly careful treatment. The event must be announced publicly, else dire results will follow. If a woman should conceal from the other people that she has had a premature birth, they might come near her, or even eat in her hut of the seals procured by her husband. The vapour arising from her would thus affect them, and they would be avoided by the seals. The transgression would also become attached to the seal, which would take it down to Sedna.' [2] Sedna is the mother of the sea-mammals. She lives under the sea, and the seals are her cut-off fingers. So when, in the words of an epileptic boy described by Jung,[3] ' a guilt is handed to ' a seal, Sedna gets a sore finger.

[1] Malinowski, in symposium on *Science, Religion and Reality*, 48.
[2] Frazer, *loc. cit.*, 152.
[3] Jung, *Three Lectures on Psychology and Education* in *Contributions to Analytical Psychology.*

Among some Bantu tribes of South Africa there are even more exaggerated notions of the virulent infection spread by a woman who has had a miscarriage, and has failed to confess it. 'An experienced observer of these people tells us that the blood of childbirth " appears to the eyes of the South Africans to be tainted with a pollution still more dangerous than that of the menstrual fluid. . . . But the secretion of childbed is particularly terrible when it is the product of a miscarriage, especially a *concealed* miscarriage. In this case it is not merely the man (husband) himself who is threatened or killed, it is the whole country, it is the sky itself which suffers. By a curious association of ideas a physiological fact causes cosmic troubles ! " ' In the language of the natives themselves, ' She has spoiled the country of the chief, for she has hidden blood which has not yet been well congealed to fashion a man.' [1]

Dr Boas' investigations of the Eskimo have brought to light much psychological material of extraordinary interest.[2] Sedna seems to be a sort of fractional Great Mother. It is from her severed fingers that whales, ground seals, common seals, and the like originate. Some of the rules enjoined after killing one of these animals are the same as the taboos imposed after killing a human being. After despatching one of these sea-mammals it is forbidden to scrape the frost from the window, to shake the bed or to disturb the shrubs under the bed, to remove the drippings of oil from under the lamp, to scrape hair from skins, to cut snow for the purpose of melting it, to work upon iron, wood, stone, or ivory. Furthermore, the women are forbidden to wash their faces, to comb their hair, or to dry their boots or stockings. This looks as though the natives felt some mystic peril hovering about, on account of which it was advisable to lie low and to leave

[1] Frazer, *loc. cit.*, 152.

[2] Frazer, *loc. cit.*, 208. Cited from Boas, *The Central Eskimo* (Sixth Annual Report of the U.S. Bureau of Ethnology, 1888, pp. 584–595) and *The Eskimo of Baffin Land and Hudson Bay* (Bulletin of the American Museum of Natural History, XV, Part I, 1901, pp. 121–4).

the affairs of daily life pretty much in suspension. ' All
these regulations must be kept with the greatest care
after a ground-seal has been killed, because the transgression of taboos that refer to this animal make the
hands of Sedna very sore.'   There are various other
taboos, too numerous to mention here.

These taboos must be stringently kept for the souls of
the sea-mammals remain for three days with the body
before returning to Sedna, who has special charge of
them.   If any taboo is broken, the transgression becomes
attached to the soul of the animal and returns with it
to Sedna and in some mysterious way makes her hands
sore.   Such a happening angers the goddess and she
then punishes the transgressor.

These Eskimos believe that contact with a corpse
causes objects to assume a dark colour and that flowing
human blood gives off a vapour which adheres to persons
coming in contact with it.   Neither the dark colour nor
the vapour are visible to ordinary people, but they are distasteful to sea-animals, whose souls are endowed with
special powers, and can see both.   Consequently these
animals avoid a hunter who has been in contact with a
corpse or with flowing blood either directly or through an
intermediary who has touched either.   To prevent such
misfortune to hunters, everyone who has touched either
of these distasteful objects and women in their periods
or after a miscarriage must announce the fact to the
community.

Dr Boas considers that these ideas have led to the
rule that requires a man to confess all breaches of a
taboo, so that the community might not suffer from the
evil influence of contact with the evil-doer.   From this it
has been but a step ' to the idea that a transgression, or,
as we might say, a sin, can be atoned for by confession.'
This belief is held by the Eskimo.   If hunting prove
fruitless, a sorcerer is called in to determine the cause.
If he find it to be due to the transgression of a taboo,
confession on the part of the evil-doer will put all right.

The dark colour or the vapour of a transgression which becomes attached to the soul of the transgressor and of all those who come in contact with the transgressor, is, by the help of his guardian spirit, visible to the sorcerer, who is able to free the soul from its attachments; if this is not done the person must die. But an integral part of this process of freeing is confession by the transgressor.

It is not amiss to point out that this primitive doctrine survives, and is even perfected, in the religious beliefs of civilized Christians. Sin is simply the violation of a taboo, of an ordinance accepted as authoritative by the group. Note that it is not the self—*i.e.*, the entire man—who suffers from the breaking of a taboo : it is only his soul. The guilt attaches to his soul, not to himself. The soul becomes red : ' Though your sins be as scarlet. . . .' The purification is of the soul alone : body and mind are not purified, because the sin has not made them unclean, but only the soul. It is the soul that must be ' saved ' by repentance, confession, and atonement. It must lose its red colour by being washed ' white.' It is from such deep springs, through which the collective subconscious forces its rich primitive imagery to the surface of consciousness, that Christianity and every other religion is nourished and made to flower.

Frazer finds that he ' can hardly agree with Dr Boas that among these Eskimo the confession of sins was in its origin no more than a means of warning others against the dangerous contagion of the sinner ; in other words, that its saving efficacy consisted merely in preventing the innocent from suffering with the guilty, and that it had no healing virtue, no purifying influence, for the evildoer himself. It seems more probable that originally the violation of a taboo, in other words, the sin, was conceived as something almost physical, a sort of morbid substance lurking in the sinner's body, from which it could be expelled by confession as a sort of spiritual purge or emetic.'

In support of this criticism, Frazer gives examples of

confession among savages of Africa, American Indians, and natives of Columbia, Guatemala, Madagascar, Borneo, and other places.   As to the Africans, Frazer says : ' Amongst them, we are told, " Sin is essentially remissible ; it suffices to confess it. Usually this is done to the sorcerer, who expels the sin by a ceremony of which the principal rite is a pretended emetic : *Kotahikio*, derived from *Tahika*, to vomit." Thus among these savages the confession and absolution of sins is, so to say, a purely physical process of relieving a sufferer of a burden which sits heavy on his stomach rather than on his conscience.' [1]

The belief that guarding a guilty secret results in sickness is very prevalent among primitives ; and persons who have studied the modern psychology know that the savages are absolutely correct in this belief. Of course modern psychologists do not go so far as the savages do in this matter ; for the latter attribute every kind of illness to sin which has not been confessed, or wished upon a scapegoat, or expiated by sacrifice or purificatory ceremonies. Still, I cannot help wondering, if conventional morality continues to melt away among the civilized, and is replaced (as I believe it will be) by a biomorality which has as its aim the affirmative doing of those things which keep the individual and society efficient, healthy and happy, shall we not come back to this primitive idea that sickness, preventable sickness at least, is the result of sin ? Of course, if we make the change from an objective standard of virtue (consisting in not violating laws imposed from without) to a subjective one (consisting in developing oneself to the highest possible degree) we shall also have to make the definition of ' sin ' more subjective. Sin then would become a violation of oneself by oneself, or a failure to bring one's individual pattern to full flower and fruition.

Frazer holds that the primary motive of the confession of sins among savages was self-regarding ; in other words, the intention was rather to benefit the sinner himself

[1] Frazer, *loc. cit.*, 213 *et seq.*

than to safeguard others by warning them of the danger they would incur by coming in contact with him. With my aversion from trying to limit psychic phenomena to any single cause, I believe that both motives enter into the matter. Since taboo is primarily the avoidance of a person or thing containing dangerous mana, it is clear that Boas' explanation—that the sinful state is a definite, infectious psychic condition (if we use the language of psychology) and that it is a menace to the whole group —certainly must be accepted. Whether the offender wishes to humiliate himself by confession or not, he must confess : for, as we have seen, the safety of the group is the supreme subconscious aim of all savage customs and the social instinct overrules all others.

But there is also something inherent in the psychic constitution of the individual which forces him to confess. Most moderns cannot keep a guilty secret without becoming ill, cannot break any of the taboos of society to which they personally assent, or even an individual taboo which they have adopted for themselves, without becoming involved in a psychic conflict that may be actually dangerous ; and as we know that civilized sinners— taboo breakers—feel subject to a compulsion (arising from the unconscious) to confess, it is clear that Frazer is also right. The breaking of a convention is a very serious thing to the primitive's mind : his ideas of right and wrong are clear-cut and immutable ; white is white and black is black with him ; there are no delicate shades of grey between them, as with the civilized. He lives under a code of morals. When he obeys the code, he is pure and lucky ; when he infringes the code, he is out of luck and unclean—subject to mystic dangers. To know that he has broken a commandment puts him at once in a state of terror ; it splits him psychically ; and he naturally flies to the priest to unburden himself of his guilt. With these ideas firmly fixed in his mind, I have no doubt whatever that he really falls physically ill under the weight of a guilty secret, and that he recovers when the burden of sin is removed. It is not uncommon among savages for delayed childbirth or especially hard labour to be regarded as due to the commission of some sin, usually adultery by the woman. In such case, confession either to a medicine man or to the midwives is believed to be the only means of bringing about the delivery and of saving the life of the mother and is always insisted on.[1]

To such stories, the analytical psychologist would say, ' What could be more natural ? The records of the civilized are full of similar instances, in which psychic conflicts are symbolically expressed by physical symptoms. The man whose unconscious cannot swallow his betrothed may get a neurotic contraction of the throat which prevents him from swallowing food. The miser is likely to suffer from constipation. In this case the woman is striving to hold something back—her guilty secret—and under this symbolism she holds back her child.'

Now to go back to the elements which we found in a conventional case of religious conversion. The first of these was a psychic split, evidenced by weariness and disgust, growing to the point of repentance. For weariness and disgust, in the case of the savage taboo-breaker we can substitute fear, fear frequently mounting to terror, and sometimes resulting in death. That this fear destroys that unity of the self of which James speaks, is not to be doubted. Neither can one doubt that, in the grip of his fear, the savage repents. One striking difference exists, however, between the civilized and the savage sinner : the savage is not a habitual taboo-breaker ; his transgressions are occasional, and often merely inadvertent ; while the civilized sinner who is ripe for conversion is getting away from a habitual mode of life and thought, from a habitual onesidedness. In the autobiography of Crashing Thunder, edited by Dr Radin, the subject is a full-blooded American Indian ; but his conversion to the cult of the Peyote is really a white man's form of conversion : Crashing Thunder is tired of his dissipated

[1] Frazer, *loc. cit.*, 216.

mode of life. It is a true change of attitude, a meta-
morphosis of the man's character. The real savage, on
the other hand, is more like a devout Catholic : he never
dreams of questioning his articles of faith ; he slips
sometimes, and then he must make all speed to cast off
the burden of his sin by confession and penance ; but
he needs no conversion. The act of confession is the
same psychologically, it seems to me, whether the con-
fessant be a savage or a cultured modern, and whether
the confessor be a shaman, a priest, or an analyst. The
confession to the analyst, as has been remarked, has the
advantage of covering a broader field than religious
confession : it is not limited to sins, but embraces all
sorts of thwarted hopes and unhappy experiences and
present needs, both those of which the patient is conscious
and those of which he is unconscious. On the other
hand, the mighty solace of religious confession is not to
be had in an analysis of the psyche ; there is no conviction of forgiveness, that one is right with the supreme
power that rules the universe. Instead, there is only the
relief which would come from unburdening oneself to any
trusted friend. The spiritual purge or emetic of confession
in the course of an analysis is only incidental ; for the
rôle of the analyst is not that of the absolving priest—
it is more like that of the expert accountant whom a
business man calls in to go over his books, in order that
he may discover what lines of endeavour are profitable
to him, and where there are leaks and wastes of money
which can be stopped. It is the owner of the business
who must change his business methods after he sees
clearly what ought to be changed. Similarly, it is the
subject himself who, after the analysis has shown him
where his libido is being wasted, and where it is tied up
in non-productive psychic investments—complexes—who
must make his own change of attitude. But in all three
examples of confession, an inherent psychic need is
satisfied.

As breaking a taboo makes the offender himself taboo,

he is, until the transgression has been cured, cut off from the tribal communion. The ceremony of confession, taking it objectively, or the ceremonies whereby the guilt is transferred to a scapegoat or to some inanimate object, make the savage once more a member of the brotherhood. There is little difference between this and joining a church, except that the savage rejoins a communion he was born into. The effect of a successful analysis is the same : the patient who has been isolated from humanity and unable to take part in the life around him because of his nervous malady finds that he can rejoin human society and play his part once more in human affairs.

The Eskimo's fear that his misdeeds will make sore the finger of Sedna,[1] the great goddess, is closely paralleled by a very prevalent idea among civilized races : that is, that God is doing the best He can, and that a man who does right is helping God ; while a man who does evil is, in his small way, blocking the beneficent efforts of God. Very many modern thinkers have adopted this view, which offers an escape from the absurdity of supposing that a deity who permits evil to exist is himself both good and also omnipotent. As evil abounds in the world, the philosopher has a dilemma presented to him : either the power or the goodness of God must be finite, for otherwise He would abolish evil. It is more sympathetic to our human nature to suppose that God's power is limited than to admit any evil in Him. William James takes this point of view : ' I hold to the finite God.' ' Having an environment, being in time, and working out a history just like ourselves, he (God) escapes from the foreignness from all that is human, of the static timeless perfect absolute.'[2] This makes the good man a partner in God's work. But the transgressor, the evil-doer, thwarts his will—and doubtless causes him pain. I fail to see much difference between these eminently respectable modern philosophic views and the Eskimo theory that violating taboos makes Sedna suffer from sore fingers.

[1] Frazer, loc. cit., 218–9.
[2] W. James, A Pluralistic Universe, 124 and 318.

In analytical psychology we call such ideas as this of helping the good deity, and avoiding giving him pain, and such ideas as Fechner's of the divine earth-soul, archetypes. This means that they are images (the original meaning of the word *idea* is archetype, pattern, and it is derived from the Greek verb *to see*) which spring into the mind unbidden because of the very constitution of the psyche itself. They are not the product of conscious reason. On the contrary, conscious reason cannot avoid them. They are part of our psychic inheritance, with something categorical about them. They seem to be nearer to psychic functions than to mere psychic contents ; for though, when they rise into consciousness, they are mental contents, they are also modes of apprehension and thinking—quite as much as any of the Kantian categories. These archetypes mould even our most original thinking (and other behaviour as well) for, in addition to being instinctive and therefore paths of least resistance with great unconscious energy attached to them, they are also to an extent not clearly known limitations upon the freedom of the human mind. In earlier chapters we have taken up details of the primitive's psychic processes, and have found them practically indistinguishable from our own. Now I shall go even further, and say that it is not only in details of the responses which savages and we ourselves make to like situations that primitive and civilized are alike in kind—but that in the higher reaches of religion, philosophy and science we still think in the terms of primitive archetypes. We dress in the language of reason the same images which the savage decks out in the language of imagination, of poetry and myth. I have given Fechner and James as examples of the primitive archetype set out in the dress of philosophy, and I could give other examples : indeed, I do not believe I have ever come across any system of philosophy or religion that was not founded upon primitive archetypes. Who, for instance, is Nietzsche's suffering Superman but Prometheus ? In the field of modern religion, we have touched upon Christ and the Christian communion where his body is symbolically eaten and his blood drunk ; and the ideas of the totem and the ritual eating of the totemic animal must have struck the reader as being very close parallels. Such comparisons should not cause distress to the most devout believer : for do these examples not prove that it is an inherent tendency, necessity even, of the human psyche to envisage thus the human brotherhood, and the individual's aspiration to metamorphose his own character ? Then there is the field of science. We have a theory that the solar system condensed out of cosmic dust, by the force of gravitation. Well, the ancient Greeks had the same idea : the only difference being that they did not call the force which drew the scattered particles of Chaos together gravitation, but Eros. In the old mythologies those personifications of energy, the gods, grow old and die. We say that kinetic energy tends to become static, that the solar system is running down. The idea, the archetype, is the same in savage myth and in modern science, religion and philosophy. It is only the manner of presentation, the dress, that changes. The primitive—even the primordial—man is alive today in every one of us. This truth is not altered by the fact that we have wrapped our primitivity in a thin but shining garment of culture.

CHAPTER XXII

CONCLUSIONS

In this last chapter I shall refer but briefly to what has gone before, and shall consider what meaning the facts related may have for the civilized man or woman of today. Let us take for granted, for the purposes of this closing discussion, that the facts both anthropological and psychological are as I have stated them to be.

We are constantly being reminded that ever since the last war we have been in a transition period; that the old moral and religious sanctions have lost their force; and that youth today is frankly contemptuous of the old pious catch-words and dull banalities which, for the fathers and mothers, too often took the place of individual judgment as guides to conduct. No doubt every period is one of transition; and the present time is remarkable solely because the evolution of ideas is proceeding at such a pace that one cannot shut the eyes to it. And the primitive in us says, Alas that anything should ever change, and that we should have to encounter anything new—alas that youth should think! Sad as it is, however, we cannot blink the fact that some of the old, conventional morality is already in the dust-bin, and more will probably follow. All we can do is to speculate as to what goal of conduct a more critical and honest point of view will reveal. Of one thing we can be sure: any new theory of morality will have to be based upon a firmer foundation than superstition or conventional ethics; it will have to be capable of withstanding the most searching hostile criticism; and it must promise to bring satisfactions—a profit, as William James would call it—here and now to those who practise it.

Analytical psychology does not pretend to have solved the ultimate problems of cosmic causation or to offer a complete philosophical *Weltanschauung*. It does, however, assert that the observed facts of human behaviour are strong evidence against materialism and determinism. To us who regard the work of the Zurich school as rather in advance of any other attempt to systematize known psychological facts, there is no psychic action which cannot be treated—and correctly treated—as having a goal, as well as a point of departure. That is, every psychic action is purposeful as well as caused. For illustration of what is meant, let us suppose that Freud, Jung, Adler and Watson were standing together beside a road and a traveller should come up to them. How account for his presence ? Freud and Watson would say, ' He is here because he set out from the neighbouring town of X.' This would express the usual causal-scientific point of view, which assumes that any phenomenon is completely explained when the past history of it has been discovered. Jung, on the other hand, would say, ' It is true that he set out from X ; but that is not a complete explanation. We must add the fact that our traveller desired or needed to go toward Y, whither this road leads.' And Adler, according to his latest writings, would agree with Jung. For it is clear that the traveller might have stayed all his life in X without leaving the town at all, unless he had had some aim, some goal, in departing from it. The new german *Gestalt* psychology has brought to light a mass of evidence which leaves almost no reasonable doubt that the psychic processes of even very young infants, and of animals as well, are purposeful—thus confirming the earlier contention of analytical psychology.

Man is the outcome of an evolutionary process, during the course of which his physical organs and his psychic capacities and tendencies have unfolded together. This division into physical and psychical is an artificial one :

it is convenient to make the separation for purposes of study ; but a man himself is a unit, even with all his complexity. The self is the entire man, physical and psychical. The self is a polity and thrives when all the lesser units composing it function in a balanced manner. Each self, in turn, is a unit in the group ; and the welfare of each individual is most intimately bound up with that of the group to which he belongs, for human society is far and away the most important feature of every man's natural environment.

The further back toward primitivity we trace human society, the more do we find that it survives only through unhesitating co-operation and mutual burden-bearing. The less culture a group has, the closer must this symbiosis be. The more primitive a group is, the more, of necessity, must its members in order to survive devote themselves to what are often called the virtues of altruism and self-sacrifice. Since these subconscious urges to co-operation are found among various animals and plants, which are mutually helpful, a broader term is needed than altruism or self-sacrifice ; and it is convenient to call such mutual helpfulness biomorality. Biomorality is a direct product of evolution, of the struggle to survive : it has only an indirect relation to conventional morality, which is merely a matter of the accepted fashion in a given group.

All the anthropological evidence available goes to show that man has always been a social animal, and that it is not until he has acquired a comparatively complex culture that egotistical tendencies begin to appear and lead him to satisfy selfish desires at the expense of his original biomorality. The evidence presented by the so-called law of recapitulation is in entire accord with the findings of anthropology, and shows that the deepest and oldest layers in the psychological heritage of the individual are social and biomoral ; moreover, a very definite gulf occurs between the appearance of these qualities and the appearance of egotistical and anti-social tendencies. The Terrible Father of Freud is a psychological metaphor, and the Caveman sponsored by Freud is a myth. Precisely as Jung has demonstrated that the Terrible Mother who tempts her son to incestuous longings is a metaphor expressing a man's temptation to avoid his duties and surrender himself to childishness, so Malinowski's researches have proved that the Terrible Father is a metaphorical expression of the child's resistance to discipline. The latter stands for the aversion from duty, and the former for a desire to do almost anything else but duty. At bottom they are the same.

The time when a child begins to develop egotistical tendencies is precisely the time when it commences to comprehend that it is an ego, the period when self-consciousness dawns. A child cannot set its own will consciously against the will of its parents before it begins to be conscious of itself as something distinct from its family group. Its social virtues develop during the period of its original identity with its parents ; its rebellion against the family group appears as this identity is dissolved by psychic unfolding from within. Thereafter the child is prevented from becoming an irresponsible egotist only by a system of prohibitions and rewards imposed by the family group. Exactly the same course of evolution has been followed by the human race : so long as the primitive and original condition of identity with the group persists, the social qualities are supreme ; and the all-powerful social instinct easily confines other instincts within ritual channels. But when this identity begins to wear thin the group unconsciously develops a system of taboos and rewards. That is, certain conduct is accepted as being correct, entitling all who conform to it to the fullest confidence of the group and all the help the group can give ; while transgression of this conduct makes the sinner taboo. This marks the birth of conventional morality, which aids the *apparently* dwindling biomorality. The conventional morality, in so far as it consists of duties that must be performed, and the taboo, which is the prohibition of acts that must not be committed, are the positive and negative aspects respectively of custom. Custom covers what we moderns have divided into good manners, legal rights and duties, and religion.

Custom, in its social aspect, promotes the unity of the group, and, by preventing dissension among the members, makes the group better able to present a united front to its environment. The psychological effect of obeying custom upon the individual actor is that he feels fortified by the sense of being at one with the group, with its united power behind him. The subjective effect of neglecting duty, on the other hand, or of breaking a taboo, is that the individual is demoralized by a sense of isolation.

So soon as a group has advanced to the point where the members consciously recognize themselves as forming a distinct group, the fact of group-unity is likely to be symbolized by the members calling themselves by the name of some familiar animal or plant from which they have not yet differentiated themselves. This object is thereafter the totem. Ordinarily the totem is sacred and taboo; but at times it must be eaten in a sacred communion. Psychologically this makes each savage in the group at one with the totem and at one with all others who are at one with the totem. With the appearance of the totem, custom begins to split into religion proper (or sacred custom) and profane custom. Law and polite usage and conventional morality are the remainder which remains after sacred custom proper has been set into a separate compartment in the savage mind; and, as Malinowski has shown, savages often violate a profane taboo when they are reasonably certain of not being caught and punished by the group.

Religion and profane custom are probably never wholly differentiated in any psyche, however, savage or civilized. We can call those customs religious where the urge to be at one with the totem (or the accepted deity) and hence with the human brotherhood, is clearly operative.

In our study of taboos we have seen that *what* the taboo is—in the matter of sexual relations, for instance—makes absolutely no difference at all. The only important thing is that there shall be *some* taboo, some ritual division of that desirable object, woman, among the men, so that the group be not weakened or scattered by dissension. Whether the rule is monogamy, polygamy, polyandry, unlimited promiscuity before marriage with monogamy afterwards, the custom of wife-lending to a friend or an honoured guest, or any other form of conventional morality, the one vital thing is, for imperfectly conscious savages, that there should be *some* conventional morality, some standard insuring uniformity in conduct. So long as consciousness has not developed to such a point among the members of a group that individuality can be tolerated, so long as the dead level of savage socialism is the most workable form of social organization, conventional morality there must be. For without individuality there can be no individual responsibility toward the group, no individual morality. All social groups feel the *horror novi* toward any member who varies from the norm, and all groups therefore discourage that surpassing of the norm which constitutes individuality : the more primitive a group the more sternly does it repress individuality. Individuality means a high degree of consciousness on the part of the subject, which necessarily involves the dissolution of many mystic participations between objects and of many identities between the subject and objects—including the most important identity, that between the subject and the group. In self-defence the group resists individuality. It is possible for a man to develop his consciousness to the point where he *consciously* turns his interest upon the group, as the factor of supreme importance to his environment, and gives his love and labour to this super-personal entity. But this means a very high degree of individuality, consciousness, on his part—a true individual morality. The evolutionary path from unconscious biomorality up to conscious individual morality is very long indeed ; and when the former urge is obscured by the rise of egotistic tendencies, and the latter is not yet strong, society must restrain its variant members by the discipline of a fixed norm of behaviour, a code. In this view, conventional morality is seen as a means of canalizing the libido so that it shall express itself in social rather than anti-social acts—a control imposed by the group upon its members which was not needed when mankind was truly primitive, and which is no longer required for those who have passed far enough along the road of individuation so that their egotistical tendencies are under conscious control.

In so far as I can interpret the evidence of anthropology and psychology, I believe this to be the general course of man's psychic evolution : He begins with unconsciousness, when he is biomoral simply because the instinct to co-operate is stronger than any other instinct : he becomes imperfectly conscious, whereupon anti-social, egotistical urges appear, and make it necessary for the group to establish and enforce norms of conduct, or conventions ; and more and more he will approach full consciousness, full individuation, and full individual self-control and responsibility. As he does this—as the race itself becomes adult—the necessity for being morally controlled from without will progressively disappear.

Even in this day, which is supposed by some to be given over almost entirely to the mad rush to get money and the egotistical gratifications that the possession of money makes possible, there are many who have passed through that secondary stage of the race's development during which they had to be controlled in their conduct by moral conventions and taboos imposed by society. These have reached a degree of individuation where they consciously serve some social group and control their egotistic impulses in order that they may contribute to the welfare of the society which supports them.

It does not matter in the least that the subject rationalizes this super-personal transference (as it is technically called) and claims that he subordinates his egotistical desires to the welfare of society because it is his duty, or because his religion demands it, or because he wishes to imitate his favourite hero, Buddha or Christ. The simple fact is that we have lost none of our primitive instincts, and that we experience a relief from nervous tension and an ensuing tranquillity and feeling of self-satisfaction whenever we have given one of them due expression : this is true of the instincts to eat, to sleep, to wake, to play, and the sex-instinct, and it is no less true in regard to allowing an outlet for that instinct which subordinates all the others, the social or symbiotic instinct of co-operation with one's fellows. Indeed, as this instinct is clearly *primus inter pares*, we are obliged to accept the word of those who tell us that there is no self-satisfaction equal to that of helping others, or doing creative work from which society may conceivably profit. We psychologists seldom take seriously the rationalized excuse which is given for performing an instinctive act. Similarly, one should not attach too much weight to extraneous reasons given for indulging the symbiotic instinct, even when the subject himself believes them. Every instinct has its own motive energy, its libido, ear-marked for spending ; and the satisfaction of any instinct is its own reward.

Nevertheless it is clear that anyone who rationalizes his own instinctive act has, to this extent, failed in becoming as conscious as he might. When a man can say, ' I rule my sexuality and my will-to-power and all my other appetites and desires, and give them expression only within such bounds as I deem wise for me, and I do this because my supreme interest and greatest satisfaction is to do creative work which serves society '—that man has gone far along the road of individuation. It is, by the way, the aim of analytical psychology in the re-education of neurotic patients, to help them find their way to this super-personal transference. Many do arrive at it, turning their interest, their love and anxiety, away from themselves and their personal affairs ; and these get well. They withdraw their energy from neurotic manifestations, and allow it to flow through the ancient, race-habitual channel of the symbiotic instinct. These neurotics—the ones who are wholly cured—are those in whom the tendency and need to progress thus in individuation has been developing subconsciously, or 'incubating,' to use James' expressive verb, until they are ripe for the character-metamorphosis.

It is perhaps sad that Nature takes very little account of conventional morality, and frequently inflicts penalties upon those who follow the collective code most faithfully. Or perhaps it is sad that humanity clings to conventions which are no longer necessary to promote the welfare of the group. Thus there is very little danger any more of disrupting the unity of any society by allowing grown-ups to form any sexual relationships they may desire. A very great part of our population has discarded the view that all sexual intercourse outside of marriage is wrong and that all sexual intercourse within matrimony is right ; and there has been no evidence so far that all the men are about to leave their occupations and fall violently upon each other in a rage of sexual acquisitiveness. In the philosophy of another great fraction of the people, the old sexual taboo is still in full force, however ; and among these conventionally moral citizens there are many chaste women whose lives are made miserable by neurosis. There are even some men whose conventional morality in matters sexual has been penalized by Nature. Similarly, one could run through the whole list of race-habitual activities which appear in the individual as an instinct, urge, or 'drive,' and find persons who are being punished for not giving one of these urges due expression and outlet. Or (it would be more accurate to say) these persons are punishing themselves, making themselves ill, keeping themselves undeveloped and incomplete.

This is one way of expressing the matter, disjunctively, taking the hereditary urges one by one and saying that health and happiness cannot be had except when each is given a due measure of satisfaction. Another way to say the same thing is to regard the whole man, conjunctively, and to point out that he is deficient and hampered to the extent that he fails to develop any psychic element which is part of his racial heritage. This may be one of his functions of adaptation, as thinking or feeling, sensation or intuition, or it may be any one of those constellations of energy (as sex, to take but one example) which furnish the drive to express himself in relation to the pattern of his environment. When a man develops himself evenly all around, he brings up into consciousness all the psychic elements which call for expression, and subjects them to conscious control. Here again we are back to the concept of individuation : it is, as has been said, a development of consciousness ; and it involves growing up in a balanced and well-rounded way to the full stature of one's possibilities. This growing up to one's full pattern results in psychic health, and efficiency and balance in conduct— which tends toward happiness and success in life. On the other hand, the suppression of a psychic element which is pressing for its place in the sun means that the conscious individuality is deficient and crippled ; and a neurosis very often results from the division of the self, from the conflict between consciousness and the element in the subconscious which is trying to get recognition. In addition, the suppressed element in its undeveloped, infantile form finds some form of expression in action, often making the subject's conduct irrational in the extreme.

Finally we can sum up the results of our study. The race tends to progress from unconsciousness toward consciousness and during this progression three stages may be seen : first, an unconscious bio-morality, in which the primitive members of any social group co-operate instinctively ; second, a period of savagery, in which the rise of egotistic tendencies requires that the group shall force the members to conform to a norm of conventional morality ; and third, a stage (not yet reached by any society, though many individuals in civilized societies have attained it) in which the members of the group consciously co-operate for the common good, and consciously restrain their egotistic desires in order to do so. The psychic life-history of every individual who reaches full individuality passes through these three phases of psychic development.

INDEX OF TOPICS

INDEX OF AUTHORS